# PRAISE FOR
# *The Power of Infinite Love & Gratitude*

*"Powerful and timely! Darren Weissman's book, **The Power of Infinite Love & Gratitude,** offers a compelling new model for disease and the role it plays in our lives. Through a beautiful synthesis of ancient insight and modern science, Dr. Weissman gives our mind a reason to accept what our heart already knows—that love is the great healer of life, and the power to love into wellness lives within each of us. This book is a "must" for any library of science and healing in the 21st century!"*

— **Gregg Braden,** the *New York Times* best-selling author of *The Isaiah Effect, The God Code,* and *The Divine Matrix*

*"Dr. Darren R. Weissman demonstrates that exercising free will and making the choice to release all judgments will result in proven molecular changes throughout the body. He doesn't just hypothesize it, he proves it. The power of the mind is infinite, and love is the greatest power of them all. I highly recommend this book."*

— **Gary R. Renard,** the best-selling author of
*The Disappearance of the Universe* and *Your Immortal Reality*

*"This book is a must-read for anyone interested in self-healing. It is not only rich with valuable information, but it addresses two of the most impactful healing tools available—love and gratitude. Darren has done an exceptional job of integrating contemporary science with the ancient traditional methods of healing, and has done so with the true essence of a healing master."*

— **Carol Ritberger, Ph.D.,** medical intuitive; author of
*What Color Is Your Personality?* and *Love . . . What's Personality Got to Do with It?*

# THE
# POWER
# OF
# INFINITE
# LOVE &
# GRATITUDE

# Hay House Titles of Related Interest

# THE
# POWER
# OF
# INFINITE
# LOVE &
# GRATITUDE

An Evolutionary Journey
to Awakening Your Spirit

## DR. DARREN R. WEISSMAN

**HAY HOUSE, INC.**
Carlsbad, California
London • Sydney • Johannesburg
Vancouver • Hong Kong • New Delhi

*Published and distributed in the United States by:* Hay House, Inc.: www.hayhouse.com • *Published and distributed in Australia by:* Hay House Australia Pty. Ltd.: www.hayhouse.com.au • *Published and distributed in the United Kingdom by:* Hay House UK, Ltd.: www.hayhouse.co.uk • *Published and distributed in the Republic of South Africa by:* Hay House SA (Pty), Ltd.: www.hayhouse.co.za • *Distributed in Canada by:* Raincoast: www.raincoast.com • *Published in India by:* Hay House Publishers India: www.hayhouse.co.in

*Editorial supervision:* Jill Kramer • *Design:* Bryn Starr Best

**Reprinted with permission:** "Darren/Halo," charcoal on paper, 26 x 20 inches, by Rick Outten, with permission from the artist, **www.screaminredhed.com**. / "Our deepest fear . . . automatically liberates others," from *A Return to Love* by Marianne Williamson, Copyright © 1992; reprinted by permission of HarperCollins Publishers, Inc. Portions reprinted from *A Course in Miracles*, Copyright © 1975 by Foundation for Inner Peace. All chapter openings are from *A Course in Miracles*. / Excerpts and photographs from *Messages from Water* by Dr. Masaru Emoto, Copyright © 1999, used with permission of I.H.M. Co, Ltd., authorization number ihm0604030576. / Excerpts from *Psycho-Cybernetics* by Maxwell Maltz, M.D., F.I.C.S., Copyright © 1960; reprinted by permission of the Psycho-Cybernetics Foundation, Inc., **www.psycho-cybernetics.com**. / The poem "Autobiography in Five Chapters," from *There's a Hole in My Sidewalk*, Copyright © 1993 by Portia Nelson; reprinted by permission of Beyond Words Publishing, Inc., Hillsboro, Oregon, USA. / Excerpts from *Why People Don't Heal and How They Can* by Caroline Myss, Copyright © 1997; reprinted by permission of Three Rivers Press, a division of Crown Publishers, Inc., Random House, Inc. / Excerpts from *Your Body's Many Cries for Water* by Fereydoon Batmanghelidj, M.D., Copyright © 1997; reprinted by permission of the author. / Excerpts from *Your Body Speaks Your Mind: How Your Thoughts and Emotions Affect Your Health* by Debbie Shapiro, Copyright © 1996; reprinted by permission of the author. / The poem "Treasure of Love" by Kristin Ryan, Copyright © 2002; reprinted by permission of the author. / The poem "The Awakening" by Ranel Gretebeck; reprinted with permission from the author. / Excerpts from *The Mastery of Love* by Don Miguel Ruiz, Copyright © 1999, with permission of Amber-Allen Publishing. / Excerpts from *Chiropractic Philosophy* by Joseph B. Strauss, D.C., Copyright © 1980, with permission from the author. / Quote from Louise L. Hay; reprinted with permission from the author. / The LifeLine Technique Flow Chart™ and Optimal Health Chart, Copyright © 2002 by Dr. Darren R. Weissman and Infinite Love Press; reprinted with permission of Infinite Love Press.

The author of this book does not dispense medical advice or prescribe the use of any technique as a form of treatment for physical, emotional, or medical problems without the advice of a physician, either directly or indirectly. The intent of the author is only to offer information of a general nature to help you in your quest for emotional and spiritual well-being. In the event you use any of the information in this book for yourself, which is your constitutional right, the author and the publisher assume no responsibility for your actions.

**Library of Congress Cataloging-in-Publication Data**

Weissman, Darren R.
  The power of infinite love & gratitude : an evolutionary journey to awakening your spirit / Darren R. Weissman.
      p. cm.
  Includes bibliographical references and index.
  ISBN-13: 978-1-4019-1717-3 (tradepaper) 1. Love. 2. Gratitude. 3. Spiritual life. 4. Mind and body. I. Title. II. Title: Power of infinite love and gratitude.
  BF575.L8W43 2007
  158--dc22                                              2006021355

**ISBN:** 978-1-4019-1717-3

10  09  08  07   5  4  3  2
1st edition, February 2007
2nd edition, June 2007

Printed in the United States of America

*For my beautiful wife, Sarit;
and our daughter, Joya Ruth;
with Infinite Love & Gratitude*

*With deepest appreciation to:*

The barefoot doctors of China
Edgar Cayce
George Goodheart, D.C.
Victor Frank, D.C.
Scott Walker, D.C.
Jon Sunderlage, D.C., Dipl.Ac., L.Ac.
Ralph Alan Dale, Ed.D., Ph.D.
Steve Ciolino, D.C.
Lord Pandit Professor Dr. Sir Anton Jayasuriya
Louise L. Hay
Bob Warwick
Bruce Lipton, Ph.D.
Richard Bandler
John Grinder
Masaru Emoto, M.D.
Francine Shapiro, Ph.D.
Candace Pert, Ph.D.
Wayne W. Dyer, Ph.D.
Caroline Myss

Without your courage, determination, and commitment
to explore the frontiers and expand the boundaries
of holistic medicine, my work would not be possible.

The LifeLine Technique follows in the
footsteps of the Masters, carving out a new road.

To extend and expand the path that the
mentor has graciously opened is the disciple's mission.

# CONTENTS

## PART II: OWNING YOUR POWER

All stories in this book are true; however, all patient names are fictitious to maintain patient confidentiality.

# FOREWORD

The experience you're going to read about is my journey through the dark night of my soul—it's the path I took to reconnect to my power, my will, and a new passion for living. When all I wanted to do was die, the power of Infinite Love & Gratitude saved me by giving me hope in the midst of life's greatest horror. It was my evolutionary journey to awakening my spirit.

My favorite uncle called me "Spitfire" when I was a child. I earned the nickname because, as soon as I could talk, I was outspoken: I said whatever I felt like saying to whoever was brave enough to listen. I always spoke my truth.

But before I turned four, I lost my voice to the "shushes" of my parents. My directness shamed them; it threatened their social standing in our community. Every time I opened my mouth to say something, their response was: "Be quiet, Gail. Don't talk like that."

From that point forward, I learned that to live I had to be quiet. I turned inward, internalizing my desire to speak until I could no longer hear my own voice. A darkness of depression became the blanket under which I smothered my own light.

Ironically, I was drawn to a career of listening to other people who needed to speak *their* truth—I became a licensed clinical professional counselor. I'm also sure that it's no coincidence that my own daughter would be born a "Spitfire" as well.

From the time that she could talk, my beautiful Rebecca didn't hold anything back. She was an intuitive, bright, and insightful child who needed less than a minute to size up any person or get to the heart of a conversation. Her outspokenness got her into trouble at school, and she had a hard time making new friends. There were times when her father and I would implore her to be quiet. Even though our "shushes" brought back memories of my own parents' demands for silence, I thought that I was *protecting*, not *silencing*, our daughter, shielding her from a world that refused to embrace difference, individualism, creativity, and sensitivity. But Rebecca wouldn't listen. She continually spoke her mind, shared her experience with people, and fought hard to be free of societal limitations and restraints.

Meanwhile, the embers of my own "fire" weren't doused . . . they still smoldered within me. As life went on, I developed an assortment of health challenges—including chronic pain and numbing fatigue—whose source couldn't clinically be determined. Later, I was diagnosed with acute thyroid disease. Despite wrestling with a broad array of symptoms, I continued my life routine as if everything were normal.

Then my mother-in-law died unexpectedly, and suddenly my health began to deteriorate. I developed an irregular heartbeat, which led to my being hospitalized due to the threat of a possible heart attack. I began to develop other symptoms that one doctor deemed alarming—as well as puzzling—because none of the medications he prescribed made any difference. I was rapidly losing weight, my hair was falling out, and I suffered from irritable bowel syndrome. The fatigue made it impossible for me to stay awake during counseling sessions. I felt hopeless, and helpless in my efforts to regain my health. It was then that I sought the help of Dr. Darren Weissman, whom I had been referred to by one of my clients.

When a person has been chronically ill and learns about an individual everyone is calling "a true healer," not only is there a glimmer of hope—there are high expectations. But as I was to learn during our first session three years ago, the compassionate holistic physician I met wasn't the person who would be doing the healing work. What Darren taught me was that the *true* healer responsible for the transformation of my health was *me.*

Using The LifeLine Technique as a guide to release trapped emotions within my subconscious mind and body, I partnered with Darren to learn The Five Basics for Optimal Health: water, food, rest, exercise, and owning my power. It was by taking full responsibility for my choices that my body and life began to regain balance. Reconnecting to my voice and owning my power was the most difficult—but liberating—work of all.

Within a month, my family, friends, colleagues, and clients noticed the difference, often commenting on the "new Gail." The doctors were at a loss to explain my newfound health. Not only did the medical doctor I was seeing significantly reduce the thyroid-medication dosage, but the irregular heartbeat disappeared.

I found myself turning 60, bursting with energy and awakened passion, and I felt as if I were in the prime of my life. As a result of treatments with The LifeLine Technique, I learned that the chronic numbing pain was my body's way of telling me that it was time to stop suppressing my feelings, time to stop smothering my voice. The moment I began owning my power and speaking my mind, the pain ceased.

But my newly discovered light was snuffed out less than a year after I first began my healing journey: My only daughter, Rebecca, took her own life at the age of 30, after suffering with bipolar disease. The utter shock of losing her so suddenly took my breath away; a piercing, unspeakable pain squeezed my heart. I was deeply wounded and, I believed, irreparably crippled—my will and desire to live vanished with the waning light.

Still, the first call I made from the hospital that night was to Darren. I knew that there was nothing he could "do," but I needed to tell him what had happened and connect with him on a deeply spiritual level in this time of unimaginable horror. He didn't disappoint me . . . he came to my home and did a LifeLine treatment during the most difficult period of my traumatic loss. I now realize that I was yearning to find a way to hold on. I needed to reconnect to the hope of being whole that I had only so recently resurrected.

Over the course of the 18 months that followed Rebecca's death, I struggled to feel the meaning and purpose of *my* life. There were times when I could barely get out of bed to visit Darren's office for treatments. But I kept going with the belief that one day I would not only be able to accept and understand my daughter's choices, but also somehow find a way to create something valuable from the ashes of this horrific tragedy.

Through The LifeLine Technique treatments, I found myself compelled to own my power and inner strength, and I had a new determination to help others find theirs. In 2005, my husband,

Norman, and I established the Rebecca Lynn Cutler Legacy of Life Foundation under the auspices of the Depression and Bipolar Support Alliance (DBSA) to enhance communication among people living with bipolar disease, their family, friends, and co-workers, so the isolation of those diagnosed might be eliminated. Our mission is to eradicate the shame felt by so many who suffer from the disorder and to help them find their voices. The logo for our foundation is a phoenix rising from the ashes. In addition, I've begun following a new career path, becoming a grief and recovery counselor. I vow to never be silent again.

In the spring of 2006, my sister and I took a trip to the Serengeti National Park in Tanzania on the continent of Africa. In the language of Swahili, *safari* simply means "journey," and it was during our "journey" that I realized how much my energy had shifted from focusing on Rebecca's death to carrying on the legacy of her life. I realized how much stronger I had become under unthinkable emotional stress.

At the end of our trip, our guide took us on one last midday safari across the veld. We were surprised to see a lion, our first during the entire trip, asleep beneath an acacia tree. While we watched, the animal rolled over on his back . . . he was missing his right hind leg! Our guide informed us that this lion had inadvertently become snared in a villager's trap intended for smaller animals. He not only lost his leg, but the snare also became embedded in his neck, cutting off his voice. By the time the rangers found the lion, he was nearly dead. But somehow he hadn't lost his will to live, surviving hyenas, vultures, and other predators who hovered patiently, awaiting his death.

The wounded lion immediately became a symbol of courage and hope, and scores of people rallied to save him. With their help, the lion learned to run on three legs, and his roar and command of life were revived.

I realized that the lion metaphorically represented my journey inward to owning *my* power. He taught me three profound lessons that day: (1) It takes courage to live life powerfully; (2) it is a decision, a choice, to face the next day; and (3) we need each other to heal, survive, and thrive.

I returned from the safari with renewed hope—and more than 100 pictures of that lion—grateful for the gift of my daughter's life and my awakening to the meaning of all these experiences. I wouldn't be able to accomplish the work I'm doing today had it not been for The LifeLine Technique and the power of Infinite Love & Gratitude.

The world keeps on turning and the sun continues rising daily. Each moment provides us with opportunities to embrace life with open arms and a full voice—or to endure it with closed hearts and silence. This book is for all people looking to discover the potential of their minds . . . a way to heal the wounded lion within their own hearts. I hope that in these pages you'll choose to own your power and take the journey of awakening your spirit amidst life's pain, fear, and challenges.

With Infinite Love & Gratitude,
— **Gail W. Cutler, M.A., L.C.P.C.**

# PREFACE

I t has been said, "At the point of complete darkness is the beginning of light." My journey, like that of so many, began as a "wounded healer."

I have memories as a child of feeling hopeless, suffering from multiple food and environmental allergies, asthma, and chronic ear infections. I received weekly allergy shots and used bronchial inhalers both preventively as well as during moments of labored breathing. At the age of seven, I had my tonsils and adenoids removed, and tubes were surgically implanted in my ears to "cure" the recurring infections that multiple rounds of antibiotics hadn't helped. There were many occasions when I was rushed to the emergency room for life-threatening asthma attacks. My eating choices consisted of fast food, Wonder Bread, Cocoa Puffs, pasta, soda, and many other foods that had a high sugar content.

My paradigm of health was shaped by my experiences and the beliefs and values of the society I was raised in. My parents, along with most people, used the medical model of taking a pill for every symptom as their primary frame of reference. Consequently, before I was old enough to learn my multiplication tables, I knew the names of more than a dozen medications that I was taking for symptoms I suffered from day in and day out. The pediatrician said that I'd be an asthmatic for the rest of my life.

Fortunately, my parents raised me with the belief that every challenge is an opportunity. I'm grateful for the health challenges that I experienced during my childhood—it's because of those adversities that I chose to step beyond the boundaries of what I knew to discover the answers that would truly enable my body and mind to heal. My journey to heal myself has taken me throughout the United States and around the world to Sri Lanka, China, and Belgium.

I've been on a mission to study with the most renowned healers and doctors of our time. I've been a sponge for information—reading books, watching videos, attending seminars, and learning from life's experiences. Everything I discovered became a stepping-stone for my own healing from the asthma and allergies, as well as an inguinal hernia, a left testicular mass, bulging discs, addiction, a ruptured Achilles tendon, learning disabilities, parasites, vitiligo, and a slew of other symptoms and challenges. Using natural healing modalities, I faced and conquered each of these seeming roadblocks. As a consequence, I developed a new and deeper understanding of the nature of symptoms. The culmination of my exploration has led me to awaken to a system of healing, the philosophy of which is the basis of this book. My journey to healing has helped me recognize that there is always hope in life . . . you just need to have determination, trust your intuition, and open your heart to find it.

For me, hope began with a telephone call. During the second semester of my sophomore year at the University of Kansas, where I was taking courses to prepare for medical school, my brother Howie was involved in a serious car accident. He initially was treated with muscle relaxants and anti-inflammatory drugs, but Howie soon discovered that the medications were unsuccessful and there were other unwanted side effects.

One month after the accident, he called to share an amazing experience: His body had completely recovered as the result of treatments by a chiropractic physician. I will always remember his exact words to me: "Darren, you've got to check out chiropractic! I think this is the profession for you."

I'd never been to a chiropractor and had no idea what they did. I looked in the telephone directory and began to call local practitioners in Lawrence, Kansas. Twenty calls later, I reached Dr. James Dray, who told me that he was in the process of relocating his office. If I helped him with the packing and moving, he said that he would teach me about chiropractic. I jumped at the opportunity.

After getting Dr. Dray settled into his new office, I spent time every day talking with him about chiropractic philosophy and the body's innate intelligence. He explained that the body is a self-healing organism, and that when the nervous system is in proper balance, it heals on its own. I remember Dr. Dray saying, "The power that created the body heals it. It happens no other way."

My passion was ignited, and I knew that pursuing a career in chiropractic was the right path for me. I majored in human biology and applied to the National College of Chiropractic, located in Lombard, Illinois. While in school there, I met Dr. Rei, an acupuncturist and chiropractor who helped me appreciate the natural connection between Chinese medicine and chiropractic. It was while I was studying acupuncture that I first began to understand the true nature of symptoms and the connection between the central nervous system and the acupuncture meridians—the pathways of energy where chi (life force) flows. I learned that the body speaks with symptoms when chi doesn't flow harmoniously through these meridians.

Upon graduating from chiropractic school, I began working in a multidisciplinary health center with Dr. Steven Ciolino, another angel along my journey. He helped me appreciate the work of Dr. George Goodheart, the founder of applied kinesiology (AK); and Dr. John Thie, the founder of Touch for Health. Through these practitioners, I learned about the intricate connection between the acupuncture meridians and the muscles of the body—how each individual muscle is associated with a complementary meridian, as well as specific organs of the body.

This insight helped me understand the body's functional and mechanical balance. I did my postgraduate work with Dr. Jon Sunderlage, a renowned chiropractor most noted for his pioneering electroacupuncture treatments. Dr. Sunderlage created a system of electroacupuncture based on the work of Robert Becker, M.D. Dr. Becker, author of *The Body Electric* and *Cross Currents,* is known for his research using electricity to facilitate regeneration. Dr. Sunderlage integrated Dr. Becker's work with electroacupuncture and Chinese medicine to aid the body's ability to regenerate.

If I hadn't seen it for myself, I would never have believed the effectiveness of Dr. Sunderlage's work. Even witnessing it, it was still hard to comprehend that his patients were able to regenerate fingers after gangrenous diabetic neuropathies. I shadowed Dr. Sunderlage on a weekly basis for two years. He's an exceptional person, teacher, and doctor with a heart as big as a whale.

In 1995, I developed an inguinal hernia, a condition that usually requires surgery. I began treating myself using Dr. Sunderlage's electroacupuncture system, which initiated the healing process. However, the real catalyst that led to my body's rapid recovery was meeting Dr. Steve Popkin, who had studied acupuncture with the late Lord Pandit Professor Dr. Sir Anton Jayasuriya of Sri Lanka, one of the most renowned holistic physicians in the world. Dr. Popkin's therapy consisted of placing two needles in specific points of my body. I continued to use these two points as part of my self-treatments, and the inguinal hernia healed in record time and without surgery.

Dr. Popkin and I immediately became great friends. He invited me to attend an international conference for holistic healers where Dr. Anton was the featured speaker. The weekend I spent at the conference was life changing. In addition to hearing Dr. Anton talk about his work in Sri Lanka, I met Dr. Ralph Alan Dale, an acupuncturist distinguished for his research and understanding of The Five Elements and holographic body parts. Afterward, I knew that I had to go to Sri Lanka to study.

Dr. Anton headed Medicina Alternativa, the alternative-healing department at the Kalubowila Hospital in Colombo, Sri Lanka. Calling it the "alternative"-healing department was quite ironic, however, because it was the busiest section of the entire facility! Students and doctors traveled from around the world to study with Dr. Anton, and the training was both intense and illuminating.

There were 20 students present during the time I trained at Kalubowila. We worked seven days a week, between the hours of 8 A.M. and 10 P.M., seeing anywhere between 300 and 500 people daily. All were treated for free, and the patients were afflicted with every symptom imaginable, including common colds, allergies, Parkinson's disease, diabetes, traumatic injuries, kidney disease, tennis elbow, sciatica, inflammatory bowel disease, schizophrenia, alopecia, cancer, and elephantiasis. We cared for everyone with natural modalities: acupuncture, chiropractic, craniosacral therapy, homeopathy, herbology, laser therapy, homeopuncture, Ayurvedic medicine, essential oils, chakra balancing, and BioGeometry using pyramids. Most of the patients had phenomenal results.

I was very fortunate to be the only chiropractor working at the hospital during the training: Every musculoskeletal condition was referred to me, and I had the amazing opportunity to get to know Dr. Anton on a personal level. Working with him expanded my perception of the possibilities for helping the human body heal with the integration of so many natural healing modalities unified at one center.

In 1996, I participated in the World Congress of Alternative Medicine. At the Congress I was introduced to lamas, Tibetan monks, shamans, and many other indigenous healers from around the world. These men and women were examples of a long tradition of people who had learned the ways of the universe and both recognized and accepted the infinite potential that human beings have to heal and become whole. I was in awe of the diverse group who had traveled from more than 60 countries to participate in the World Congress. There were lectures about every aspect of healing, covering the spectrum from color therapy and chakras to pranic healing and plant alchemy.

On my journey home from Sri Lanka, I visited Drs. Thomas Bayne and Ingrid Maes in Belgium. Tom ran a chiropractic practice in Ostend with Ingrid and helped manage the largest nutritional company in all of Europe. His specialty was (and still is) natural healing using wholefood nutritional supplements, including herbal botanical products that assist the body with detoxification.

One of the great treasures of Belgium is its chocolate, and I ate several pieces the first day that I arrived. I hadn't had any chocolate during the time I studied in Sri Lanka, and my body responded with a stomachache. Despite not feeling well, I went to dinner with Tom and Ingrid at the home of their friend Dr. Philippe Lanckriet. After the meal, Philippe told me that he could get rid of the pain I was experiencing. Although I didn't tell him what I'd eaten, within minutes of using a healing modality called Total Body Modification (TBM), not only did

Philippe inform me that my body was having a reaction to chocolate, but the stomachache was gone. I was very excited by the experience and asked Philippe several questions. After explaining the process, he encouraged me to study with Dr. Victor Frank, the developer of TBM, noting that this was the key to understanding "the root of healing."

Shortly after returning to the U.S., I sought out Dr. Frank and began to learn about TBM. Over the course of six years, I studied it with great enthusiasm and became very close to Dr. Frank—I still consider him a second father. He's worked tirelessly to share with the world TBM's incredible potential for healing the body. He is a living testament to its power and efficacy, having used TBM treatment to confront and defy death multiple times.

In 1997, I returned to Sri Lanka to continue my training and to participate in the World Congress of Alternative Medicine for a second time. I introduced TBM to the healers and doctors in the Congress and received wonderful feedback. Incorporating the knowledge I'd acquired from my diverse training, this modality became the catalyst for my awakening. Every year at TBM research seminars, where holistic physicians from around the world gathered and shared their discoveries, I presented what I'd learned from synthesizing my knowledge and developing treatments for those who came to me with health challenges. I received multiple awards for these presentations, as well as acknowledgment of how the techniques I taught were helping people throughout the world. It was also through TBM that I met Dr. Scott Walker, the developer of Neuro Emotional Technique (NET). I attended many of Dr. Walker's seminars, and his work has helped me understand the relationship between emotions and symptoms.

My first major test since being introduced to the many disciplines of holistic medicine was disguised as a mass in my left testicle. Despite the negative thoughts that filled my mind, I held true to the belief that every symptom and challenge is an opportunity for change and healing. I was determined to discover the meaning of why my body had developed a growth within my testicle, and to do whatever it took to heal.

Dr. Frank recommended that I see Bob Warwick, a man who has been nicknamed "the Wizard." Bob became my mentor and friend, further opening the doors of my mind. My body reabsorbed the mass completely on its own and without surgery. It took approximately a year, and I continued to study and train with Bob for the next three— I now know why he's called the Wizard.

~

Ultimately, my endeavor to discover the true cause of symptoms began as a child. My journey through the darkness of health challenges took me around the world to train with some of the greatest minds in holistic healing. My studies and experiences, along with my work with countless patients, culminated in my awakening to the power of Infinite Love & Gratitude. The process, including how and why the dots connect, is explained in detail in this book.

The use of the words *Infinite Love & Gratitude* as a healing modality is both new and revolutionary. Called The LifeLine Technique, this treatment not only pinpoints and corrects the *source* of imbalance in the body that manifests as symptoms, disease, or personal challenges— the internalized, denied, or disconnected emotions stored in your subconscious mind—it helps the body heal. Many times the results are *immediate.* From releasing old traumas and embracing life with passion to creating optimal health and increasing your potential for wealth, opening your heart to the power of Infinite Love & Gratitude will provide you with all the resources and tools necessary to achieve optimal well-being.

To some people, these claims may seem blasphemous. I understand. During the course of my study and in my own work with patients, there have been times when the outcome of the treatment so defied the traditional medical paradigm that it was soul shaking. Nevertheless, I have continued this effort because the actual *proof* is in the results. The health and well-being of thousands of people have been transformed. Let me share a few of their stories with you:

— Jake, who is in his late 40s, was diagnosed with diabetes. He was prescribed insulin, and as soon as he began to take it, he started to lose his vision. He underwent multiple laser surgeries to slow or reverse the retinal damage that had occurred in his eyes. Unfortunately, they were unsuccessful, and Jake was diagnosed as legally blind. After a month of my treatments, his blood-sugar metabolism was perfectly balanced, and he no longer needed to take insulin. Jake's eyes have begun to regenerate, and he is now able to drive during the day. He's been off insulin for three years.

— Sharon, a woman in her early 30s, had seen a number of fertility specialists to help her discover why she and her husband weren't able to conceive. After five years of tests, medications, and psychological trauma, Sharon was feeling hopeless and frustrated. However, following two months of treatments, Sharon became pregnant and now has two beautiful children. (I've been blessed to help nearly 50 couples have kids—parents who were once told they were infertile.)

— Lana, age 35, had suffered from chronic depression her entire life. Despite years of psychotherapy and taking a variety of antidepressants, nothing lifted away the gray cloud above her head. The Lifeline Technique enabled Lana to release the subconscious roadblocks that were at the root of the physical and emotional pain she was feeling. Using The Five Basics for Optimal Health (water, food, rest, exercise, and owning her power), Lana is now empowered with the tools to experience a life of joy and gratitude. She realizes that she's not a victim of depression—rather, the condition was the way her body let her know that she had disconnected from her truth.

— Phyllis, a woman in her late 40s, had been suffering with a severe case of psoriasis since she was 19. She had attempted to cure it by using many different forms of medication and natural remedies, but nothing seemed to help the very uncomfortable skin condition. By using The LifeLine Technique, we determined why her body was *communicating* through the symptom of psoriasis and corrected the imbalance. In less than a year, Phyllis's skin had healed 95 percent.

— Liam, a newborn baby of two weeks, had an extremely traumatic birth. The doctors had used metal forceps to remove him from his mother's womb, and his brachial plexus (the nerves in the neck that travel into the arms) were torn. Liam was unable to lift his left arm or turn his head. His mother brought him to my office after consulting with a neurosurgeon. The doctor had told her that Liam would need multiple operations to correct the damage from the injury, but that her child would still remain permanently disabled. Within two months of being treated, Liam healed without ever needing surgery. The only remnant of the traumatic birth is a slight winging of his left scapula.

— Arlene, a woman in her late 60s, was challenged with macular holes in both her eyes, a condition that is self-limiting and results in blindness. After three weeks of treatments, her ophthalmologist stated that the macular holes had healed 100 percent.

— Jodi was a woman in her late 40s who had lost her will to live. She had been severely abused physically and sexually by family members when she was a child. She coped with the emotional and sexual trauma by cutting herself, using the pain to numb and cover up the severe anguish of her early experiences. Because of the horrifying memories, she wouldn't allow herself to become involved in an intimate relationship. Since being treated, Jodi has ceased to have thoughts of cutting herself. Not only is she no longer haunted by the trauma of her childhood, she's been in a healthy relationship for the past two years.

Every day I experience miracles like these, witnessing people's transformations as they discover how their subconscious thoughts, feelings, and limiting beliefs have impeded their ability to heal or achieve greatness. Infinite Love & Gratitude is the key to unlocking the subconscious prison that has trapped us for far too long. Once the portal is open, we are free to soar—free to embrace our unlimited potential and live healthy, fulfilling lives.

My ultimate goal in writing this book is to teach and empower people. More important, I believe it is my moral obligation to share the simplicity and profundity of the power of Infinite Love & Gratitude so that we can all heal our lives and thus create a more peaceful world.

Thank you in advance for joining me on this journey.

— **Dr. Darren R. Weissman**

# PART I

# THE AWAKENING

*Whispers from above, beyond,*
*beckoning the heart that sighs*
*lost in slumber, gaining strength*
*from the mires now to rise,*
*first a breath, then to see*
*all that one was meant to be*
*has always been,*
*though in disguise, now the Light to realize,*
*then resonates my soul to sing*
*. . . it's time for the Awakening.*

— Ranel Gretebeck

# CHAPTER 1

# THE WORLD IS
# NO LONGER FLAT

It's only been a few years since the beginning of the 21st century, which was hailed as a new dawn for humanity. And yet, these are paradoxical times. From the catastrophe of war, terrorism, pestilence, disease, and pollution to the extinction of many forms of life on the planet, we have become eyewitnesses to the greatest changes and challenges humankind has ever faced. We can no longer pretend that the world is the same. Our perception—the way we experience our environment—is forcing us to look around with wide-open eyes.

This transition isn't without precedent. In 1491, most people believed that the earth was flat. Anyone who sailed a ship into the sunset, it was thought, would likely reach the end of the world and tumble into the depths of hell. That perception changed in 1492 when Christopher Columbus discovered the New World, along with the fact that the earth was actually round. What a difference a year can make!

Think about Isaac Newton: When an apple fell on his head and he wondered, *Why did that happen?* he discovered the law of gravity. Some time later, Galileo discovered other aspects of gravity, such as the different rates of speed at which objects fall and the impact of wind resistance. Perhaps a better, more accurate word than *discovered*, however, is *awakened*. After all, the law of gravity existed before Newton and Galileo, just as the New World existed before Columbus arrived.

With a new awareness of gravity, some people began to look to the sky and see birds in a different way. They started to fold paper in unique configurations, creating objects that could float in the air. Their perception changed . . . they *awakened*. Human beings, they realized, had the potential to fly—so they made wing-shaped contraptions and began jumping off cliffs (some to their deaths). Everyone called them crazy. But after many disasters, the Wright brothers developed the Flyer I in Kitty Hawk, North Carolina, and took to the skies. In December of 1903, Orville and Wilbur changed the course of humankind by awakening to the potential of powered flight. Think about it! It's only been a little more than 100 years since the famous flight of the Flyer I. The brothers didn't realize at the time that they were learning what the birds already knew: the law of aerodynamics—the right combination of velocity, lift, and pressure corresponds to the ability to fly (or crash).

It was Albert Einstein's *awakening* to the theory of relativity, $E = mc^2$, that has become the bridge between modern-day physics and what we now call energy healing (which The LifeLine Technique is based on). Einstein was seeking to understand the gravitational force on a falling object when he *awakened* to this powerful formula. $E$ refers to energy, $m$ defines mass, and $c$ is the speed of light. The closer an object's mass moves toward the speed of light, the greater its density and the gravitational pull on it. Einstein's theory states that if the object doesn't have enough potential energy to arrive at the speed of light, then the density and gravitational pull acting on it causes it to stop. However, when the mass *reaches* the speed of light, it's converted into energy.

The science of quantum physics further demonstrates that everything in the universe is composed of energy and is always in motion. The varying states of matter—solid, liquid, and gas—represent the different frequencies of energy, and the rate at which energy moves determines the physical state of matter. How life flows through us determines the nature of the stream of energy through the body.

There is a "pinnacle" law, like the law of aerodynamics, that reinforces Einstein's theory of relativity and quantum physics. It is The LifeLine Law of Transformation and Creation: *Emotions transform energy; energy creates movement; movement is change; and change is the essence of life.* The body is very much like a computer: It responds in a binary (on/off) manner. Every time you experience an emotion, your brain produces an electrical frequency that instantly sends signals and patterns throughout its mass, as well as to every cell in your body. Depending on the positive or negative—optimistic or pessimistic—content of that emotion, its vibratory frequency creates movement or blocks it within your physical body. Consequently, the direction of your health is dependent upon the unfettered flow of energy to and from the brain. The challenge is that 98 percent of the mind is subconscious. *When life experiences move freely through the subconscious mind, the body is able to heal.*

It's interesting to note the connection between physics and linguistics, and how they segue to help us understand the process of healing. Energy in motion is literally *E*-motion. How the body is transformed by emotions depends on the regenerative or degenerative cycle in which it expresses itself—that is, a cycle of health or of disease. The trillions of cells that form the body are constantly breaking down and rebuilding in a circadian rhythm . . . this process is called *life.* In order to heal, light or energy must be able to flow through the physical body unimpeded. As in Einstein's theory of relativity, when this energy does so, the density or gravitational pull on the body increases. This increase forces the body to go through a process of detoxification or purification. The poisons, toxins, and blockages that have accumulated over time are released, and the body is able to regenerate.

Contrary to conventional medicine's paradigm of symptom relief, it is energy that promotes the body's self-healing potential. In Chinese healing, energy or life force is referred to as *chi;* in the Ayurvedic tradition, it's called *prana.*

The LifeLine Technique works by balancing the energy of the body to help people release stress and signs of illness. Symptoms are a result of stored poisons, toxins, or blockages caused by the subconscious internalization or denial of—and disconnection from—emotions. It's by reconnecting to the feelings that have been trapped within the subconscious mind that we can achieve optimal health.

### The New Frontier of Healing

Energy healing facilitates the movement of the spirit, creating a more harmonious connection between the body and the universe. The more balanced your connection is to the world around you, the better you'll feel . . . the better your life force will flow. Just as we use energy from the earth to make our lives easier—from cell phones and satellites to e-mail and television—as human beings, we harness energy to both assess and optimize health.

We evaluate wellness by measuring the body's electrical potential. Think about it: An electrocardiogram (EKG) measures the electrical activity of the heart. When an EKG is "flatline," an individual's body no longer has the potential to maintain its energetic life force, and that person is pronounced dead. The brain's activity is assessed with an electroencephalogram (EEG). Muscles are gauged with an electromyogram (EMG). It's because of the body's electromagnetic field that we're able to view different anatomical parts with magnetic resonance imaging (MRI).

Now take a moment to visualize clouds floating across the sky and waves moving over the surface of water. The energy that pushes the clouds or water is the same force that manifests itself within the physical movement of your body. By learning to unleash the blocked energy within, you'll unlock your infinite potential to achieve optimal health and well-being.

What I know to be true and what the power of Infinite Love & Gratitude and The LifeLine Technique has proven is this: *The greatest obstacle to your health and well-being is the subconscious disconnection from your emotions.*

### Learning the Body's Language

Paying attention to symptoms is the key to understanding what's going on in your body. They are how the body "speaks." Some of them may be quite obvious, while others are so subtle that you regard them as normal functions. Either way, symptoms are symphonies that the body composes to get your attention.

Your body speaks only when necessary, and symptoms are the way it says: "I don't want this in me any longer," or "I'm not happy with the way you're treating me." Your body loves you; it communicates to help you appreciate that you're in danger. I tell all my patients that symptoms are gifts from their physical selves. These gifts, however, arrive in very strange wrapping paper. Whether they include headaches, stomach pain, diarrhea, nausea, fatigue, low-back pain, depression, panic, anxiety, inflammatory bowel disease, or cancer, symptoms are the body's way of saying, "I am out of balance."

These imbalances occur emotionally, structurally, biochemically, or spiritually. When you indiscriminately take a pharmaceutical drug to address a symptom, you're basically telling your body to "shut up," impairing its ability to heal. Emergency medicine is superb for saving lives in times of crisis. However, popping a pill for every ailment without addressing the underlying cause inhibits the body's natural capacity to heal itself. It's the same as taking the battery out of a fire detector in your home: Without the battery, the alarm can't alert you to danger. Even worse, the problem escalates—by suppressing symptoms, you mask the body's ability to warn you of danger lurking within.

Emotions can be defined as the energy that moves us. Considering that energy is always in motion, when we disconnect from, internalize, or deny an emotion, that energy takes a wrong turn that often keeps us stuck in a maze. Every time these buried emotions are triggered, the body becomes compromised and has to compensate, leaving it at risk for injury or opportunistic pathogens. Recurrent symptoms and chronic stress are the warning signs that emotions are trapped within the subconscious mind.

Symptoms start long before we become conscious of them. They usually begin as an uncomfortable feeling. When ignored, that uncomfortable feeling—that is, the emotion that we internalized, denied, or disconnected from—manifests in the body as an imbalance. This leads to stagnation or leakage of life force, which results in symptoms, depending upon where the problem is located. If left unchecked, the imbalance becomes a pattern of "dis-ease," and eventually pathology, that will devastate the body on every level.

The current medical-industry paradigm is to treat and suppress symptoms. For every symptom, your allopathic (medical) doctor is likely to write a prescription for you. Yet chronic diseases are at an all-time high—very few people are getting well. In our nation alone, hypertension, diabetes, and obesity are rampant in *every* age-group. Not one medication on the market cures these illnesses. Insulin, for example, doesn't eliminate diabetes. And doctors never say that chemotherapy, radiation, or surgery cures cancer; instead, they state that the cancer is "in remission."

Of course, the doctor's intention is to alleviate the symptoms and help people get well. Many of the medications they prescribe, however, have what physicians refer to as *side effects.* I think that's a funny term: They're not "side" effects—they're the *direct effects caused by the pharmaceutical drugs,* and they create additional symptoms for which you're usually encouraged to take *more medication.* At that point, you're taking additional drugs for *symptoms caused by the original medication.* The cycle has spiraled out of control. What happens in the interim? By not listening to what your body was telling you in the first place, you've made it weaker and more vulnerable.

Just remember that nobody knows more about you than you. No one sees life through your eyes, hears with your ears, smells through your nose, tastes with your mouth, feels through your skin, or is aware of your intuition as acutely as you are. Once you embrace the fact that the natural state of the body is health and wholeness, you'll never look at a symptom in the same way again. As the late Supreme Court justice Oliver Wendell Holmes remarked, "Man's mind, once stretched by a new idea, never regains its original dimensions." Once you know, you know forever, and that means you must be authentic in how you live your life.

The LifeLine Technique locates the disruption in the flow of energy and releases it immediately, targeting the cause of disease. Sometimes the symptom will go away with one treatment. On other occasions, the process involves a journey to awaken your spirit. The LifeLine Technique doesn't work inside a vacuum. It requires that you make the necessary adjustments to your lifestyle in order to maintain your body's balance. The Five Basics for Optimal Health include the quantity, quality, and frequency of water consumption, food intake, rest, exercise, and owning your power . . . these are the keys to helping the body tap in to its innate potential to heal.

### You Can Heal

I know this to be true: You already possess the power and the ability to heal. No matter how serious the illness or how catastrophic the event, the body has the miraculous capacity to regenerate, rejuvenate, and revitalize itself. What does it mean to heal? I like the definition written by author Debbie Shapiro in her book, *Your Body Speaks Your Mind:*

> To be healed means to become whole. . . . Becoming whole means bringing all of ourselves into the light, leaving nothing in the dark, no matter how disturbing or painful it may be. It is an embracing of all the parts we have ignored, denied, tried to push away or eliminate. Healing brings all of this into the conscious mind, into our hearts, into our lives.

When I was a child, the pediatrician told my mother that I had asthma, a condition that he said I would suffer with for the rest of my life. The process of treating it included very painful shots for many years, and I was told that I had to use bronchial inhalers to prevent asthma attacks. I internalized the belief that being diagnosed with asthma made me weaker than other people.

The last asthma attack occurred when I was 22 and in chiropractic school. I'll never forget struggling to study for an exam while I waited in the emergency room to be administered an adrenaline shot because I was gasping for air. It was the asthma, along with other health challenges, that propelled my journey to become whole. Ultimately, I realized that there's no such thing as a "cure" in the world of allopathic medicine, and if I was going to truly heal, I would need to embrace all the parts of myself that I'd internalized, denied, or disconnected from.

You are your own healer. Once you *awaken* to how your subconscious mind impacts your life, as well as to The Five Basics for Optimal Health, your body will be able to create balance and naturally mend itself. The process of healing is a spiritual journey, the evolutionary voyage to awakening your spirit. And the first step begins with *choosing* to own your power and to feel.

I've been engaged in an ongoing process of study and practice to help individuals understand the power they already have within themselves to heal from dis-ease and lead healthy and fulfilled lives. Through my work as a holistic physician and doctor of chiropractic healing, I've incorporated multiple traditions and treatment modalities, ranging from the ancient medicine of the barefoot Chinese doctors to the frontiers of energy medicine. These experiences have culminated in *my* awakening to the power of Infinite Love & Gratitude and The LifeLine Technique—which corrects the emotional, structural, and biochemical imbalances of the body and reconnects it to the spirit, facilitating the healing process.

Awakening to the power of Infinite Love & Gratitude was akin to understanding that the world isn't flat and that humankind has the ability to fly. Infinite Love & Gratitude is the connection—the thread that weaves together the complex matrix of the mind, body, and spirit. It enables you to embrace the internal matrix that exists in everyone, linking you to nature and the laws of the entire universe.

One person's ability to believe in the power of his or her own imagination can, and indeed has, changed the course of the planet. Look up in the sky on any given day and you'll see airplanes and helicopters. Turn on the news and you'll receive your information via satellite and hear about spacecraft venturing in search of new worlds. All of that is possible because people believed in themselves and their dreams.

For those who understand engineering, physics, and chemistry, the achievements launched by the Wright brothers' vision may seem quite simple. In many ways, The LifeLine Technique is a product of that simplicity, and that's why it's so effective. It may take some time to master it, but the basic principles of healing are very straightforward: love, balance, and authenticity. Once awakened to The Five Basics for Optimal Health and The LifeLine Law of Transformation and Creation, both laypeople and healing-arts professionals can easily comprehend and utilize these principles.

### Healing the World

I'm not a spiritual guru professing to know the way. Rather, The LifeLine Technique is part of the continuum of natural-healing knowledge that began with the ancient arts of Chinese and Ayurvedic medicine. That chain includes acupuncture, chakras, shamanism, homeopathy, chiropractic, applied kinesiology, Total Body Modification (TBM), Neuro Emotional Technique (NET), Neuro-Linguistic Programming (NLP), psychoneuroimmunology, Eye Movement Desensitization and Reprocessing (EMDR), and many other forms of energy healing. It is based on thousands of years of empirical investigation, documented research, and biomedical evidence.

Along with my colleague and collaborator, Dr. Tom Bayne, my journey toward further development of The LifeLine Technique continues. At our health center, The Way to Optimal Health, we have successfully treated the energy imbalances of thousands of people in a clinical environment, leading them on a path to balance and healing. I believe that it's imperative to teach people how to take full responsibility for their lives and heal themselves. My goal is to enable you to understand the language your body uses to communicate and to empower you with healthy lifestyles. My mission is to help heal the world, one person at a time.

The LifeLine Technique enhances the current paradigms of allopathic *and* holistic medicine. It's the key to restoring the health and vitality of everyone . . . to both imagining and creating a world full of awareness, health, respect, and love. It's the key to *our awakening* to the magnificent and unlimited capacity we possess as human beings, and it's the bridge to a bright future.

During their first treatment, people who are referred to my office often display the attitude *I'm here, but I'm a skeptic.* I like skepticism; I believe it's healthy—it means you're at least open. You'll ask questions, you won't follow simply because someone tells you to, and you'll more than likely pay attention to your gut. No matter what, you'll make your own decision.

I encourage you to approach this book with skepticism. But once you've read it, after you witness the phenomenal power of Infinite Love & Gratitude and The LifeLine Technique, you'll know that you have unlimited options for healing . . . and your world will never again be flat.

~ ~ ~

# Chapter 2

# Awakening

Looking back, I realize that each experience and teacher, and everything I studied, ultimately played a part in my awakening to the power of Infinite Love & Gratitude. Each modality I learned and used provided a piece of my personal puzzle: How could I best help the people I treated? Based on what I already knew, the patients I treated made progress . . . however, there was still something missing.

During the summer of 1998, my cousin Rob Morgan worked as an intern in my office in preparation for becoming the first deaf chiropractor ever to graduate from the Palmer College of Chiropractic. After a full day of observing my work with patients, Rob turned to me and held up his hand in a gesture that I was later to learn means "I love you" in sign language. I was amazed by the warm, powerful, and peaceful feeling I experienced as Rob made this sign. Intrigued by my internal reaction, I asked Rob to hold his arm up as I assessed different reflex points on his body using a muscle test. Depending on what's being measured, this type of test uses an indicator muscle to evaluate the balance or integrity of the body. When the muscle becomes weak after being pressed, it's a signal that there's an imbalance present or the body's integrity is being compromised.

When I found a weak reflex point, I held my hand next to his body in the "I love you" sign mode. The reflex in Rob's arm instantly became stronger. I didn't realize then the impact of that moment. . . . It would take another three years for all the pieces to fall into place.

To my amazement, the missing link that eventually tied it all together came via e-mail. I logged on to the Internet to check my messages: There was one from my friend Greg. In the subject line, he wrote: "This is going to fascinate you." The body of the e-mail said: "Darren, of everyone I know, I thought you would appreciate this the most." I clicked on the URL at the bottom of the message, and a picture of a crystal—one of the most delicate and uniquely formed that I'd ever seen—popped up on my screen.

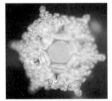

Love and Gratitude

I studied the photo for a long time, drawn to the intricacies of its core and the brilliance of its facets. Even on the computer screen, it seemed to twinkle. It was the work of Masaru Emoto, a doctor of alternative medicine and a visionary researcher based in Japan. Dr. Emoto had made an amazing discovery:

> Human vibrational energy—thoughts, words, ideas, and music—affects the molecular structure of water. It is the very same water that comprises over 70 percent of a mature human body and covers the same amount of our planet. Water is the very source of all life on this planet; its quality and integrity is vitally important to all forms of life. The body is very much like a sponge and is composed of trillions of chambers called cells that hold liquid. The quality of our life is directly connected to the quality of our water.

For more than a century, scientists and researchers have been seeking to understand the "true" nature of water and its value for living beings. Naturalist and scientist Johann Grander was one of the first to note that water is like a liquid tape recorder, storing information and vibratory frequencies. Viktor Schauberger's research took this a step further, revealing that water in its natural state moves with a spiraling, or vortex, action, which gives it its vitality or "livingness."

Dr. Emoto built upon existing knowledge about water's characteristics. He demonstrated not only its vitality, but also how environment affects its molecular structure. Using a dark-field microscope that had photographic capabilities, he documented his work in his monumental book *Messages from Water*. Dr. Emoto conducted numerous series of experiments in which he froze samples of water in vials, extracting some of the frozen crystals and examining them under the dark-field microscope, where he photographed his results.

In his first samples of the water from different cities in Japan, Dr. Emoto found tremendous discrepancies:

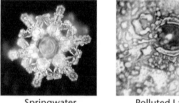

Springwater          Polluted Lake

The crystals from heavily polluted water were distorted and random, while water from pristine mountain streams and springs showed beautifully formed geometric designs in crystalline patterns. Based on his initial findings, Dr. Emoto decided to expose the water to sound, using Mozart, Bach, Beethoven, Kawachi folk music, and heavy-metal music.

Mozart's Symphony          Bach's          Beethoven's
no. 40 in G Minor          Air for G String          *Pastorale*

Kawachi Folk Music      Heavy-Metal Music

Following this series of experiments, Dr. Emoto and his team of researchers examined how thoughts and words affected the formation of untreated, distilled water crystals. He typed words in different languages onto paper and then taped them to glass bottles. The bottles were frozen, and the next day water crystals were extracted, examined under a dark-field microscope, and photographed. Once again, Dr. Emoto's results showed variation in the formation of each and every crystal, depending on the words used.

Distilled Water

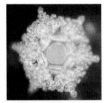

Love and Gratitude     Thank You     Beautiful

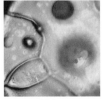

You Make Me Sick     You Fool     Dirty
I Will Kill You

In another group of experiments, Dr. Emoto's team of researchers placed water on a table. Seventeen participants stood in a circle around the table, holding hands. Each person spoke a beautiful word of his or her choice to the water, such as *unity, love,* or *friendship.* The team took before and after photographs of the water crystals. Not only did the crystals change, the team was excited to discover, but the results were instantaneous.

Tap Water Before
Positive Intention

Tap Water After
Positive Intention

Dr. Emoto's work provides tangible evidence that thoughts, words, ideas, and sound affect the molecular structure of water. He has demonstrated how easily water takes on the vibrations and energy of its environment. Moreover, his studies document that the effects are immediate. Because we're composed of 75 to 90 percent water, his research shows that our bodies are extremely sensitive to emotions, thoughts, the music we listen to, and the food we eat. I knew immediately that Dr. Emoto's research had tremendous implications for understanding the emotional, structural, biochemical, and spiritual well-being of the human body.

I forwarded copies of the e-mail to my colleague Dr. Tom Bayne and printed one for the office so that our patients could read it while they waited for an appointment. As I was to discover, Dr. Emoto's work was the missing link I'd been searching for.

Building upon existing holistic models, I'd already awakened to a wide range of natural-healing techniques to address the emotional, biochemical, structural, and spiritual components of health. I've always been able to enhance healing on an energetic level using minimal information. Many times during public presentations, I was asked when

I was going to merge all the techniques I'd awakened to into one comprehensive system.

When Tom and I first began to collaborate at The Way to Optimal Health, we spent endless hours of our free time brainstorming in an effort to find or create what we knew was out there somewhere: the single key to helping people truly heal themselves. Each innovation brought us closer, but we were at a loss as to what would unlock the giant steel door to the technique that would profoundly improve the quality of people's lives.

During dinner with Tom; his wife, Ingrid; and my then fiancée (now wife), Sara, the answer emerged.

"Well?" prompted Ingrid.

"Well, what?" responded Tom.

"So what's the new technique?" she asked. "You've been at it for months now. Tell us about it."

Tom and I looked at each other like two puppies caught chewing on a new shoe.

"Not yet," I said.

"We're still working on it," Tom added.

"Can I be honest with you, Darren?" Ingrid asked.

"Yeah, of course," I replied.

"I think the reason you haven't come up with the technique is because you're just too scared of how powerful it will be."

I'll never forget that moment. We all looked at her, and the only thing I could do was nod my head.

Later that night, I paced the floor of my home and talked to Sara. Over and over, I could hear Ingrid's voice in my head saying: *"You're just too scared."* What happened next might sound mystical, but I know of no other way to describe it: One minute I was talking to Sara, and the next, the room suddenly froze. I could hear Sara's voice, but I was no longer able to make out her words. It was as if the top of my head opened and a surge of energy ringed it, sending shivers from my brain down to my arms and fingers. My hands felt tingly, then numb.

"I need a pen and paper!" I abruptly yelled to Sara. "Hurry, babe. I think I've got it!"

Within minutes, I drew lines, made circles, and wrote words without saying anything. Sara would later tell me that when I finished, I looked so calm and peaceful that my face was "iridescent."

"Will you let me use it on you?" I asked, looking up from the paper where I had just scribbled what was to be called "The LifeLine Flow Chart."

Sara had been having neck pain for quite a while. I asked her to pinpoint the discomfort and describe it on a scale of 1–10. I told her to hold her arm at a 90-degree angle from her body to do muscle testing, and then I began to go through the flow chart. Every time Sara's arm went weak, I would hold my hand in the "I love you" sign and say the words *Infinite Love & Gratitude.* The pain in Sara's neck changed locations and decreased in intensity. I ran the flow chart again. Minutes later, the pain was gone.

"What *is* that?" Sara asked in amazement.

"I'm not sure," I responded. "It came through me like a lightning bolt. I just know this is *it!*"

Although I didn't have any symptoms myself, I decided to run the flow chart on myself, using Sara as a surrogate for muscle testing. When I finished, I felt strong, clearheaded, and focused. There was a powerful energy running through my body.

The next day at the office, I took Tom aside to explain the flow chart before we saw our first patients. I knew that I was standing at the threshold. He was very excited and ready to use it, but I first wanted to see how the morning patients responded. I promised to report back to him after lunch. I treated 20 patients who had a multitude of issues, including sinus infection, cold, neck pain, fatigue, headache, knee pain, and panic attack. Everyone responded instantly, leaving the office that day virtually symptom free.

After finishing with the morning patients, I taught Tom the technique. For the rest of the day, and in subsequent weeks, we used the flow chart as our primary modality for rebalancing the energy in our patients' bodies. We compared notes and continued to modify and refine the flow chart every time we learned something new. Within a week, our office manager designed the flow chart on the computer.

The moment The LifeLine Flow Chart channeled through me, I realized that every system of natural medicine I'd previously studied was actually just a piece of the puzzle. This was the missing thread necessary for weaving all the pieces together into a unified system of healing. But more than just a systematic approach, The LifeLine Flow Chart provides the narrative for explaining what's *really* going on by translating the language of the body and subconscious mind—symptoms—into simple and accessible information that can be used to heal.

Since first awakening to the power of Infinite Love & Gratitude, I've treated thousands of patients and have been on a mission to teach people the simplicity of The Lifeline Technique. Every single day I learn something new, and that's part of the beauty and wonder of the treatment. The moment one door is opened, there's another one behind it. I'm humbly honored to be both a trailblazer and a witness.

I wrote this book from both these perspectives. My goal is to share the philosophy behind every aspect of The LifeLine Technique with you—from the independent and interdependent mechanism of each system, to how they harmoniously and completely unite to balance the mind, body, and spirit. Throughout these pages, I'll share different examples of treatments using The LifeLine Technique and the *subconscious* story behind the symptoms that each patient experienced. Some of this information will be viewed as heretical, or even blasphemous. However, keep in mind that, from the shape of our planet to our ability to walk on the moon, every revolutionary idea that's changed the course of human history has been met with skepticism, denial, and cries of heresy.

# The Way to Optimal Health LifeLine - Flow Chart™

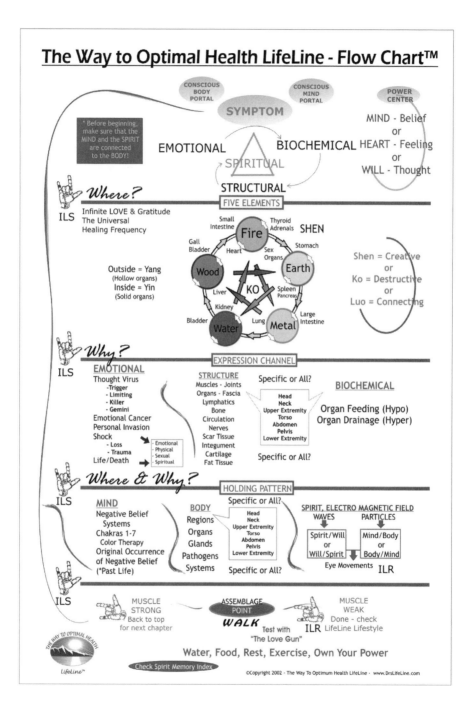

CONSCIOUS BODY PORTAL

CONSCIOUS MIND PORTAL

POWER CENTER

SYMPTOM

MIND - Belief
or
HEART - Feeling
or
WILL - Thought

* Before beginning, make sure that the MIND and the SPIRIT are connected to the BODY!

EMOTIONAL    BIOCHEMICAL

SPIRITUAL

STRUCTURAL

**Where?**

ILS

Infinite LOVE & Gratitude
The Universal
Healing Frequency

FIVE ELEMENTS

Small Intestine    Thyroid Adrenals    SHEN

Fire

Gall Bladder    Heart    Sex Organs    Stomach

Outside = Yang
(Hollow organs)
Inside = Yin
(Solid organs)

Wood    Earth

Liver    KO    Spleen Pancreas

Kidney

Bladder    Lung    Large Intestine

Water    Metal

Shen = Creative
or
Ko = Destructive
or
Luo = Connecting

**Why?**

ILS

EXPRESSION CHANNEL

EMOTIONAL
Thought Virus
-Trigger
- Limiting
- Killer
- Gemini
Emotional Cancer
Personal Invasion
Shock
- Loss
- Trauma
Life/Death

- Emotional
- Physical
- Sexual
- Spiritual

STRUCTURE
Muscles - Joints
Organs - Fascia
Lymphatics
Bone
Circulation
Nerves
Scar Tissue
Integument
Cartilage
Fat Tissue

Specific or All?

Head
Neck
Upper Extremity
Torso
Abdomen
Pelvis
Lower Extremity

Specific or All?

BIOCHEMICAL

Organ Feeding (Hypo)
Organ Drainage (Hyper)

**Where & Why?**

ILS

HOLDING PATTERN

MIND
Negative Belief
Systems
Chakras 1-7
Color Therapy
Original Occurrence
of Negative Belief
(*Past Life)

BODY
Regions
Organs
Glands
Pathogens
Systems

Specific or All?

Head
Neck
Upper Extremity
Torso
Abdomen
Pelvis
Lower Extremity

Specific or All?

SPIRIT, ELECTRO MAGNETIC FIELD
WAVES          PARTICLES

Spirit/Will      Mind/Body
or          or
Will/Spirit      Body/Mind

Eye Movements    ILR

ILS

MUSCLE STRONG
Back to top for next chapter

ASSEMBLAGE POINT

WALK

Test with
"The Love Gun"

MUSCLE WEAK
Done - check
ILR  LifeLine Lifestyle

Water, Food, Rest, Exercise, Own Your Power

LifeLine™

Check Spirit Memory Index

©Copyright 2002 - The Way To Optimum Health LifeLine · www.DrsLifeLine.com

### Overview of The LifeLine Flow Chart

Each aspect of The LifeLine Flow Chart will be addressed in greater detail throughout the book. However, I want to begin by providing you with an overview.

The first tier of The LifeLine Flow Chart involves symptoms. Symptoms (which are fully explained later on) are the way the body "speaks." Their sole purpose is to notify you that you've subconsciously disconnected from an experience. A symptom may be pain or dysfunction anywhere in the body. It could be an uncomfortable feeling when you're around certain people. It might occur while you're giving a speech, driving on the highway, eating a new food, or doing anything outside of your comfort zone. But rather than being an obstacle, symptoms are perhaps your greatest asset. (You'll learn why as you read each chapter.)

All symptoms occur because there's an imbalance somewhere in the body, which originates in what's called the **Triad of Health.**

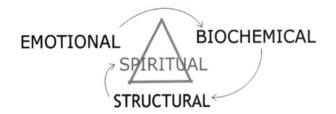

EMOTIONAL     BIOCHEMICAL

SPIRITUAL

STRUCTURAL

The Triad represents the emotional, biochemical, structural, and spiritual aspects of the body. The body actually begins to leak or lose life force or energy when an imbalance is present. It's that loss of life force that triggers the body to speak with a symptom—the door or portal through which we *discover* what our subconscious mind is saying, and in this light, it's also the means of reconnecting to our truth.

The *root cause* of imbalance in the Triad of Health, which leads the body to lose energy or leak life force, is located in the **Power Center.**

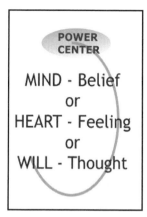

*Consciously*, this process begins subtly; however, on a *subconscious* level, imbalance occurs when life experiences create emotional chaos. At that point, it's common that we have a disconnection within the subconscious mind and the Power Center: beliefs (mind), feelings (heart), or our thoughts (will). The brain automatically and subconsciously internalizes the chaos and keeps the emotions of that experience trapped in a cycle of disconnection.

Like a metal detector, The LifeLine Technique zeros in on the location of the imbalance in the body and its cause. In addition, it helps you reconnect to the emotions that you've subconsciously detached from so that your body can regain balance and heal.

The **Five Elements** demonstrate the flow of life force through the body's 12 major acupuncture **meridians**.

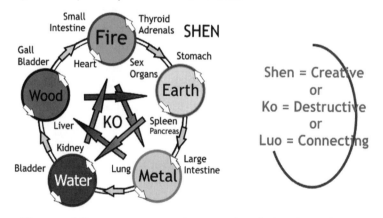

The meridians are a complex matrix of circuits, which provide energy throughout the body and connect us to the universe that we're all a part of. Because emotions are *energy in motion*, blockages within the acupuncture meridians occur when we're in a state of subconscious disconnection. Blockage anywhere along the meridian pathway causes the body to respond with symptoms, and by restoring balance within the meridians, it's able to heal on its own. The Five Elements guide The LifeLine Technique practitioner in the discovery of the exact location of that blockage of life force. The Five Elements help us appreciate and view the subtle connection between the macrocosm of the universe and the microcosm of the body.

The **Expression Channel** explains *why* there's a decreased flow of life force through the acupuncture meridians.

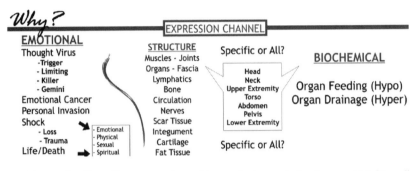

*Expression* literally means "speaking what one is feeling or thinking." The Expression Channel is the body's way of communicating what's going on emotionally, structurally, or biochemically. For example, a patient might come to my office with a stiff neck. Traditionally, it's been assumed that this condition could be caused by strained or injured muscles. The Expression Channel of The LifeLine Flow Chart, however, provides someone with the opportunity to probe even deeper and determine *why* there was a strain or injury in the first place. By running The LifeLine Flow Chart, the patient is able to reconnect to the subconsciously internalized, denied, or disconnected emotions that are creating a blockage in his or her acupuncture meridians. When the Expression Channel is cleared, the subconscious emotion is released, increasing the potential for the body to heal effortlessly and completely.

The next step of the chart is to locate the **Holding Pattern.**

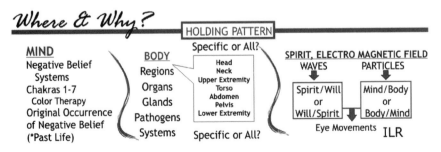

The Holding Pattern answers the questions *Where?* and *Why? Where?* is the holding pattern that's inhibiting the person from becoming conscious, and *Why?* isn't he or she able to release it? The holding pattern can be discovered in the mind, body, or spirit:

- If it's located in the mind, it's the result of limiting beliefs inhibiting the person from perceiving the infinite potential and possibilities that exist in every moment.

- If it's found in the body, it's due to long-standing sub-conscious disconnections that have resulted in a mutation or physical breakdown of a specific region, organ, gland, pathogen, or system.

- If it's in the spirit or electromagnetic field of the body, it's caused by a trauma that's sustaining a disconnection between the spirit and will or the mind and the body. This rift is associated with the eyes and their inability to process trauma during REM sleep.

When the Holding Pattern is located, the body is released from the grip of limiting beliefs, physical disconnection, or trauma, which enables it to heal. Letting go of the subconscious emotions that are stuck in a Holding Pattern allows people to create a new view toward life's challenges, overcome addiction, and reconnect to their truth.

The LifeLine Flow Chart next guides the practitioner to the **Assemblage Point**—the specific anatomical location within the microcosmic orbit (superconscious) where a person originally disconnected within his or her subconscious mind, thus creating the attractor field for the symptom or challenge.

By locating the Assemblage Point, the practitioner, in a shamanic-type fashion, is able to seal the leaks in the patient's energetic field or reassemble the electromagnetic field of the body. Once he or she reconnects to the emotions of the subconscious mind, it's necessary to assess the lifestyle changes that the person needs to make.

### Water, Food, Rest, Exercise, Own Your Power

It's of utmost importance that the body be nurtured and nourished so that it's healthy enough to integrate and conduct its life force. Like a laser, The LifeLine Flow Chart will guide you through the journey of discovery and of understanding the root cause of every symptom or stressful situation. This book is the map, complete with descriptions explaining every road you'll travel on.

# CHAPTER 3

# THE FUSION OF SCIENCE AND SPIRIT

Two weeks after Tom and I began treating our patients using what we now called The LifeLine Technique, I suggested to him that we conduct a live blood cell analysis of one of our patients, both before and after a LifeLine treatment. We used a dark-field microscope, the same type of instrument that Dr. Emoto used to conduct his experiments on water. The patient I had in mind was a man who had been diagnosed with hepatitis C.

Tom took a sample of the patient's blood and looked at it under the dark-field microscope. The sample revealed severe liver distress: The man's red blood cells were sticking together and not moving. His blood also displayed signs of lymphatic congestion and abnormal numbers of white blood cells, which were unhealthy in shape and function. We observed the slide for 20 minutes and then returned to the patient to perform The LifeLine Technique.

It took less than ten minutes to run The LifeLine Flow Chart, after which we drew blood again. We stared at the slide, astonished by the results: The patient's blood had undergone a complete transformation! All of his red blood cells were now moving freely and were perfectly spaced and shaped. The lymphatic stagnation had cleared up, and the pathogenic imbalances that were initially present had improved.

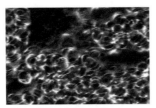
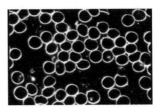

Blood Before LifeLine Treatment    Blood After LifeLine Treatment

"That's incredible!" I said to Tom. "I think we're on to something."

Dr. Emoto's work showed that water's molecular structure is impacted by every aspect of its environment. In his word and crystal experiments, the most intricately formed crystal was extracted from the frozen vial on which the words *love* and *gratitude* were taped. What links this experiment to our health is the fact that the human body is 75 to 90 percent water.

In one moment, all the pieces of the puzzle fused into a beautiful image. I immediately understood the impact of the experience I'd had three years earlier with my cousin Rob. All of Rob's water molecules, which make up each cell of his body, responded to the vibrational frequency of love when I held the "I love you" sign next to his body. The autonomic reflex of the muscle test improved as the water molecules transformed.

It was a moment of clarity: I had transcended belief and entered the realm of knowing. The energy of Infinite Love & Gratitude has the potential to affect the highest of frequencies, which means that it has the power to harmonize the body and help it restore balance.

As human beings, we're affected by every experience we encounter through the molecular structure of water in our bodies. However, most significant is the subconscious mind's *response* to the events of our life. Subconscious limiting or pessimistic thoughts, feelings, and beliefs will result in the stagnation of our cells, eventually leading to symptoms and disease. Remember that 98 percent of our perception is subconscious.

When *Infinite Love & Gratitude* is written or spoken aloud, as documented in Dr. Emoto's research with water, these profound words have instantaneous effects on the molecular structure of water—the same substance that permeates each cell in the body. Using The LifeLine Technique, Tom and I have witnessed, and participated in, phenomenal healings that we've been able to objectively measure. People who come to our center for holistic healing, The Way to Optimal Health, or our seminars, are empowered to take charge of their lives through the use of The LifeLine Technique. The beauty and truth is that healing is all about love and gratitude.

Using live blood cell analysis and a dark-field microscope, we've continued to document this phenomenon at The Way to Optimal Health. Instantaneous molecular-healing changes have been consistently observed within the blood after Tom and I perform The LifeLine Technique. One of the greatest results of Dr. Emoto's work and the advent of The LifeLine Technique is the documented and tangible evidence of the healing power of Infinite Love & Gratitude. Why does love heal? That's a question that has withstood the test of time but now can be answered thanks to Dr. Emoto's work and the diagnostic tests that Tom and I have conducted as documentary proof of The LifeLine Technique's effectiveness.

After using The LifeLine Flow Chart, muscle testing, and the words *Infinite Love & Gratitude* on our patient with the hepatitis C diagnosis, we observed the alterations in the molecular structure of his blood. If I hadn't seen it for myself, I wouldn't have believed it! Instant molecular changes had occurred. I'm not a hepatitis C specialist, nor do I treat this disease. On the contrary, I help individuals whose bodies are imbalanced and expressing themselves with *symptoms.* By using The LifeLine Technique and the power of Infinite Love & Gratitude, I'm able to help people regain balance in both their minds and bodies, thus creating the perfect environment for healing to occur. Within a year, the viral load in the patient's body had decreased by more than 90 percent.

Because the body is two-thirds water and water acts as a liquid tape recorder, it's very sensitive to both its internal and external environment. As demonstrated by Dr. Emoto, love and gratitude enhance water's molecular structure and function, thereby enabling the body to release its optimal healing potential.

When the molecular structure of our cells is healthy and intact, they conduct electricity better and therefore regulate homeostasis more efficiently. Tom and I have documented that when the words *Infinite Love & Gratitude* are spoken or experienced, the molecular structure of the body's cells immediately undergoes a healing change.

Valerie Hunt, the author of the book *Infinite Mind,* states, "Theoretically, I accept that the mind is the most powerful force in the world, more powerful than the split atom because it is beyond physical force." The essence of love can't truly be captured by reading a book . . . it must be experienced within the mind. The power of the mind and of love is that they are both one and infinite. To perceive them, all judgment must be released. The power of Infinite Love & Gratitude is an experience—a moment of being present, of defying logic and embracing intuition and the heart.

Helen Keller once said, "The best and most beautiful things in the world cannot be seen or even touched. They must be felt with the heart." It is in each and every moment that we're faced with the ultimate choice, that of faith—faith that the universe is a perfect creation and that every moment is a "big bang," an instant of infinite possibilities. Right now, if you choose to be ruled by fear, what will the consequences be? If, on the other hand, you opt to embrace this moment with love and gratitude, what will be the outcome? Your heart knows the difference. It feels each moment that you've disconnected from love and gratitude. Consequently, every fear-driven beat of the heart plays a symphony of victimization and suffering.

Love is a state of openness, the essence of acceptance. The frequency of love amplifies *conductance.* This term literally means "movement." And movement, as we know from The LifeLine Law of Transformation and Creation, is change, and the essence of life. When we disconnect from love, fear is more apparent. So living in a constant state of fear occurs when we've disconnected from love, and in this state, we create boundaries for protection. We construct illusionary lines and differences between people, places, and things. It's by recognizing that we're all connected through love, and discovering unity within the diversity of life, that these boundaries begin to melt away.

The following poem, "The Treasure of Love," was composed for my wedding ceremony by my wife's cousin, Kristin Ryan:

*Love . . . .*
*Simple and at times complicated in its expression*
*Defined over the ages by many,*
*No two definitions the same.*
*The truth of love being found*
*By each of us in different ways.*
*Warmth . . . Peace . . . Selflessness . . . Nurturing . . .*
*Guidance . . . Joy . . . Comfort . . . Strength . . .*
*Loyalty . . .*
*Thoughtfulness & Tenderness.*
*Surrounded by these, you will know Love.*
*Love is a treasure*
*More precious than we can measure.*
*Too often locked away*
*Kept safe, not used.*
*But the value of Love*
*Is in the life that it gives*
*It needs to be shown.*
*At the core of Love is expression.*
*Love is both giving and receiving.*
*More than a feeling . . .*
*A decision,*
*A choice to care for another*
*As well as you care for yourself.*
*Experience Love,*
*Express it often,*
*Care for each other,*
*Enjoy the treasure of Love.*

Love is the subtle web that maintains connections. From the beginning of time, it has guided and enlightened searchers of the truth. This emotion is a power that uplifts and transforms people who have lost their will. Love moves the waters and shapes the mountains. Its ethereal nature bonds families, races, and species and potentiates the harmony of all humanity.

One thing that any experienced outdoors enthusiast knows is never to get caught between a mother bear and her cub! Love causes us to act and react in ways that are beyond prediction. All life-forms—humans, animals, and other things of nature—will do whatever is necessary to maintain their connection with love, because it's the life force that feeds and nourishes all living beings at their core. Without it, we literally die.

The lack of self-love is the final, destructive blow. It results in a "lifeless" life—one without passion; reason; and ultimately, without connection to self or nature. Author Don Miguel Ruiz, a shaman and healer, writes in his book *The Mastery of Love:*

> We can talk about love and write a thousand books about it, but love will be completely different for each of us because we have to experience love. Love is not about concepts; love is about action. Love in action can only produce happiness.
>
> Fear in action can only produce suffering.
>
> The only way to master love is to practice love. You don't need to justify your love; you don't need to explain your love; you just need to practice your love. Practice creates the master.

Love is a learned behavior. Author Richard Carlson, Ph.D., once wrote: "Love begins in our own hearts. It is a choice . . . each choice we make along the way becomes an important step on the path of love." Just as the process of life is the continuum of many experiences, love is the product of fully embracing our experiences without judgment. Life provides endless resources and opportunities for learning how to master love. It's the choice we make to embrace our magnificence . . . it's the choice we make, as Don Miguel Ruiz says, to become masters.

The simplest component of The LifeLine Technique is the treatment itself: saying the words *Infinite Love & Gratitude* and holding your hand in the universal sign-language mode for "I love you."

.

You don't need a doctorate, a medical degree, or any holistic-health training to perform The LifeLine Technique. Whether you're an executive, nurse, grocery-store clerk, salesperson, messenger, or homemaker, once trained in The LifeLine Technique, you'll have all the tools necessary to face any challenge.

For example, a woman of 83 years young who had taken just one of The LifeLine Technique training seminars had an amazing experience. She'd been feeling dizzy and even thought that she was going to pass out while riding the train. The next morning, she was still feeling dizzy and decided to test her blood pressure: It was 161/85—it had never before been that high. Then she treated herself with The LifeLine Technique. The treatment took about 15 minutes, and she checked her pressure again: It was 151/75. It dropped ten points on both the systolic and diastolic pressures, and the dizziness totally went away.

It's my hope that one day this type of training—not just the technique, but also the philosophy, of which The LifeLine treatment is a part of the continuum—will become integrated into the school curriculum for children, signaling a profound shift in the way we view symptoms, healing, and life.

# CHAPTER 4

# CONVERSATIONS
# WITH THE BODY

B ecause we've been taught that imbalances such as allergies, hypertension, and diabetes are hereditary conditions, we feel as if we're victims of our environment and prisoners of our genes. We believe that we don't have any power over illness and disease. The advent of The LifeLine Technique provides a liberating alternative to those beliefs by demonstrating that we have 100 percent control over our health. The first step is to learn to talk to the body.

In 1964, George Goodheart, Jr., D.C., awakened to applied kinesiology (AK), or muscle testing, as a diagnostic and therapeutic tool. He integrated muscle testing into his treatment procedures. Through his ongoing research and the results of his work, Dr. Goodheart discovered the relationship between the body's major muscle groups and the acupuncture meridians.

Many other innovative practitioners elaborated upon Dr. Goodheart's original work. Using his powerful intuition, Dr. Victor Frank awakened to and developed Total Body Modification (TBM), a technique that utilizes kinesiology to assess the functional, physiological health of the body. Dr. Frank learned that he could communicate with the body through muscle testing. Expanding the boundaries of TBM, Dr. Scott Walker awakened to the Neuro Emotional Technique (NET), a kinesiological way to understand functional, emotional imbalances.

All of these doctors balance the body with kinesiological-based treatments. AK focuses on the structural features of the body; TBM emphasizes the functional, physiological components; and NET addresses the body's emotional aspects. These magnificent techniques overlap with one another in a beautiful mosaic, creating the totality of energetic healing at its best!

The LifeLine Technique uses muscle testing as the diagnostic and therapeutic tool to reveal the root cause of all symptoms. By connecting the emotional, biochemical, and structural aspects of the body to the spirit through Infinite Love & Gratitude, this technique facilitates the body's healing process in an extraordinary way.

The LifeLine Flow Chart provides a guided journey through the subconscious mind, helping you to understand how your body manifests what's in your mind. That's why symptoms are a gift: They're the body's way of saying, "The subconscious emotions you're internalizing, denying, or disconnecting from are hurting me."

Take some time right now to close your eyes and think about a friend. Let whatever emotions about that person come into your mind. Now, think about when you were in the fifth grade. Remember your teacher, the house you lived in, your friends, and whatever other memories are associated with that time and let the thoughts just flow. Now, contemplate your mother, allowing your mind to experience her through whatever thoughts, feelings, and beliefs arise. Open your eyes and see that your friend, your fifth-grade experiences, and your mother aren't present. However, they're still within your subconscious mind.

Every emotion that you've ever experienced is imprinted in your mind, whether or not you're aware of it. With The LifeLine Flow Chart and muscle testing, you now have the ability and the power to connect to the subconscious mind and heal it. With this knowledge, there are no limits—anything and everything is possible.

A landmark study by Daniel Monti, M.D., et al., measured the effects of cognitive factors on muscle strength and demonstrated the validity of muscle testing. The investigation conclusively showed how thoughts and statements elicit changes within a muscle-test reflex.

The body has an innate intelligence that can be assessed with this method to determine whether it's maintaining balance. Just like the autonomic nervous system, muscle testing is a polarity-dependent mechanism where a muscle will maintain its strength as long as there's a congruency with the function, adaptability, and survival of the entire organism. When there's *in*congruency, an indicator muscle will test weak.

A specific organ, pathogen, system, acupuncture meridian, chakra, muscle, or belief can be used to assess congruence or incongruence through the "locking out" or "giving way" of the muscle test. When a muscle locks out, it's an indication that whatever is being evaluated is congruent with the overall balance of the body. When a muscle gives way, it's a sign that what's being tested is incongruent with this balance.

The LifeLine Flow Chart, used in conjunction with muscle testing, enables you to discover the incongruent patterns within the subconscious mind that have manifested as imbalances or symptoms in the body. For example, when you touch a painful area of the body, an indicator muscle will sometimes give way, signaling incongruence with the function of that particular area. The LifeLine Flow Chart can then be used with muscle testing to balance those patterns within the subconscious mind that have resulted in the pain or are the reason why it hasn't healed. With muscle testing, The LifeLine practitioner never has to guess: With each question asked, the muscle will either stay locked or give way.

Muscle testing involves the use of an indicator muscle, which is created by extending either the left or right arm at a 90-degree angle to the body. To assess for a strong reflex, the arm is held in a locked position while the practitioner uses his or her hand to press against it. A good way to test the difference is through the use of a declarative statement. When a person states his or her name, for instance, the indicator muscle will remain locked. However, if the person says a name that isn't his or her own, the muscle will give way or test weak. For example, if I make the statement "My name is Darren," the indicator muscle will stay locked. However, if I state, "My name is Jeri," the muscle will test weak.

Here is a great exercise to show the validity of muscle testing. Place a package of sugar next to the body. The muscle will instantly become weak because sugar is a poison. The self-preservation mechanism of the body discerns whether a substance is harmful through the strength or weakness of a muscle. Say the word *love* and an indicator muscle will be strong; say the word *hate* and it will instantly become weak.

For some people it will take a little practice to feel the difference between a locked and a weak muscle. Even working with 25 to 30 patients daily, it took me about a year before I felt as if I'd mastered muscle testing. Once you get the feel for it, however, you'll be able to recognize the sometimes subtle differences between a muscle that stays locked and one that gives way.

A surrogate (that is, another person's arm) may be used to evaluate a very young child, an elderly person with disabilities, or anyone who's unable to use his or her own limb. There's no difference between using a surrogate or the patient's own arm during the evaluation, since an electrical circuit is created between them. The person performing the muscle testing needs to be focused on the individual he or she is testing, not the surrogate.

It's important never to guess while muscle testing! If you're unable to tell the strength or weakness of the muscle, use a surrogate. There are many reasons why a person's muscle may feel "boggy." (Usually it's due to dehydration.) During muscle testing, it's imperative that both the tester and the patient remain in Present Time Consciousness (focused intent). To stay in tune with the process, have the person being evaluated resist while testing is performed so that the strongest muscle possible will be assessed.

The LifeLine Technique uses muscle testing as a tool to evaluate balance or imbalance and to detect the emotional, structural, biochemical, or spiritual source of a symptom. It's the vehicle through which we communicate with the body and find out what's *actually* going on. Diagnostic tools, such as blood tests and urinalysis, don't show dysfunction until there's at least a *40-plus percent* breakdown in the body. With muscle testing, however, we can determine imbalance within *1 to 2 percent* of dysfunction, which means that you don't need to have a symptom to find a weak muscle. The body's innate intelligence hones in on minute changes before they actually become a significant health challenge.

When there's a change in the indicator muscle—that is, when a strong muscle gives way—it's a signal that an imbalance is present. The LifeLine Technique corrects this immediately, and changes can be observed with the use of muscle testing. The previously weak indicator muscle will test strong immediately after a correction has been made. All it takes is saying the words *Infinite Love & Gratitude.*

The LifeLine Technique doesn't *cure* anything. In fact, no "healer" ever actually *heals*—it's the body that performs the process of regeneration. The healing-arts practitioner is like a mechanic who knows the steps necessary to remove any barriers to the smooth running of a car. The intent of the practitioner is vital: A positive attitude, along with a vision of health and love, is imperative while working on someone or on yourself. In addition, it's crucial that you harbor no preconceived notions about whether the muscle will become weak or strong in response to the questions asked—after all, you may be wrong. It's best to let the body's innate intelligence guide you. You'll be amazed by the laser-like accuracy that muscle testing reveals.

# CHAPTER 5

# GOING WITH THE FLOW

Thousands of years ago, Chinese philosophers awakened to the *Wu hsing,* or The Five Element theory, which explains the natural flow of the universe. Based on this natural law, everything in the cosmos has a relationship that's interdependent in some way. These relationships exist between the **Five Elements—** *Fire, Earth, Metal, Water,* and **Wood.** *Element* in Chinese means "movement" and "change," which explains the interconnection of the Five Elements.

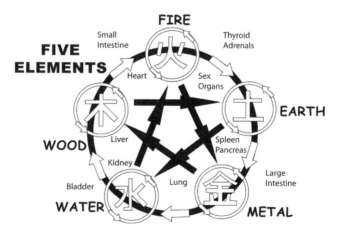

Early philosophers realized that there was a specific pattern that existed between the elements of the universe. Through this observation and their experience, the Five Element theory was devised to help them understand how human beings maintain balance within themselves and the universe that they're a part of. They observed that the cycle of the seasons was infinite in the expression of life and death.

From spring to summer, and then from autumn to winter, they realized that there was a universal energy that cycled over and over again. It was in this cycle that the mind-body-spirit danced in a symphony of life. The lesson the philosophers learned through observation was that nature moves via the law of least effort. Water takes on the form of its vessel. Metal flows like water when heated by fire. Water also has the capacity to extinguish fire; at the same time, if a fire is hot enough, it has the ability to evaporate water. The Five Elements are simply intricate and intricately simple.

The Chinese observed that there were three distinct patterns or cycles to how the Five Elements interacted. They called these the *Shen, Ko,* and *Luo.*

The **Shen** is the creative cycle of nature in which each one of the elements naturally created the next in a continuous circle of life. From fire came the "big bang" out of which the earth was created. From Mother Earth, when we dig deep within her, we discover precious metals. These metals, when melted, flow like majestic waters. Water, in turn, when poured onto the earth, brings life in the form of trees. And when two pieces of wood are rubbed together, the friction creates fire, beginning the Shen cycle all over again.

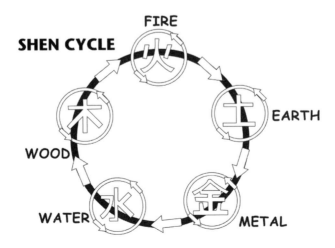

The **Ko** is the controlling or destructive cycle. Beginning with the fire element, a blazing fire will melt metal, as in the process of forging a sword. Metal destroys wood, such as when an ax chops down a tree. Wood controls the earth, as when a tree grows out of the ground. Earth surrounds and directs water, as in a lake or a river. Water controls fire by extinguishing it, completing the Ko cycle.

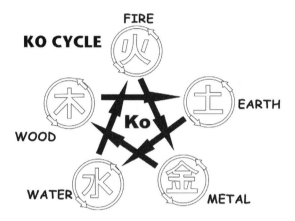

The **Luo,** or connecting cycle, relates to the principle of yin and yang. In the yin/yang symbol, one half is white and the other is black. Within the white, there's a small dot of black; within the black, there's a small dot of white. This represents the interdependency of polar opposites. In the Five Element theory, each element has a yin and yang component as represented by a particular acupuncture meridian. The Luo cycle represents the yin and yang component and demonstrates the interdependence and balance between the acupuncture meridians within an individual element.

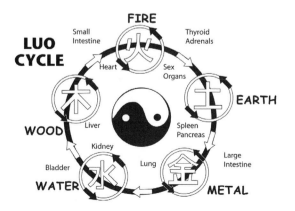

It's within all these cycles that regeneration and rejuvenation occur. From new to old and back again, each cycle occurs within a year's time, much as a tree forms a new ring. The more balanced the tree is, the sturdier and healthier it will be. Whales will migrate, bears will hibernate, and caterpillars will transform into butterflies, all with the specific patterns of the Five Elements and the seasons.

Since the dawn of technology, human beings have attempted to control and harness the planet's resources for energy. The results have been catastrophic for the earth and her inhabitants. Destruction of coral reefs and rain forests, holes within the ozone, and melting of the polar ice caps are but a few of the obvious consequences. As a result, the devastation to the earth has left the animal kingdom in chaos. For example, the natural migratory patterns of whales have been disrupted, causing many to beach themselves.

The same chaos occurs within the body when you don't recognize the importance of flowing *with* the universe, rather than against it. Your body appreciates the outdoors and the increase in activity and sunlight during the summer, just as it appreciates slowing down and internalizing in autumn and winter. When you deny or disconnect from the natural cycle of the seasons, your body becomes imbalanced, leading to symptoms and disease. The symptoms are the warning signals that you've strayed.

There are 12 pathways of energy or life force within the body, called *meridians*. Each one of these corresponds with an individual organ and carries life force to and from it. It's literally a network of invisible wires that enable your body to function. These meridians will always show imbalance long before the actual organ has a disease. For example, not all people who have a gallbladder meridian imbalance have an ailment in their gallbladder.

However, everyone who has a diseased gallbladder has imbalance within that organ's meridian. Taking out the gallbladder doesn't correct the imbalance in the meridian—it only removes the diseased organ. The imbalance in the body will persist if the cause of the imbalance in the gallbladder meridian isn't addressed. Therefore, maintaining wellness in your meridians is imperative to ensure an optimally healthy life.

Dianne Connelly, Ph.D., wrote a phenomenal book called *Traditional Acupuncture: The Law of the Five Elements.* I read this volume at the beginning of every season. It helps me keep in tune with the natural flow of the seasons. With this awareness, I'm able to maintain Present Time Consciousness more efficiently and adapt appropriately to the shifts that are occurring.

Life is about change; nothing that lasts ever remains the same. It's easy to get stuck in a pattern of internalization, denial, or disconnection. When we do, however, the energy or life force that moves within our meridians becomes affected. It's with the power of Infinite Love & Gratitude that we're able to view our challenges from a new perspective, empowering us to make the necessary changes for both survival and learning.

Your experiences are the treasures of your life. The feelings that result from them will guide you through comfort and discomfort: You must feel to heal. When you're authentic in your expression of your emotions, you'll find it easier to go with the flow. It's very simple— although it might seem challenging—so have faith in the process. May your spirit move like the wind . . . may it flow effortlessly like the Five Elements.

~ ~ ~

# CHAPTER 6

# THE POWER OF WORDS

"Sticks and stones may break my bones, but words can never hurt me." It's a familiar childhood taunt that we once thought was true. But as we learned from Dr. Emoto's work, words have an energy frequency that affects the molecular structure of water. Because the body is 75 to 90 percent water, we *are* affected by words. Not only can words hurt us emotionally, but the ones that we choose to use represent the flow of our subconscious mind.

One of my patients, Jennifer, was 13 in 1967 and excited about being invited to her first "teenage" party. When she told her friend about the invitation, her companion responded, "No boy will ever want to dance with you." At the time of those remarks, Jennifer and her friend were eating tuna salad. When Jennifer began dressing for the party hours after the conversation, her nose and lips started to swell. Her parents took Jennifer to the emergency clinic, and the doctor declared that she was allergic to fish. From that point forward—over the next 35 years—Jennifer never ate fish, and if she was around while it was being cooked, she had an allergic reaction.

Using the words and intention of *Infinite Love & Gratitude,* I harmonized the internalized thoughts, feelings, and beliefs associated with Jennifer's memory. She no longer has any allergic reaction to fish and enjoys eating it on a regular basis.

Words can have a profound, life-altering positive impact—or they can create intensely negative, devastating effects. Think about the words used when you have a disagreement with your spouse or significant other, or when you receive criticism from your parents or praise from your boss. How do words affect you when your siblings, friends, or co-workers tease you? If you don't respond to them right away, what energy frequencies are rumbling around your body as a result?

Some words that you use every day have a similar impact. Close your eyes and say the words *my, try,* and *can't.* What feelings do they evoke for you?

Let's start with the word *my.* It means "belonging to or done by me." So what happens when you use *my* to describe a symptom or disease? "*My* migraine headache is killing me." "*My* allergies are making me sneeze like crazy." "*My* arthritis won't let me stand up for long periods." "*My* diabetes is acting up."

When you use the word *my* when speaking of a symptom or a disease, you create an identity as if the condition defines you. That's dangerous! Adding the word *my* means that the symptom belongs to you. The truth is that the ache or other dysfunction is a sign that there's an imbalance in your system, and your body is attempting to get your attention. When you qualify the headache by calling it "*my* headache," it sends a negative message to your body, and the cycle of breakdown continues. In addition, when you participate in verbal patterns of communication that are pessimistic or limiting in any way, the body has to take on another opponent—you. It's hard to defend against yourself. It's like shadowboxing: The opponent ducks every time you do.

This is what I recommend: When you talk about a symptom, make it *the* pain instead of *my* pain—*the* pain in my head, *the* pain in my stomach, or *the* pain in my back. At the same time, you should own your body parts—that is, *my* head, *my* stomach, or *my* back. But don't say *my* arthritis, *my* multiple sclerosis, or *my* Parkinson's disease. When you do, you're just solidifying dysfunction as being a part of you.

Why is this important? The founders of Neuro-Linguistic Programming (NLP), Richard Bandler and John Grinder, have spent their lives studying the impact of language on the nervous system. *Neuro* refers to the mind and the way you externally experience and internally represent the world through your senses. *Linguistics* corresponds to the use of language with other people and yourself. *Programming* relates to the sequence or patterns of your behavior that can be changed like reprogramming a computer. Bandler and Grinder discovered that language "programs" the nervous system. And what does your nervous system control? Everything!

Words are powerful. When you speak, in effect you're programming yourself, and you'll manifest the physical results. Think about what happens when you say, "If you don't put on your hat, you're going to catch a cold," or "You make me sick," or "You always mess up everything."

Bandler and Grinder developed NLP in California during the 1970s, based on their study of three exceptional communicators: the eminent family therapist Virginia Satir; the originator of Gestalt therapy, Fritz Perls; and the hypnotherapist Milton H. Erickson. Bandler and Grinder noted that these communicators were achieving outstanding results with their clients, and had much in common in the way they related—the language patterns they used, for example, and the beliefs that guided their behaviors. Bandler and Grinder also drew upon the work of others to develop a set of principles and techniques that allowed them to help people change their lives.

There are several core beliefs that are the foundation of NLP. The most commonly referenced are:

- **The map is not the territory.** You respond to *your* map of reality, not reality itself.

- **Mind, body, and spirit are one system.** The mind, the body, and the spirit are inextricably linked—change one and the others must change.

- **Having choice is better than not having choice.** Having the greatest number of options in any interaction provides you with the opportunity to exert the greatest amount of influence over it.

- **Excellence can be modeled.** If one person can achieve something, anybody can learn to do it.

- **All human behavior provides you with an opportunity to create something positive.** Both positive and negative behaviors present the opportunity for you to learn lessons. What may seem to be negative conduct only appears so because you don't yet know, or you haven't yet experienced, the positive effect. Behavior is the result of an adaptive positive intent.

- **The meaning of communication is the response you get.** The response may not be the one you intended. If you don't get the result you want, do something different.

- **You have all the resources within you to achieve what you want to achieve.** You have all the resources necessary to make any desired change. No one is wrong or broken.

Based on the theory of NLP, if you say, "I can't do that," you won't be able to do it. The word *can't* is like having your hands and feet bound together behind your back. Short of that, anything is possible. What do you think happens when you act as if these suppositions are true?

You can always do your best. There is no failure, only opportunity. Let me say that again: *There is no failure.* What our society defines as failure or an obstacle, with all the negative connotations, is actually an opportunity—a chance to learn important life lessons and create something positive.

*Can't* is a word that places artificial limitations on yourself, or that other people use to define you. Where would the world be if Albert Einstein had listened to his grade-school teachers, who told him that he would never do well in science? Where would the National Basketball Association be if Michael Jordan had listened to his high-school coaches, who said that he'd never play pro ball? And what would we do if billionaire talk-show host Oprah Winfrey had listened to everyone who ever told her that her weight would prevent her from having a successful career on television? There are endless stories of great people throughout history—from the Wright brothers to Martin Luther King, Jr.—who refused to accept other people's limiting beliefs about their dreams. Not only were they able to achieve their goals, but they accomplished more than they ever imagined possible and helped millions of people in the process.

I have a patient who once told me that he had "quit-itis"—he never followed through on anything. *Can't* was a word that he often used. This patient complained of an assortment of aches and pains, as well as overall fatigue. One day he came into the office and said that he was ready to quit being a quitter! Using The LifeLine Technique, we discovered the root cause of his self-destructive behavior and corrected the imbalances that were affecting how he felt about his own life. In addition, he made a commitment to follow The Five Basics for Optimal Health—quantity, quality, and frequency of water, food, rest, exercise, and owning his power. On his next visit, he reported a marked improvement in both his health and attitude. Over the past year, he's faithfully maintained a healthy balance with The Five Basics and continues to strive toward optimal health. He has indeed quit being a quitter.

*Try* is defined as "an attempt to succeed." However, the subtext of the word is that we *expect* to fail. For example, you might say, "I'll *try* to eat right," but you mean, "Sugar is very hard to resist." Or you state, "I'll *try* to go to the gym," but you mean, "It's so difficult to get out of bed in the morning." Or you say, "I'll *try* to remember to take my supplements," when you actually mean, "I hate to take pills."

The difference between trying and succeeding is staying in the present moment, making a *commitment,* and using your *will* to do your very best. Your will is the driving force that allows you to expand your potential to succeed. Free will is the infinite number of choices you have in any given situation, and ultimately the one you make based on what's right for you.

It's your lack of will—along with a denial of free will, of self, and of love—that are the motivation behind your use of *my, can't,* and *try.*

This isn't a judgment. What you're actually doing is embracing fear. When you deny your will—from the most magical experiences to the most challenging, hurtful, depressing, spiteful, grievous situations imaginable—you're embracing fear.

During a recent service of Rosh Hashanah (Jewish New Year), our rabbi gave a wonderful sermon. He talked about a little boy who showed his teacher a picture of the earth. As an experiment, the teacher tore it into little pieces and instructed the boy to put them back together again. In a short amount of time, the child came back with the picture taped together.

"How did you do it so fast?" the teacher asked.

"On the other side of the earth was the picture of one person," the child responded. "Putting that one person back together helped me put the earth back together."

In order to heal the earth you must first put yourself back together—you must heal your own life. The words *my, can't,* and *try* are representative of the state of imbalance and dis-ease in your subconscious mind. *My, can't,* and *try* are symptoms of the subconscious mind's perpetration of harm against the body. Own your power by doing your best: Unconditionally respect, honor, and love yourself by choosing to take responsibility for the words you use. The impact of your choice will send a ripple outward to heal the earth, one person at a time.

~~~

# CHAPTER 7

# THE JOURNEY OF YOUR SPIRIT

The journey of your spirit is to reconnect with the power of Infinite Love & Gratitude. *Infinite* means "the universe," or "the collective conscious," which has no beginning or end. *Love* is the universal power that propels life, fueling your will and enabling you to face and overcome challenges. *Gratitude* empowers you to go through life without judgment—with this feeling, you see the value of any experience as an opportunity, rather than being a victim of your circumstances.

From Dr. Emoto's work and our exploration of The LifeLine Technique, we know that the intention, words, and acts of Infinite Love & Gratitude transform the molecular structure of water—the same water that makes up our cells. This transformation enables the electromagnetic field of the body to flow freely. This field is the energy that nourishes the body, facilitating its ability to heal. When it's unimpeded, you'll find that your ability to create your reality through your intention and achieve optimal health occurs effortlessly.

The law of conservation states that energy can neither be created nor destroyed; it just changes form. Because you're an energetic being, there's a part of you that's eternal . . . it wasn't born, nor will it ever die. Energy has polarity, a positive and negative charge that radiates an electromagnetic field. Your body's field is your spirit. Keep in mind that when I refer to "spirit," I'm not talking about religion— I'm referring strictly to the electromagnetic field of the body. Many people recognize this as life force. In the Preface, I discussed it briefly in relation to Einstein's theory of relativity. When the electromagnetic field flows freely, the physical body detoxifies and heals on its own.

The electromagnetic field has what's called a *superconscious*. The superconscious is where the mind resides and where all emotions begin. Every experience is attracted into your life through the electromagnetic attraction or repulsion of the superconscious mind. These frequencies of energy travel through protein receptors within the senses and the skin, and are then processed within the primordial centers of the brain.

In the 1950s, neurologist Paul MacLean, M.D., considered to be one of the world's greatest brain scientists, proposed that the skull held not one brain, but three. He called this the "triune brain." Dr. MacLean, who is the former director of the National Institute of Mental Health's Laboratory of Brain Evolution and Behavior in Poolesville, Maryland, says the three brains operate like "three interconnected biological computers." His research has found that each has "its own special intelligence, its own subjectivity, its own sense of time and space, and its own memory." These three brain centers are referred to as the neocortex, or neo-mammalian brain; the limbic system, or paleo-mammalian brain; and the brain stem and cerebellum, or reptilian brain. Each of the three is connected by nerves to the other two but seemingly operates as its own brain system with distinct capacities.

It had previously been assumed that the highest level of the brain, the neocortex, dominated the other, lower levels. Dr. MacLean, however, has shown that this isn't the case. His research has demonstrated that the physically lower limbic system, which rules emotions, can "hijack" the higher mental functions when it needs to.

The oldest brain—the reptilian—includes the brain stem and the cerebellum. In animals such as reptiles, these parts dominate. In humans, the reptilian brain has the same type of archaic behavioral programs as snakes and lizards. It's rigid, obsessive, compulsive, ritualistic, and paranoid. It's "filled with ancestral memories" and repeats the same behaviors over and over again, never learning from past mistakes. This brain controls muscles; balance; and autonomic functions, such as breathing or the rate at which the heart beats. This part of the brain is always active, even during deep sleep. Examples of reptilian-brain behaviors are road rage, checking one's appearance in a mirror, long multiplication, and putting together a jigsaw puzzle.

Dr. MacLean was the first to coin the name *limbic system* for the middle part of the brain. The limbic system is concerned with emotion, attention, affective (emotionally charged) memories, instincts, feeding, fighting, fleeing, and sexual behavior. Everything in this system is either "agreeable" or "disagreeable." Survival depends on avoidance of pain and repetition of pleasure. It helps to determine valence (whether we feel positive or negative toward something), salience (what gets our attention), unpredictability, and creative behavior. According to Dr. MacLean, the limbic system is the seat of our value judgments, instead of the more advanced neocortex. It decides whether our higher brain has a "good" idea or not—whether it feels true and right.

The neocortex, also known as the superior brain, comprises almost the whole of the cerebral hemispheres. The higher, cognitive functions, which distinguish humans from animals, are in the neocortex. In humans, it takes up nearly two-thirds of the total brain mass. The neocortex is divided into hemispheres—the famous left and right brains. The left half of the neocortex controls the right side of the body, and the right half governs the left side of the body. The right brain is more spatial, abstract, musical, and artistic, while the left brain is more linear, rational, and verbal.

The unification of the three brains enables the electrical frequency of our thoughts, feelings, and beliefs to be integrated into behavior. The reptilian system will respond in a reflexive manner to an experience for survival purposes. Once processed through the reptilian brain, the electrical frequency of an experience is transformed by the limbic system into emotion and memory. When an experience is perceived as nonthreatening, it will be sent to the neocortex for processing. If a situation is perceived as life threatening or beyond the higher brain's capacity to adapt to or cope with, the limbic system will inhibit the emotion from being processed by the neocortex.

Overwhelming feelings and painful experiences are downloaded and stored in the limbic brain. This takes place automatically and on a subconscious level in a single millisecond of time, capturing all the sensory data, feelings, and perceptions of the traumatic experience. Since the 1970s, through the work of famed hypnotherapist Milton Erickson, we've known that trauma triggers a spontaneous state of self-hypnosis that binds us to the emotional pain of the initial event. In other words, overwhelming emotional experiences induce a natural hypnotic state as a way of containing pain and fostering survival. These states form the basis of disease and suffering within the body, mind, and spirit. This is the way the subconscious mind disconnects from emotions, and it's that subconscious disconnection that inhibits the journey of our spirit.

Every thought, feeling, and belief that you have originates from the collective conscious. Your electromagnetic field, or spirit, attracts specific frequencies of energy that are filtered through your sensory receptors into your body. The limbic system transforms these thoughts, feelings, and beliefs into emotion. Emotion is energy *in* motion—its natural state (whether it's within the collective conscious or inside your body) is to stay in motion. Ultimately, to enable your body to function optimally, emotions need to be felt and then expressed. Your emotions are the intermediate state between your mind and body. They're associated with your limbic system, which integrates the neocortex and the reptilian brain. When you have a subconscious disconnection from an emotion lying dormant within the limbic brain, it will continue to maintain a separation between your conscious mind (neocortex) and the body (reptilian brain).

From my experience with The LifeLine Technique, I've come to the conclusion that the limbic system acts as a stopgap to prevent trauma or shocking experiences from being processed by the neocortex. Instead, the traumatic event waits to be released. When the subconscious memory of it is triggered by any one of the senses, a signal is sent from the limbic system directly to the reptilian brain center.

The signal is blocked from connecting to the neocortex due to the emotions in the subconscious mind. The body doesn't know the difference between reality or imagination. When the trauma is triggered, the body will begin to respond as if it were experiencing it for the first time. The body won't break the holding pattern of reacting in a survival-like fashion until the trauma is processed.

The reptilian brain can only function as the reptilian brain . . . it's only able to support the survival mechanisms of the body, such as the basic physiological functions of circulation, respiration, digestion, and elimination. It's also involved in mating, territorial behavior, pecking order, defense, aggression, and the emotions of anger and fear. Subconsciously, the reptilian brain keeps the body functioning and behaving in a maladaptive way, creating a holding pattern of imbalance between the mind and body. On a conscious level, the person never learns from previous experiences because the trauma locked in his or her limbic system will trigger the same response over and over again.

When the limbic system processes an event, a signal is sent to the neocortex. This experience occurs during sleep when the eyes are going through rapid eye movement (REM) cycles, and it's when the REM patterns are inhibited that emotions stay locked in the subconscious aspects of the brain. This signal of information to the neocortex facilitates the processing of a short-term memory into a long-term one, which then enables the person to learn a lesson from the traumatic experience and consequently stay in Present Time Consciousness.

~

Lena came to see me the day after having a mammogram. The test revealed two invasive masses in her left breast. On the day of her appointment with me, Lena was scheduled to have another mammogram and an ultrasound in order to determine the extent of the masses. When I placed my hand over Lena's right breast, her indicator muscle stayed intact. When I put my hand over her left one, however, her indicator muscle immediately became weak. Lena was frightened by the response of the muscle test and wanted to know if it meant that she had cancer.

"I don't know," I responded. "I don't diagnose cancer. However, your body is showing that you're leaking energy from your left breast."

I ran The LifeLine Technique to this area until the weak indicator muscle-tested strong. While I was working with her, Lena said to me, "I knew that I'd get cancer."

I asked her how she knew that, and she replied, "I told my husband, 'If I don't divorce you, I'm going to get cancer.'"

I applied The LifeLine Technique to release Lena's limiting belief that she would get cancer unless she divorced her husband. Afterward, I used it again to create positive-attractor fields of health and well-being by having Lena make positive, declarative statements. The entire treatment took 15 minutes. Lena left the office feeling lighter, stronger, and empowered.

Six hours later, I received a call from Lena: Her doctor had taken six mammograms and two ultrasound tests of her left breast, but he didn't find any sign of the masses. These follow-up results astonished and confused him. He told Lena that the first test had probably been misinterpreted. But Lena had seen the pictures. She told me that she felt physically different following the treatment we did with The LifeLine Technique. She knew that the masses went away as a result of it.

The internalized emotion of "I know that I'll get cancer if I don't divorce you" created a holding pattern between the limbic and reptilian brains, leading to a decreased flow of life force in Lena's left breast. With The LifeLine Technique, we released the stopgap that was inhibiting Lena's limiting belief from being processed by her neocortex. Once it was removed, the healing occurred all on its own.

The authentic expression of your emotions creates the opportunity for you to find or stay on your true path. It's through feelings of pain or discomfort that you recognize your need to reconnect to your true path. When your emotions that have been internalized within the subconscious mind are triggered, the molecular structure of the water that makes up every one of your cells instantly begins to change and break down, which diminishes your body's ability to conduct energy. It's truly the health of the water in your body's cell composition that enables your electromagnetic field (spirit) to flow without resistance.

Infinite Love & Gratitude enhances the molecular structure and beauty of your cells, thereby providing the perfect environment for health and well-being.

With The LifeLine Flow Chart and the power of Infinite Love & Gratitude, current challenges, past traumas, and shocking experiences can be released from the subconscious centers of the limbic brain and get processed by the neocortex in an instant. You'll be able to face health issues, past hurts, relationship challenges, and financial difficulties with a fresh perspective. What you choose to do from this point of view is your choice . . . your free will.

# CHAPTER 8

# THE PASSION OF FREE WILL

The concept of *free will* has been misunderstood and taken to mean doing whatever you please. But it's more complex than that. Free will is the choice you have to express your thoughts, feelings, and beliefs. It means being authentic, not only by living your truth, but also by how you treat others.

Lack of communication is widely regarded as the number one source of conflict in society—from familial relationships and marriages to international relationships among countries, religions, and different races.

The key to fully expressing your free will is maintaining rapport. This entails listening, understanding, showing empathy, and extending compassion, while allowing another person to do the same. Even if you disagree with that individual, respecting his or her free will directly impacts your ability to exercise yours. Rapport permits the expression of free will on both sides, even when two parties don't see eye to eye.

Compassion can be defined as *com,* meaning "with," and *passion,* meaning "to suffer." Compassion gives you the opportunity *to suffer with* a person, sharing his or her experience without judgment, even though you may have a different perspective about how you would handle the situation.

So many times you have a thought that you don't share because you're afraid of being wrong, judged inappropriate, or censored. This is why rapport is so critical. It's unconditional acceptance of free will—your own and that of others. Many people expend far too much energy in acts of resistance: harboring fear as opposed to love; hatred of people because of their race, gender, age, sexual orientation, or religion; or disbelief about things that they don't understand. Establishing rapport in and of itself is a healing response, as it enables you to live authentically while honoring someone else's right to do the same.

Everyone's journey is different. It's of the utmost importance to recognize and honor the emotions created from your own experiences. Doing so opens a direct link to your subconscious mind. This awareness empowers you to make the appropriate choice when you feel comfortable or uncomfortable in any given situation.

The challenge is to express your emotions—even when it's difficult—so as not to create subconscious patterns that result in dysfunction, and eventually symptoms, in the body. If the emotions we've subconsciously disconnected from aren't released, a disease pattern is set into motion.

Consider that thoughts are your free will and that they create feelings. Feelings guide you in every moment, creating either an emotional (internal) or sensory (external) reaction. When you deny your free will (thoughts), you deny yourself the opportunity to react authentically in the moment. For example, when you touch a flame, the feeling/reaction is "Wow, this is hot!" The emotion may be fear or anger that you touched the flame. At the same time, the sensory experience is to instantly move your hand away. The difficulty arises when you don't recognize your feelings. At this point, pain changes to suffering: You continue to keep your hand in the flame, screaming while it burns. That's the denial of your free will.

The trick is not to wait until your hand is in the flame to feel the fire. Once it's there, it's too late—you've already burned yourself. Your hand will need to heal once you remove it, and it's going to take some time. However, when you increase your sensitivity to Present Time Consciousness (PTC), you become aware of your feelings and are able to feel the flame when it's subtly warm. In this way, the flame becomes an asset. You're able to create a healthy boundary with the fire by being in tune with the feelings that you're currently experiencing. All of a sudden, what had the potential to be a destructive inferno transforms into a beautiful and meaningful bonfire. It can be used as a meeting place for friends and family and is a location to roast marshmallows, sing songs, and create wonderful memories.

The healing of your will begins with the acceptance of what you've denied, internalized, or disconnected from. Before you get to where you're going, you have to be okay with where you are. Even when it's uncomfortable, that's the starting point.

Take, for example, addictions or self-destructive behavior. The denial is that you're numbing yourself from feeling the true essence of an experience. The starting point for healing and reconnecting to your will is acknowledging that you're addicted or that your behavior is self-destructive.

Another example of denied free will is choosing to live as if you're a victim of your circumstances—for example, poverty, race, gender, religion, education, or state of health. You've become compliant in accepting whatever situation validates your limiting/negative beliefs. How many times have you heard people say, "I've always been overweight, and that's just the way it is," or "Women are always treated like second-class citizens, and there's nothing I can do about it!"? You may not be able to pick your circumstances, but you can *choose your reaction* to them. That's your free will.

Every human being has a choice. My idea of a completely harmonious world is one where we're unencumbered in our expression of free will and where we don't impose that will on other people. Because there's truth from every angle, it's ultimately about love and gratitude—the unconditional acceptance and respect of free will . . . your own and that of others.

The same holds true when you have feelings about a person or concerns about your health. If there is an immediate feeling of comfort or discomfort, it's very important not to deny your feelings so that the potential pain doesn't evolve into suffering. For example, what happens when someone offers you what sounds like an amazing opportunity but you get an uncomfortable sensation in your gut that contradicts what's being said? By expressing your emotions about the situation, you'll prevent this internal conflict from creating an imbalance in your body or a struggle in your life.

According to the precepts of Chinese medicine, different emotions have specific vibratory frequencies that electrically travel through the acupuncture meridians. For example, the emotion of grief travels through the lung meridian. Feelings of anger flow through the liver meridian. Fear moves through the kidney meridian. Every emotion is associated with a specific one. When we're living in a state of subconscious denial of our will, the body is thrown into a subtle level of imbalance that creates particular symptoms depending on the acupuncture meridian that's being affected. Based on Chinese medicine and the Neuro Emotional Technique (NET) developed by Dr. Scott Walker, the chart on the next page is a list of each acupuncture meridian and its corresponding emotions.

Conscious and subconscious triggers constantly stimulate your emotions. Your will is the engine that propels your spirit along its journey, and it's your spirit that feeds your body and makes it possible for it to adapt and heal. However, without an engine, or your will, your spirit is unable to move. Passion—the authentic expression of emotion—is the fuel for that engine. Your passion is what connects you to your purpose and enables you to use your intention to create abundance in your life. Embracing your experiences with passion is the key to acknowledging and honoring your emotions. Resistance occurs when you don't genuinely respond to your circumstances . . . when you attempt to control how life flows through you and how *you* flow through life.

I had a client whose blood pressure was 150/100. During a treatment, it became clear that she was attempting to control every aspect of her life. She recognized the connection between her need for control and the symptom of high blood pressure. By clearing out the subconscious emotions of fear and anger, her blood pressure went down to 124/84 within two days.

As life moves through you, make appropriate changes in the moment—express your emotions—so that you aren't dragged down by life's undercurrent. Staying true to your purpose and embracing your circumstances with passion helps you stay focused on achieving a desired outcome. Passion maximizes your ability to adapt to even the most unforeseen obstacles and actually uplifts your spirit so that you're able to create a new view with new possibilities.

High blood pressure has many causes. However, I believe that the core reason so many people are taking blood-pressure medications is that they fight rather than flow with life. They struggle with each experience, creating resistance not only in their lives, but in their bodies, too. In Chinese medicine it's said that blood follows chi. *Chi* is life force or the energy that moves us—that is, emotion. It's when we attempt to control our emotions, rather than feel and express them, that we increase the pressure in our lives . . . as well as in our cardiovascular systems.

When there's increased resistance, there's *de*creased conductance, leading to the stagnation of your spirit. This experience results when you keep taking the same path, even though your emotions are telling you to go another route. Stagnation denies Present Time Consciousness (PTC), your authentic self, and is a manifestation of the denial of your will.

Owning your power and living true to your feelings facilitates the chi or life force that feeds and nourishes your body, which enables it to adapt and heal. The journey to awakening your spirit proceeds by expressing your free will, by living in PTC, and by being open to the need and right of others to experience their own journey.

# CHAPTER 9

# SYMPTOMS:
# GIFTS FROM YOUR BODY

One morning while I was on a cruise, talking with my wife, Sara, I began to think about how, as human beings, we've captured and filtered the earth's energy to create an easier way of life. For example, everything that happened on the cruise ship depended on the harnessing of energy and the interdependence of all its parts. The same relationship is at work in the body. Applying The LifeLine Law of Transformation and Creation *(emotions transform energy; energy creates movement; movement is change; and change is the essence of life)*, what happens to the body when your emotions are somehow stifled? What does the body do with *that* energy?

The subconscious is the storehouse of your experiences. When you stifle, stymie, ignore, deny, or internalize your emotions, they get locked away. Because *emotions transform energy, energy creates movement, movement is change, and change is the essence of life,* they don't just sit in the storehouse waiting for permission to be released. They keep moving, banging up against the locked door, sending out below-the-radar messages to your physical body through the autonomic nervous system (ANS). When the body gets these messages, it searches for places to put them. It's when the emotions of the subconscious mind are triggered that the ANS begins to respond in a survival-type fashion. What's important to recognize is that *subconscious* means "automatic." You're not able to rationalize the behavior of the subconscious mind, since its intention is aimed toward survival. However, the situation that's triggering the response doesn't warrant this type of reaction. The result of a prolonged subconscious response is complete and utter exhaustion of the body due to the constant triggers of internalized emotions.

The longer your emotions remain disconnected, the greater the impact they have on the physical body, resulting in it becoming imbalanced. The only time you're aware of your subconscious mind is when it uses a symptom to get your attention. Occasionally that symptom is so deeply buried that it first appears as something as trivial as a headache or elbow pain. But unless you're in tune with your body, you may be missing what the subconscious mind is telling you . . . you could be overlooking the connection to how your body is *expressing* itself. Awakening to The LifeLine Technique helped me realize the subconscious connection between imbalances within the body—due to trapped, unexpressed emotions—and symptoms.

When you have a symptom, such as a headache, nausea, or back pain, it's the body's way of creating dialogue. Symptoms are a language, just like French, Hebrew, Spanish, or English. A symptom is really dis-ease, and dis-ease is the voice that the body uses to express imbalance. It's not the same thing as a breakdown . . . when the body is leaning in one direction or the other, *that's* an imbalance. For example, diarrhea, vomiting, and fever are signs of imbalance, as they're the body's innate intelligence triggering the need to purge poisonous substances. When you're able to bring the body back into balance, it prevents the dis-ease from becoming pathology (diagnosable disease).

Symptoms are a gift. Pain is a gift. They're the body's way of saying that it's time to heal whatever emotions you've internalized, denied, or disconnected from. With this in mind, when you're experiencing symptoms, instead of saying, "I'm getting sick," keep the dialogue going by stating, "My body is beginning to heal." You're actually being provided with an opportunity to listen. This attitude of gratitude enables the molecular structure of your cells to be in a healthier state, shortening the time it will take for your body to regain balance.

The five most dangerous words you can ever say to yourself are: *Maybe it will go away.* When you're confronted with physical or emotional symptoms and choose merely to hope that they'll disappear—rather than determining why your body is communicating with you in this manner—you're putting your life at risk. You're missing the opportunity to engage in an internal dialogue of health on both a conscious and subconscious level.

Unfortunately, we've been taught by our parents, teachers, medical doctors, and now by the pharmaceutical companies through TV advertisements to look upon symptoms as the enemy. We've been told that the body produces symptoms because it's at war with itself, and the secret weapons to deal with illness or disease are pharmaceutical drugs. But taking them beyond the scope of emergencies could worsen or actually silence the symptoms, inhibiting the body's innate ability to heal. As a consequence, the original imbalance is now prone to become a diagnosable disease, commonly referred to as *pathology.* Taking medications for every symptom stops the crucial dialogue between the body and the subconscious mind.

For example, as reported in major media throughout the U.S. in the spring of 2004, the FDA's Center for Drug Evaluation and Research sent a letter to drug manufacturers requesting label changes on antidepressants warning of possible suicide, as well as worsening depression, anxiety, and panic attacks in adults and children. Ten of the most often prescribed antidepressants were on the list: Prozac (also sold generically as fluoxetine), Zoloft, Paxil, Luvox, Celexa, Lexapro, Wellbutrin, Effexor, Serzone, and Remeron.

Does this mean that antidepressants aren't necessary? No. However, the indiscriminate use of them is beyond frightening and needs to be regulated much more carefully. We're so conditioned to take a pill the moment that we endure a painful, scary, or challenging experience—but the consequences are grave. It's time to take responsibility for being on medication. We need to begin by educating ourselves about the meaning of symptoms and stress. Otherwise, we'll continue to experience the devastating effects of overmedicating.

Depression is anger turned inward—anger at oneself—and it leads to a molecular breakdown in the structure of the water that makes up our cells. This causes stagnation in our life force, which results in the body communicating through symptoms.

Unless the emotion of depression is embraced as an opportunity to move through a challenging experience, it will continue infinitely until the experience is faced. For optimal health, it's imperative to allow the body to communicate rather than suppress the symptoms. It's crucial for you to become versed in the method of communication used by your body every moment of every day of your life. This book is an instruction manual in the most important language you'll ever need to learn—human body language!

A new patient came to see me one week after she was told that she no longer had cancer. She had been diagnosed with a grade-four squamous cell carcinoma of the left tonsil that had metastasized to her lymph nodes. She underwent radical surgery to remove the tonsil and 22 lymph nodes in her neck. She also endured 8 weeks of chemotherapy while concurrently receiving 12 weeks of radiation. She stated that the treatments had left her without the ability to produce saliva, to taste, or to swallow effectively. She now has a feeding tube directly connected to her stomach and a main line in her chest to administer medications. She takes morphine every evening to sleep and is on an experimental chemo pill that's supposedly going to prevent recurrence of the cancer. Her doctors recommended that she use a nutritional supplement that's loaded with sugar. She stated, "I feel like a train wreck."

During our first treatment session, I wanted to be sure that her subconscious mind wasn't going to sabotage her goals of optimal health. She was congruent with her goals, so I began to focus on where her body was speaking the loudest. I found that she was leaking energy from her neck and the left side of her face. The emotion of depression came up when I ran The LifeLine Flow Chart. Her body expressed a subconscious death wish that was associated with the depression.

She told me that she'd been feeling down ever since her husband left her and their three children 17 years before. She had a limiting belief about loving herself unconditionally that inhibited her from releasing the depression. We discovered that this feeling originated when she was five years and seven months old, when she was told that she had learning disabilities and wasn't able to do the things that "normal kids" could do. She bought into these limitations as if they were fact, and the depression that she'd internalized since the age of five and a half continued to devastate her mind and body to the point that it practically killed her.

When she left my office, she noticed that her neck and face felt lighter and full of life. She was empowered by the knowledge that she wasn't a victim of cancer, but rather that her body was expressing the emotional pain she had subconsciously disconnected from for so long. She was ready to heal and begin listening to the language that her body so urgently wanted her to hear.

It's important to understand the concept of *emotion* on a much deeper level. Dr. Candace Pert, a noted neurobiologist and the author of the book *Molecules of Emotion,* has proven that neuropeptides—the chemicals triggered by emotions—are thoughts converted into matter. *Webster's New World College Dictionary* defines *emotion* as "complex reactions with both mental and physical manifestations." Dr. Pert's research uncovered that emotions reside in the body and physically interact with cells and tissues.

As I said earlier, symptoms are a gift, and sometimes they have very strange wrapping paper. But once uncovered, they'll turn into exactly what's needed at that moment. One of the unique and simple aspects of The LifeLine Technique is that it empowers you to use symptoms to access the *real* source of the imbalance—the subconscious mind—and release internalized, denied, and disconnected emotions. Bringing those feelings to light and transforming them with the power of Infinite Love & Gratitude opens the body to healing. It's akin to unplugging a stopped-up drain so that the water can flow freely through the pipes.

The following chart represents the cycle between optimal health and death:

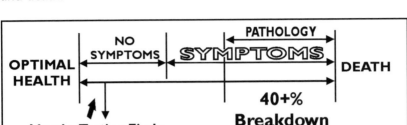

*Pathology* literally means "a diagnosable disease." For pathology to be recognized in a blood test, urinalysis, MRI, mammogram, or bone scan, the body must have already degenerated 40-plus percent. The irony is that when a diagnostic test comes back "positive," it means that you have a disease! This is the point at which most people recognize that their body is imbalanced because, prior to that, they were ignoring or covering up the subtle symptoms—the cough, rash, allergies, and headaches—with over-the-counter drugs.

What happens when you have symptoms but the test results are within the "normal" reference ranges? That's when doctors prescribe medications that have been scientifically proven to eradicate symptoms. But when you don't have a *diagnosable* disease, taking medication for the symptoms is like playing Russian roulette, often with fatal consequences.

As reported in the July 26, 2000, issue of the *Journal of the American Medical Association* (*JAMA*), a study of hospitalized patients found that an estimated 250,000 people die each year from iatrogenic causes (that is, those induced by a physician's activity, manner, or therapy), making this the third leading cause of death in the U.S., after heart disease and cancer! Figures from a Harvard Medical Practice Study, reported in a 1996 *JAMA* article, also demonstrated that widespread use of medication to relieve minor pain has caused a national epidemic. Nearly 20,000 people have died from bleeding stomach ulcers, and close to 200,000 people annually have been hospitalized as a result of using over-the-counter drugs to treat minor pain. I believe that the actual numbers are far greater than what has even been documented.

Whenever you take a pill for a symptom without looking for the underlying cause, you're telling the body, "Shut up, I don't want to hear you." By ignoring what your body is telling you, you're turning off its natural ability to heal, thus placing it in a survival mode. This denial or silencing of its communication is what slowly but surely leads to pathology.

Your body will never heal in this mode. It's working too hard just to survive, just as if it were running away from a tiger. Your body doesn't need to worry about food digestion or boosting its immune system while fleeing a predator. The survival aspect of the nervous system means that your body is focusing on the task of staying alive. Your heart rate and respiration increase, and all your blood rushes away from your internal organs, thus giving your body the instant energy it needs—in the form of oxygen, nutrients, and blood glucose—to deal with a tiger. All your muscles tighten so that you can react more quickly, either to fight or to turn 180 degrees and run away.

Your body is numb to any symptoms when you're in this state. You're fooled into thinking that nothing is wrong because you've been trained that not having symptoms is the same as being healthy. If you're always operating in a survival mode (that is, you're under a lot of stress), you don't feel symptoms until it's too late. Have you ever known someone who worked 10 to 12 hours daily and never missed a day of work? Often three to six months after retiring, the person drops dead of a heart attack. This is such a common scenario because your body is simply unable to spin at the fastest rpm for extended periods of time. It's only able to sprint efficiently for short periods and provide you with enough energy to dash away from a tiger. While it's overwhelmed by the immediate need to survive, your body can't and won't heal.

When your body is running on overload or in survival mode, the energy boost it receives is more like the one you get from drinking coffee, rather than from being well rested or from exercising. You *know* the difference. There are subtle feelings that the body creates in every experience. It's through these sensations that you'll gain insight into when it's numb and in a survival mode or just feeling great. Recognizing the distinction is one of the keys to living an optimally healthy life.

That may be difficult because of the way in which many people live—drinking coffee and diet sodas, eating fast food, and indiscriminately taking medication for every symptom. In effect, if you're numbing yourself with food, alcohol, drugs (prescribed and street), sex, shopping, or work, you're creating patterns of self-destruction that lock symptoms into place . . . the symptoms have become a prison. Before you realize it, multiple dysfunctions on several different levels are expressing themselves. Your body ends up compensating, moving symptoms around like chess pieces, and sometimes you're fooled into thinking that the "issue" or challenge is gone.

It is important to know *how* to listen to the body's *voice,* which speaks emotionally, biochemically, structurally, and/or spiritually. This is where the responsibility falls into the hands of the individual. A thorough understanding of The Five Basics for Optimal Health—quantity, quality, and frequency of water, food, rest, exercise, and owning your power—will enhance the course that your health will take.

Emotionally, the body's voice may speak with irritability, fear, or insecurity. Limiting beliefs could trigger your biochemical body to speak with hormonal imbalances or low blood sugar. Structurally, the body might communicate with low-back pain or muscle aches. Every symptom is an expression of the body's innate intelligence. Be open to feel and you'll gain access to and understand the infinite ways in which the body is ready to heal.

*Chiropractic Philosophy,* by Dr. Joseph B. Strauss, outlines three common approaches used to understand the body's language: mechanistic, pseudo-mechanistic, and vitalistic. The mechanistic approach seeks a silver bullet. *Merriam-Webster's Collegiate Dictionary* defines the word *mechanism* as "a doctrine that holds natural processes to be mechanically determined and capable of complete explanation by the laws of physics and chemistry." The true mechanist believes that only science is real, rejecting any vitalistic concept—anything that can't be empirically demonstrated.

Pseudo-mechanistic individuals acknowledge the existence of forces that they can't see or demonstrate. But in practice, they deny the ability of these forces to run the universe or the body. Most people fall into this category. They recognize that a power greater than themselves created their body and that two cells, in roughly nine months, make a human being. Then, for the next 70 years, they deny that power and allow a finite mind with a mechanistic philosophy the opportunity to run it. They're like the folks who get up every morning and ask God to watch over them before they leave the house, but then put a rabbit's foot, crystal, or some other meaningful symbol in their pocket for luck before departing. There's an inconsistency.

*Vitalism* is defined as "a doctrine that the processes of life are not explicable by the laws of physics and chemistry alone and that life is in some part self-determining." In other words, life is more than just chemical actions and reactions. If we take apart a pocket watch and put it back together properly, it will work. However, if we disassemble a living human being and reassemble it, even putting all the parts back in the right place, it will never function again. There's an inexplicable factor that can't be seen or created in a laboratory.

Dr. B. J. Palmer, the developer of chiropractic, called this factor *innate intelligence.* As I mentioned earlier, Chinese medicine refers to this as *chi.* Ayurvedic healing says that it is *prana.* In different religious texts it's described as the *Divine,* or *Spirit.* When I refer to "spirit" in this book, I'm talking about the electromagnetic field, or the life force, of the body.

The LifeLine Technique will help you understand the vitalistic essence of symptoms and facilitate the ability of your body's innate intelligence to heal. LifeLine practitioners treat people, not disease, focusing on symptoms as the vehicle to recognize the root nature of energetic imbalances. As you can see from the earlier graph, halfway between pathology and optimal health is the cutoff where symptoms begin to express themselves. Your goal should always be to strive toward optimal health and be proactive by maintaining a healthy lifestyle.

~~~

# CHAPTER 10

# BEGIN WITH SELF-LOVE

Many people are victims of chronic pain, illness, and premature death. They've been brainwashed by pharmaceutical companies to focus on eradicating symptoms, rather than taking responsibility for their health and getting to the root cause. As we now know, this view of eradicating symptoms will lead to further suffering. It's crucial that you actively participate in the conversation that your body is having with you at every moment.

Thoughts, feelings, and beliefs are a by-product of your experiences. When you embrace life with Infinite Love & Gratitude, your body has a direct connection to the collective conscious, thus enabling it to do what it does best—*heal*. The human body as a mechanism has evolved to maintain balance and mend itself. It's when we disconnect from Infinite Love & Gratitude that the vitalistic essence of the body is inhibited, causing it to break down and speak with symptoms.

The only occasion when a pharmaceutical drug is necessary is in life-threatening situations. Otherwise, the human body is the best pharmacy on the planet. It's able to produce every chemical known and unknown to humankind. The only time that this pharmacy isn't open for business is when we're disconnected. Infinite Love & Gratitude is the currency that keeps the body, mind, and spirit in business.

*You are your own best doctor.* Rather than looking at symptoms as the cause, learn to use them as a portal to discover *why* your body is talking to you in the first place. Every symptom in your body or challenge in your life is like a mosaic: When standing close to it, the picture is blurry and has no meaning; however, as you move back, you're able to appreciate how all the colors and pieces merge together to form a beautiful work of art. Every thought, feeling, and belief you have is a piece of your own personal artwork. Each color in the mosaic has meaning, as does every symptom or uncomfortable feeling through which your body speaks. The language it uses to communicate with you is an opportunity for you to heal or create abundance in all areas of your life.

Whether you have emotional or physical symptoms, they are your body's way of saying, "I'm not happy with how you're treating me. You've gotten off track—it's time to focus on The Five Basics for Optimal Health."

Author Louise L. Hay, who popularized the connection between mind/body and healing, wrote in an essay in *The Handbook for the Heart*:

> Many people contact me for help with health issues, even very serious ones. All I do is teach them to love themselves. They learn to look at what has gotten in the way of their love and health. . . . I have people look into a mirror, just look into their own eyes, and say, "I love you."

Healing begins when you love yourself unconditionally. Symptoms are an expression of your denial of the need for self-love. The first step of healing is to completely embrace who you are right now. When you neglect self-love, it's reflected in your relationships with others, your health, your work, and every other aspect of your life. The LifeLine healing process helps you see how, when, where, and why you've neglected your need for self-love. It allows you to appreciate the journey that you've already traveled on and prepares you for the road ahead.

I was in the middle of a treatment with a woman named Suzie. I noticed that she seemed distracted, and I asked her to get in touch with the conversation going on in her head.

"Right now, I'm feeling bad that you're running an hour behind and there are several people sitting in the waiting room," she replied.

I asked her to focus on her feelings about the people who were waiting to see me. As she did, Suzie began to recognize that she always put other people's needs and concerns ahead of her own. She started to cry when she realized that she *believed* no one would love her unless she put them first.

To heal, you must accept where and who you are and love yourself unconditionally for being a perfect creation. Here are a couple of analogies:

1.  You have to deposit money in a bank before you can withdraw it.

2.  When flight attendants recite safety presentations before a plane takes off, what do they say about the oxygen mask? "Put on your own mask first before assisting others."

Self-love isn't self-indulgence, selfishness, or self-centeredness. Self-love requires that you own who you are at this moment, without judgment. True happiness is discovered during the healing process; it's a by-product of the journey, not the end result.

Healing is about balance. By using the frequency of Infinite Love & Gratitude, The LifeLine Technique balances the body so that it will be able to accept and harmonize the emotions that you've subconsciously denied. Once harmony is restored, the body's natural ability to heal itself is unleashed. Balance, and therefore healing, begins with self-love.

~ ~ ~

# CHAPTER 11

# HEALING THE REAL PAIN

*The body speaks the mind.* It's very common for chronic health conditions to be triggered during stressful times. Asthma attacks, herpes outbreaks, low-back pain, and digestive disturbances all seem to be provoked when our lives are in turmoil. Symptoms become chronic when we're disconnected from our mind. They serve as a distraction from the *real* pain—the emotional hurt in the subconscious mind. Emotional pain is experienced differently by everyone. We're subconsciously programmed by our families, society, culture, education, religion, and the media to disconnect from our feelings.

Western medicine helps us further disconnect by labeling us as if we *are* the diseases. Defining ourselves as a disease, such as an "asthmatic" or a "diabetic," causes us to further numb the mind, perpetuating subconscious addictions. When I refer to addiction, I'm talking about the *continuous,* subconscious internalization or denial of—or disconnection from—a painful situation. Addiction is a symptom. We long to know our truth, but we're afraid. Our truth, according to author Marianne Williamson, is that "we are powerful beyond measure." We're frightened of our own power, so we subconsciously numb ourselves with chronic symptoms. Ask yourself this question: *Is there any aspect of my life that I'm afraid to embrace without judgment?* If so, that makes you an addict.

While we're aware of addictions that occur on a conscious level, there are stronger ones that happen on a deeper level. We've all been subconsciously conditioned to disconnect, and that traps us in a cycle of addiction. Not only are we left numb *with* chronic pain and disease, we have bought into and *defined* ourselves in terms of those illnesses.

We must first recognize that chronic disease processes are a way that the body dulls emotional pain within the subconscious mind. To heal the chronic process, we have to heal the subconscious wound. Otherwise—sometime, someplace—the subconscious mind will be activated, re-creating the pattern within the body and causing the chronic health condition to reappear. The body will react to the trigger in a classical-conditioning response, and the breakdown will begin again. Every symptom, including addiction, is an opportunity . . . a gift from the body, as well as from the mind. Whether or not a symptom becomes chronic (a subconscious addiction) is determined by our ability to stay connected to an experience when facing emotional and physical pain.

I had a breakthrough with a long-term patient who had been diagnosed with Crohn's disease and kidney stones. Peter, 45, had already undergone multiple surgeries, resulting in the removal of several feet of his intestines. He acknowledged that he hadn't been taking good care of himself and realized that this self-destructive behavior had deeper roots. However, he was unaware of the source of this behavior. Peter's body had been classically conditioned to numb itself on a subconscious level by creating inflammation in his bowel. When he would have certain thoughts in his mind or feelings in his body, this condition would be triggered.

To facilitate Peter's ability to heal, it was important to help him become aware of the subconscious patterns that first triggered the inflammation in his bowel. To begin The LifeLine treatment, I asked Peter to say: "I'm okay that I'm an addict." By making this declarative statement, Peter was able to release the subconscious holding patterns that were perpetuating chronic disease. Unless an addiction is acknowledged and brought to the surface, we remain unaware of the subconscious emotions that are manifesting as chronic disease.

The LifeLine Flow Chart led us through six layers into Peter's subconscious mind. Each layer had to do with Killer-Thought Viruses and Death Modes (which are explained in detail later in the book) that were programming his body to form chronic illness. His life force had diminished in each of the Five Elements, depending upon the layer in which we were working.

At one point, a limiting belief appeared in his fourth (heart) chakra having to do with his inability to unconditionally love himself. While running The LifeLine treatment on Peter, I discovered that the original occurrence of this belief began after two hours and 40 minutes of life. He told me that he was born six weeks premature, his umbilical cord was wrapped around his neck, and his mother almost died during the delivery. At that moment of his birth, in a state of lowered resistance and vulnerability, his subconscious mind created a limiting belief that he didn't love himself unconditionally, along with a Killer-Thought Virus of hopelessness, worry, and low self-esteem.

Through this treatment, we discovered the inflammatory bowel disease that formed in his body later in life was the result of this initial trauma. It was used as a way for him to subconsciously disconnect from the extreme pain of his birth. Peter felt a major shift in his mind and body after the treatment. He said, "I feel like you've just helped me open my mind to a healthy state of being. I'm now ready to heal." Peter has become consciously aware of his responsibility for maintaining his health. He also knows every time his bowels act up not to blame it on the Crohn's disease, but rather to embrace the symptoms as a gift and focus on The Five Basics for Optimal Health.

Owning your power and being authentic in the moment enables you to break the cycle of chronic disease and subconscious addiction. Acknowledging your experiences without judgment empowers you to accept who you are and where you are in life. Choose now to live fearlessly by embracing your truth with Infinite Love & Gratitude.

# Chapter 12

# Beliefs and Healing

My wife, Sara, and I have three cats—Floyd, Zen, and Buddha. Zen, the biggest of the three, is fairly agile, even at 23 pounds. Whenever we use our electric can opener to open the cats' food, Zen is usually the first one in the kitchen. A couple of years ago, I opened a can, but Zen didn't come bounding into the kitchen. I went looking for him to make sure that he got some food before his brother, Buddha, ate it all. I found Zen, picked him up, and placed him on the floor. When I did, he fell on his face. I thought, *Oh my God, I dropped him! He broke his leg!* I quickly realized, however, that Zen didn't have a broken leg—he was paralyzed.

I immediately began to perform acupuncture, energy work, and chiropractic treatments on Zen, but I didn't notice any improvement. The next day I took him to a veterinarian, who conducted several tests, including a sensory test in which he squeezed Zen's paw with pliers. There was no reaction. The vet asked whether Zen had exhibited any signs of pain before the onset of the paralysis. I shook my head. His diagnosis was that Zen either had a herniated disc or an embolism lodged in his cervical spine.

I've been trained in veterinary manipulative orthopedics, and I'm very much in tune with the structural health of "my boys." I knew that there was no way Zen had a herniated disc. However, I wasn't sure about the embolism.

Within a week, I took Zen to the vet again because I felt that he still wasn't improving. I was heartbroken because I thought that I was going to have to put him down. I didn't want him to suffer any longer, and if he was going to die, I wanted to be holding him in my arms. However, when the vet conducted another sensory test, again squeezing Zen's paw with pliers, Zen hissed. The vet said that the sensation in his paw showed that he was moving in the right direction. Six days later, Zen was visibly making progress. A week after that, he was walking and jumping up on chairs. The vet was as amazed as Sara and I were. Zen had achieved a complete, miraculous recovery from total paralysis. . . . Eight more lives to go!

Zen's recovery helped me realize that animals, like children, don't have limiting beliefs that impede their healing. They don't question the possibility that a treatment, even if it's nonconventional, can help them.

My understanding of the connection between beliefs and healing also came from experiences with two human patients.

Molly, who was 53, came to see me after her medical doctor said that she had one month to live. She was diagnosed with stage-four pancreatic cancer, which she'd been told was fast growing and terminal. She didn't want to die with her head in the toilet because of chemotherapy—if she was going to go, she said, she wanted to do so with her dignity and pride intact.

During our first session, I adjusted Molly's ribs, which enabled her to breathe more freely. When we began more intensive, holistic types of treatments, her body responded wonderfully. After an entire year of treatments, Molly decided to see her oncologist again, the person who had given her the "one-month-to-live" diagnosis. She wanted to get a CT scan to see what was going on. It revealed that the cancer hadn't disappeared, but it had defied her doctor's prediction . . . the tumor hadn't grown. Despite that good news, Molly had hoped and expected that the cancer would have completely disappeared. At that moment, her belief that "everybody who has cancer must die" took hold. She passed away within six months.

My heart still aches with the thought of Molly's death. However, I'm also filled with a strong sense of satisfaction and pride that as a result of our healing work together during those 18 months, the "fast-growing," aggressive cancer hadn't grown at all. Molly was able to celebrate anniversaries and birthdays and take walks in the sun with her friends with her pride and dignity intact. I grew so much as a physician and a person from my experience with Molly. I treated her prior to awakening to The LifeLine Technique, and I know that my experience with her was a huge stepping-stone to its development.

Another patient named Bill, who was in his 40s, was diagnosed with multiple sclerosis (MS) and was confined to a wheelchair when he first came to see me. After two or three months of treatment, Bill was walking laps around the office.

"Dr. D," he would say, "you're the Michael Jordan of doctors."

"It's not me—it's you," I'd respond, laughing. "It's your body that's healing itself."

One day Bill didn't show up for his appointment. I was surprised because he'd never missed a session. I called and asked if he was all right.

"I just couldn't make it," he replied.

Bill never rescheduled, and I never saw him again. I was still treating his wife, however, and I inquired why Bill no longer came to the office.

"He just doesn't *believe* in this anymore," she said.

"He was walking!" I exclaimed. "What's going on?"

She simply shrugged her shoulders.

~

What *is* going on? *You are what you believe yourself to be.* Once you've created your *identity* based on limiting beliefs, it's difficult, even scary, to accept change. What's the source of beliefs? Your life experiences help to mold them; and they're influenced by your relationships with your parents, siblings, spouses, partners, doctors, bosses, and co-workers, as well as religion, gender, race, age, the media, personal losses, traumas, and so on. With your senses—vision, smell, hearing, taste, touch, and feelings—you're able to perceive the environment. And from these impressions, your *beliefs* are created.

It's through life experiences that you learn to identify with the value of a moment. Values give the world meaning. They're the catalyst for choosing whether to transcend challenges or be overwhelmed by them. When you value the infinite possibilities and potential of each moment, there are no limits to your beliefs.

Your perceptions of the outside world send signals to all your cells, telling them what's going on so that the body can adapt to its environment. Depending upon the situation, the body's nervous system will respond in one of two ways: (1) in a sympathetic/"fright, fight, or flight" survival mode, or (2) in a parasympathetic/relaxation or healing mode.

Dr. Bruce Lipton, a cellular biologist and the author of the book *The Biology of Belief,* documented the connection between perception and health. Dr. Lipton set out to discover the "brain" of a cell. He began the process by studying deoxyribonucleic acid, more commonly known as DNA.

DNA was discovered in the early 1950s. This scientific advance was the result of the Nobel Prize–winning work of two scientists, Drs. James Watson and Francis Crick, based on the initial research done by Dr. Rosalind Franklin. Since the discovery of DNA, technology and science have found many ways of using it—from genetic fingerprinting to identifying criminals.

At the heart of the scientists' work was the idea that DNA is the *brain* of a cell. That being said, if a person has the chromosomal, genetic makeup for breast cancer, inflammatory bowel disease, or bipolar disorder, the belief was that he or she would eventually develop that disease. As a consequence, in this day and age, some women are having complete, bilateral, radical mastectomies without any physical sign of cancer due to a genetic evaluation of their DNA.

The tragedy, as Dr. Lipton's research documented, is that DNA is *not* the brain of the cell. Dr. Lipton conducted tests in which he removed the nucleus, containing the DNA, of a cell. He hypothesized that if DNA were the brain, something very predictable would happen when it was taken out: The cell would die instantly, just as people would die if their brains were removed.

However, just the opposite occurred . . . the cell lived. Dr. Lipton discovered that the brain of a cell is its protein receptors—very thin membranes that function like a cell-phone antenna, sending messages directly to the nucleus. These protein receptors are not only on the outside of a cell and in the nucleus, but also in our senses—the rods and cones in our eyes, for instance, or the cilia (hairs) in our nose and ears. All our sensory receptors are made of protein, which in an antenna-type fashion, picks up the vibratory frequencies of sound and light and sends the signal to our brain. The brain then directs a signal down the spinal cord to specific areas of the body, depending on the message.

When the protein receptors on the outside of individual cells receive the information, they send a signal to the nucleus, where the messages are encoded. From that encoding, the protein *creates* the DNA for a specific cell so that it will adapt to its environment. The nucleus, according to Dr. Lipton's research, is in fact the reproductive system of a cell—it's the center of a cell's ability to regenerate.

Dr. Lipton's exhaustive studies also sought to discover how a cell responds to stimuli, similar to the way the brain reacts to the senses. He wanted to know how the liver, lungs, or intestines respond to what's going on in the external environment.

What he discovered, as explained in his book, is the link between beliefs and our state of health: "Cellular biologists now recognize that the environment (external universe and internal physiology), and more importantly our *perception* of the environment, directly controls the activity of our genes."

At this very moment, your liver isn't conscious that you're reading this book, your lungs don't know what color shirt you're wearing, and your intestines aren't aware of the temperature outside. All your organs rely on your senses to receive external stimulation so that your internal body will adapt optimally. Your autonomic nervous system (ANS) functions in a sympathetic/"fright, fight, or flight" survival mode or a parasympathetic/healing mode. Dr. Lipton discovered a catch-22: Belief systems serve as a filter through which we perceive the environment.

Let me give an example. Suppose that you're waiting at a bus stop when a red Jeep drives by. The last time you were standing at a bus stop and saw a red Jeep, there was an accident. You had to leap out of the way to keep from being injured. On a subconscious level, seeing that particular vehicle now triggers the limiting beliefs associated with the accident—it changes your perception of the situation, and you feel as if you're in danger. That sense of alarm sends a signal inside your body to every organ, muscle, and cell. You feel the need to run because of the *subconsciously perceived* danger. The sympathetic nervous system kicks in, and the body goes into a survival mode. Inside your cells, the DNA is reproduced and continues to perpetuate patterns of fear, even though the red Jeep you see presently poses no danger whatsoever.

Your limiting beliefs filter this benign situation and keep the trauma alive, causing your body to be more susceptible to breakdown. The survival mode is good for one thing—survival. Any extended state beyond its inherent function leads to breakdown. A deer, for example, senses a mountain lion before it actually sees it, based on its innate survival skills. If the deer constantly walked around in fear of the mountain lion, it would lose its ability to *truly* recognize danger, thus creating a bigger threat than the predator.

Near the Arctic Circle, people's perception of their icy environment facilitates the creation of DNA that helps them adapt. Similarly, those who live along the equator have their own sense of their surroundings, and their DNA has changed over the generations to allow them to adapt optimally. Since September 11, 2001, we've all changed our perception about the possibility of planes crashing into high-rise buildings. That belief is embedded in our protein receptors, which send messages to cells throughout the body, creating DNA that causes many people to live in a fright, fight, or flight survival mode every time they see an airplane. Consequently, anything similar to their collective social experience will on a subconscious level re-create the limiting belief locked in by the initial trauma. This experience results in the autonomic nervous system functioning in a survival mode. Suddenly, life becomes overwhelming, and they're stricken with panic attacks, phobias, and anxiety. The fear mechanism is lost, and they're stuck in a holding pattern of disconnection and disease. The challenge is that they're unaware of the origin of the panic and anxiety and its connection to the initial trauma.

There are certain belief systems that are anchored in our being. Holocaust survivors, Native Americans, and descendants of slaves have their traumatic experiences imprinted in their protein receptors, which in turn are passed along through generations, creating certain perceptions and inherent belief systems.

The body responds to anything remotely similar to that trauma by increasing the production of the protein receptors that are keeping it alive. As a result, we continue to attract more experiences that facilitate the subconscious disconnection. For example, feelings of low self-worth, insecurity, and shame will continue infinitely in a loop of complete annihilation until they're embraced by the conscious mind. Subconsciously, we continue to attract relationships, jobs, and other life experiences that trigger these emotions. This may seem self-destructive; however, through our feelings of low self-worth, insecurity, and shame, we awaken to the patterns and emotions lying dormant within us. By recognizing the symptoms of our body or the stress in our life as the language of the subconscious mind, we're able to break the subconscious addictions to pain and suffering.

In the film *What the Bleep Do We Know!?* Dr. Joe Dispenza says:

> If I change my mind, will I change my choices? If I change my choices, will my life change? Why can't I change? What am I addicted to? What will I lose that I am chemically attached to? And what person, place, thing, time, or event that I'm chemically attached to, that I don't want to lose because I may have to experience the chemical withdrawal from that? Hence the human drama.

Because 98 percent of our reality is subconscious and 2 percent is conscious, at the sensory level, we *miss* 98 percent of what's happening around us. Right now, without *consciously* thinking about it, do you know what your feet feel like touching the floor? Are you presently thinking of your mother's maiden name or her birthday?

Are you aware of the emotions that you're experiencing in this very moment? The subconscious mind is aware of this and much more.

The conscious and subconscious minds are portals that connect us to the physical body, as well as to the collective conscious. The collective conscious is Infinite Love & Gratitude . . . it's the energy of the universe, which has been described as God by many religions. Think of the conscious mind as the tip of the iceberg, and the subconscious mind as what lies below the surface. Each time we view the pain and challenges of life as an opportunity to heal, we take one step closer to being connected to our subconscious mind.

Emotions are our *super*conscious mind. The superconscious acts as an attractor field and is a combination of both the conscious and subconscious minds. When a subconscious emotion is triggered, an imbalance is created internally. This affects the flow of our life force through our acupuncture meridians, resulting in the body expressing itself with physical symptoms and life presenting us with emotional challenges. The type of symptoms or challenges experienced is directly related to the acupuncture meridian that's not flowing freely. They aren't a form of victimization, but rather an intricate language that our body and life are using to warn us: "Stay in the moment, no matter how difficult it may be, so that you can learn from the experience and reconnect to your infinite potential." In fact, no matter how challenging or painful your emotions are, have faith and embrace them with courage and passion. When you do, you'll find that you're able to face any obstacle, achieve any goal, and overcome any trauma.

With the power of Infinite Love & Gratitude, The LifeLine Technique removes the roadblocks from the subconscious mind, creating a more conscious life. By opening the subconscious mind, the barriers to healing become more apparent, allowing us to view the potential dangers that exist more clearly. As with anything, the more you practice opening the subconscious mind, the easier it becomes to master and live life truly in the present moment.

At a recent seminar in Chicago, a woman was treated using The LifeLine Technique to help her release the limiting beliefs that were preventing her from losing weight. She first made a declarative statement about being okay with her present size, acknowledging her current weight challenge. She was previously unaware of the subconscious holding patterns that were keeping her from shedding the extra pounds. After harmonizing the internalized, denied, and disconnected emotions about her current weight, she then made positive statements about the goals that she wanted to achieve. We harmonized those subconscious patterns, and within the next two weeks, she lost ten pounds. Coupled with The Five Basics for Optimal Health of proper quantity, quality, and frequency of water, food, rest, exercise, and owning her power, she had all the tools necessary to accomplish her goal. Amazing as it sounds, it's truly that simple: The first step is to reconnect to the subconscious mind.

Dr. Victor Frank, developer of Total Body Modification (TBM) always says, "If you keep doing what you've always done, you'll keep getting what you've always gotten." Our beliefs can do us harm, even if we're not aware of them. The most important thing is to recognize that we have the power to change. So the first step is recognition. The second is speaking our truth: *I want health. I deserve to be financially secure. I am worthy of an authentic, reciprocal relationship. I love myself unconditionally. I live my life with passion. I follow my true path in life.* Be open to the fact that the moment you decide your life will change, you have the power to transform the impossible into the possible.

By becoming aware of the fear-based beliefs that filter your sensory perception, you awaken the power to create positive, love-based thoughts that facilitate and attract what you desire. In the example of the woman who attended the Chicago seminar, harmonizing her limiting beliefs transformed her energy and created movement in her life that enabled her to lose the weight she desired.

Emotions transform energy and energy creates movement. The movement that's present in your life will determine the direction in which you're headed. The subconscious patterns that may be holding you back from achieving your dreams can now be harmonized with Infinite Love & Gratitude.

# CHAPTER 13

# FREEING YOURSELF TO HEAL

There are two laws by which we live. One is made by humans. This law provides society with guidelines for structure, safety, and harmony. The other is created from the universe and is the law of nature. When followed, it reveals the path for us to find structure, safety, and harmony within ourselves.

When we break the laws of humans, we're given a fine or ticket or we're sent to jail. We're punished for not maintaining the structure, safety, and harmony within our community. In contrast, when we break the laws of nature, our bodies begin to break down. Symptoms are a sign that we haven't followed the laws of nature—we've disconnected from our emotions—and that we aren't maintaining structure, safety, and harmony within ourselves. The body only speaks with symptoms: Physically, we begin to experience pain, discomfort, and dysfunction; emotionally, we're stricken with depression, anxiety, and fear. The police and judicial system enforce the laws of humans, but we ourselves are responsible for upholding the laws of nature.

We know that there are consequences for breaking the laws of humans. However, we aren't always conscious of the repercussions of not abiding by those of nature. As is often said, we're all spiritual beings having a human experience. When we break the laws of nature, our human experience is disease. A tree whose roots aren't planted firmly in the ground won't survive. Neither will one that's fed too much or too little water. All of the laws of nature that affect a tree also influence *our* well-being.

Just as the tree has a natural rhythm that flows from season to season, so do we. Learning the laws of nature is essential for living optimally. They include providing the body with the proper quantity, quality, and frequency of water, food, rest, exercise, and owning your power—and being willing to change.

Diana, who was in her late 30s, came to see me because she was suffering from environmental illness. She was allergic to seemingly everything, and her situation was very challenging. I knew that she had the potential to heal, and there was a part of her that knew it, too. However, she had a powerful fear: that of being well and of owning her power. When I encouraged her by talking about her body's ability to heal itself and her ability to choose health, she accused me of being arrogant. Every supportive thing I said to her was met with a negative, limiting response.

"I can't heal," she said. "Everything makes me sick. You don't know what you're talking about." She had spent the last 14 years "trying to get well," she stated, and she believed that I didn't really understand what was going on with her. Diana never scheduled another appointment.

In her book *Why People Don't Heal and How They Can,* Caroline Myss writes:

> I believe that we are all born with a certain packet of perceptions, of "that which we know to be true." One of the perceptions in that packet is that if we let go of certain things, our lives are going to change. And the reality is that we are actually more afraid of change than we are of death.

Myss refers to this belief as *woundology,* a kind of "welfare state of the soul" in which we prefer to remain caught in the pain of chronic illness, disease, addiction, past traumas, and/or tragedies rather than to do the work needed to heal ourselves.

What is the source of woundology? I believe that it's both fear of healing and lack of love, particularly self-love. For most of us, the fear of healing stems from our anxieties about change. Even if our current state is uncomfortable, it's at least *familiar.* Think about people who have been diagnosed with diabetes but who continue to maintain the same unhealthy lifestyles . . . or what about individuals who stay in abusive relationships?

Fear of change keeps us driving down the same streets to work every day. These behaviors are familiar on a primordial, core level. They're at the base of our subconscious mind.

As we attempt to move toward healing on a conscious level, the mind brings in all the data of its experiences . . . it becomes aware of possibilities. But those feelings are immediately met by limiting beliefs of pessimism, triggering self-doubt. Our subconscious mind sounds an alarm: If we change, we aren't going to be loved. The radar flashes: *Beware. Change is unknown and painful.*

Hal and Sidra Stone wrote two books that address this issue, *Embracing Each Other* and *Embracing Our Selves.* The Stones believe that the human being is composed of multiple energies. The primary one inside all of us, they write, is a vulnerable (inner) child. Before babies are born, their data is raw; they are liquid computers ready to be programmed. During their gestational period, they take on the emotions of their mothers. After birth, every touch, noise, and movement—every experience—programs newborns, influencing who they will become and creating bonding patterns between them and their family. Those patterns will either stimulate or inhibit the flow of their growth.

How do you think we're affected by parents who are constantly critical or who use anger to express themselves? We very likely internalize our feelings, developing a response that's not a true reflection of what our authentic needs really are.

Disease and health are both learned behaviors. We're born with the ability to express our basic needs. When we're hungry and must be fed, we cry. When we want to be held and comforted, we kick and scream. When we're tired and have to rest, we become irritable and fussy. This expression of our basic needs is, on a core level, our way of communicating the need for love.

Love, both given and received, is the primary nutrient that feeds us and enables us to grow and adapt. When we're denied that feeling, we search for alternative ways to receive it. We've learned that certain behaviors are rewarded with love, and we turn to them to maintain the caring connection to our primary relationships. This denial of our authentic needs creates a scenario of self-destructive patterns in which we're not able to own our power. We end up disliking the part of ourselves that we've denied and even, at times, hating it. That dislike or hate (both conscious and subconscious) causes the molecular structure of the water that comprises our bodies to stagnate and become distorted.

More critically, because water conducts electricity, our life force is inhibited, increasing the possibility of breakdown and decreasing our potential for adaptation and survival. At the very root of all desire is the need to be loved. When messages from the environment tell you that being yourself could result in *losing* love, who do you become?

Because we want to be cherished, we act in a manner that assures we'll get approval. If our vulnerable child feels like singing and being playful, but the critical parent wants us to be quiet, we'll be quiet. We disavow the part of ourselves that needs to laugh and have fun. The singing, playful inner child becomes buried and disowned, retreating to the shadow side, a side that's scary to express. On the outside, we're very serious, but that isn't our authentic self. For example, people born in Israel are called *sabras*. They're named after a fruit that grows from a cactus. On the outside it has prickly thorns that protect the plant from being eaten, but on the inside it has a sweet, delicate core. Israeli sabras live in an environment where there's a constant threat of danger. Because of this, they're known for their tough countenance . . . while at the same time, their core is rich with tradition, insight, and love.

Our vulnerable child is the intermediary between our primary and our disowned selves. Because this part of us always strives to be loved, we create a primary self that assures this emotion will remain. We disown our authentic self in order to maintain a loving connection with key relationships, such as the one with our parents.

What's the foremost reason, then, why so many people are afraid of getting well? The answer is the fear of losing love as soon as we reclaim our disowned selves. There's a subconscious reaction, reminding us of the moment that we denied our authentic self.

I'm reminded of a quote that's most often attributed to Nelson Mandela, the former president of South Africa. It was actually written by author Marianne Williamson, and it appears in her book *A Return to Love: Reflections on the Principles of A Course in Miracles*:

> Our deepest fear is not that we are inadequate. Our deepest fear is that we are powerful beyond measure. It is our light, not our darkness, that frightens us. We ask ourselves, Who am I to be brilliant, gorgeous, talented, fabulous? Actually, who are you *not* to be? You are a child of God. Your playing small doesn't serve the world. There's nothing enlightened about shrinking so that other people won't feel insecure around you. . . . We were born to make manifest the glory of God that is within us. It's not just in some of us; it's in everyone. And as we let our own light shine, we unconsciously give other people permission to do the same. As we're liberated from our own fear, our presence automatically liberates others.

Fear of our own power causes us to maintain dysfunctional connections, no matter what the consequences. We've been brainwashed to believe that darkness (in other words, symptoms and challenges) is the root cause of our discontent. The truth is that the source of darkness is denying our light. Owning our power and embracing love unconditionally releases the suffocating hold of fear. Symptoms and challenges are the lighthouse in the darkness that guides us to unconditional self-love. Just as Marianne Williamson so eloquently wrote: ". . . as we let our own light shine, we unconsciously give other people permission to do the same. As we're liberated from our own fear, our presence automatically liberates others."

Every aspect of life has the potential to create challenges for us stemming from the original incident when we denied a part of ourselves in order to maintain a love connection. Although it may feel far removed, this is how we "learn" disease. When we view the symptoms related to relationship issues, health challenges, financial struggles, and spiritual stagnation as an opportunity to liberate ourselves, we're free to create the life we desire—the life we're capable of living. In the meantime, the personas we've developed are a chance to find our Holy Grail, our connection to the Divine. Each and every persona provides a journey inward to discover our authentic self.

~ ~ ~

# CHAPTER 14

# YOUR PERSONAS AND HEALING

*P*ersona is defined as "the outer personality or façade presented to others." Everyone has multiple personas. Depending upon the circumstances—whether you're with your parents, siblings, friends, co-workers, family, boss, strangers, or alone in a car listening to your favorite song—a different one emerges. Sometimes your personas become compartmentalized or disowned.

For example, David's father, Steve, constantly expressed anger. Steve was a walking time bomb ready to explode at any moment. Whenever David made a mess in the kitchen or his room, his father yelled and spanked him. If he received a grade less than a B, Steve reacted with judgment and severely punished him. David learned how to tiptoe around his dad by becoming overly tidy and making sure that he always received high grades in school. David subconsciously became aware of the subtle cues from his father and was able to sense Steve's anger by the tone of his voice and his body language.

David lived in constant fear of being yelled at, judged, and punished. In response to his fear, he embraced the persona of a "pleaser," while denying his own independent needs and desires. He learned how to maintain a superficially peaceful environment with his angry, volatile father. David disowned the child within himself who enjoyed living in the moment and acting upon his free will.

On a subconscious level, David disliked the part of himself that yearned to make his father happy. The moment David denied his own needs, a persona was developed and a dysfunctional pattern was set into motion, affecting both his nervous system and acupuncture meridians. This pattern inhibited his ability to adapt to various situations when his free will was challenged. Because of David's denial, his body began to "talk" to him with migraine headaches and hypoglycemia. His doctor gave him several medications, but none of them helped. Ultimately, the symptoms of chronic migraines and hypoglycemia provided David with an opportunity to own his power by acknowledging and honoring what he'd originally denied. With the power of Infinite Love & Gratitude, David and I harmonized his internalized emotions of anger, fear, and grief. He no longer has the headaches, and his blood sugar is now stable.

~

If you have a health challenge that isn't going away with basic treatments, the pattern of dysfunction in your body is very likely being held in a different persona. Dysfunctional patterns are created when you respond to an experience out of fear rather than faith. Unless the persona affected is specifically accessed, it will be extremely difficult to get to the core of the symptom. Through The LifeLine Technique, you'll be able to identify the number of personas an individual has and determine which ones hold dysfunctional patterns. If the persona that holds them isn't the one being worked on, then the patterns of imbalance will never be reached.

When you're acting or reacting out of a persona that has dysfunctional patterns, your electromagnetic field isn't unified. This can be recognized as limiting behaviors that continue to repeat themselves. Relationship issues, health challenges, financial struggles, and lacking passion for life all stem from a non-unified electromagnetic field. When fear is your modus operandi, you hold on to old history because it's familiar in order to maintain the illusion of safety.

When your field is unified with Infinite Love & Gratitude, you'll find it easy to accept what you've denied and tap in to the limitless possibilities of the present moment. By unifying the electromagnetic field, the subconscious denials become conscious, enabling you to own your power and transform the dysfunctional patterns. Once these are balanced, you'll be able to embrace your experiences with faith and courageously live your life with intention and purpose.

Through muscle testing, we discover at what age a dysfunctional pattern began, as well as what occurred to cause a specific persona to develop. By harmonizing this persona, we get to the original source of the imbalance in the body-mind-spirit.

The experiences you're having now are the result of the light reflected from your past, just as the illumination we receive from the stars comes to us from thousands of light-years away. Once your electromagnetic field is unified, you'll continue to experience situations that have been attracted to you from your personal history. However, there's a transition period before you begin to receive the light you reflect as a unified field.

Take a moment right now and *feel*. Scan your entire body with your mind. Begin with your head, and take note of your feelings of comfort and discomfort. When you discover an area that's holding discomfort, stop and appreciate it. Pay attention to the depth or the intensity of the discomfort. Is it sharp or dull? Is it deep or more superficial? Is it localized or diffuse? Breathe deeply into your abdomen while you continue to appreciate the discomfort. Send Infinite Love & Gratitude to that area, and pay attention to what happens to the quality of the feeling. You'll begin to notice that it dissipates as you breathe. Now, move on to your neck, shoulders, arms, hands, chest, and abdomen, scanning each area of your body. Stop when you come to a region that's holding tightness, heaviness, numbness, or pain. Breathe and observe whatever thoughts or images begin to flow in your mind. You may notice that a voice begins to speak inside your head when you get to a particular area of discomfort. Embrace the thoughts, images, memories, and voices, breathing as you send them Infinite Love & Gratitude.

You're learning how to listen to the conversation that your body is having with you in every moment. Listening is the most important aspect of communication and will enable you to focus your intention on your body's authentic needs. Many of us are engaged in a monologue when it comes to conversing with our physical self. It's a monologue of hate, judgment, and criticism of the parts of ourselves that we want to disown. When our body speaks to us with symptoms and challenges, we either ignore the messages or tell it to "shut up" by using medication or addiction. However, a healthy relationship requires a dialogue. The aspects of ourselves that we hate, judge, and criticize must be embraced with Infinite Love & Gratitude.

Learning to listen is the first step in having a dialogue. Whether it's a pain in a muscle, bone, or other region, it's our body's direct way of communicating. By paying attention to our feelings, we open ourselves up to the poetic manifestation of our body's needs. Healthy communication provides a forum for authentic expression and listening without judgment. When we dialogue with our body in this manner, we'll soon recognize our inner beauty, the flow of life, and the infinite possibilities of being.

Dialoguing with your body can be used in every experience you have in your life. Pay close attention to your feelings while talking to a friend or your spouse, or while eating a meal. Embrace *all* of your experiences, and *feel.* Notice the difference between the comfort and discomfort that you're feeling in every moment. Then own your power, creating healthy boundaries and relationships along the way.

# CHAPTER 15

# IT'S YOUR RESPONSIBILITY

Some people have experienced the most horrific or inhumane circumstances and yet have found a way to persevere. The late Dr. Viktor Frankl was a Holocaust survivor and psychiatrist, as well as the author of *Man's Search for Meaning.* Curious about why some people were able to endure horrendous circumstances and others weren't, he discovered that individuals with passion for life, a deep spiritual conviction, and optimism were survivors. He wrote: "Ultimately, man should not ask what the meaning of his life is, but rather he must recognize that it is *he* who is asked. In a word, each man is questioned by life; and he can only answer to life by *answering for* his own life; to life he can only respond by being responsible."

As a result of his studies, Dr. Frankl developed an entire school of psychotherapy known as *logotherapy.* He helped his patients overcome their terrible circumstances by working with them on regaining their passion for life, deepening their spiritual beliefs, and becoming aware of emerging opportunities by taking full responsibility for their lives.

I have a patient named Chris who was diagnosed with ulcerative colitis, which allopathic physicians consider to be an incurable inflammatory bowel disease. He first came to see me after having been hospitalized . . . his situation was so critical that he almost died. After taking down Chris's history, I realized that he was extremely dehydrated and his blood-sugar metabolism was severely imbalanced. It was also clear to me that it was difficult for Chris to express his emotions. He was having challenges in his family and didn't know how to confront them. All of these situations contributed to the inflammatory process that was devastating his colon.

After his first treatment, Chris began to embrace The Five Basics for Optimal Health. He started by drinking one quart of water daily for every 50 pounds of body weight, adopting a healthy eating program, and making time to sleep so that his body would be able to heal. He gradually added an exercise regime, and he began to confront the stressful situations in his life by authentically expressing his emotions.

Chris took full responsibility for his health and always maintained an optimistic attitude, even in the most difficult moments. Although his allopathic doctor said that he'd have this condition for the rest of his life and be permanently dependent on medication, he's been healed from ulcerative colitis for two years and is no longer taking the drugs. Chris has made the commitment to maintain healthy lifestyle choices and now sees me for maintenance health visits.

In a way, Chris's healing journey can be likened to a gauntlet—a notably difficult challenge. Many before him took up the gauntlet and won, surviving every possible situation imaginable. But when you have the attitude *I'll never make it through,* or you view yourself as a victim of your circumstances, you've given up without taking the first step.

Lao-tzu said, "The journey of a thousand miles begins with a single step." The first step to healing is to take responsibility for your life. Even if you feel as if you don't have the tools to heal (money, access to healing professionals, parents, friends, and religious/support groups), you have the power and the innate capacity to choose to get well. Begin with an optimistic attitude, and have faith that however long the journey takes, you can and will make it through. There's no right or wrong in terms of the amount of time it will take. Trust yourself to have experiences, even if they're scary.

How do you trust yourself? There's a part of you, on some rudimentary level, that can tell when something is right or wrong. Go by what you're *feeling.* You just have to believe in your instincts. Of the infinite number of roads you can take, the correct path is the one that you're on. Just keep going, and don't ever give up.

When I was 12, my dad gave me a plaque that read: "Opportunity is often missed because it is disguised as hard work." Healing is hard work; it's focus, commitment, and action. It's about the attitude you choose to maintain during difficult circumstances. How you decide to view a situation—either as an opportunity for change or for victimhood—determines the outcome. Whether you heal, and how and when you do so . . . your beliefs, attitude, and passion determine if you're ready to take full responsibility and embrace the changes your life needs for optimal health.

# CHAPTER 16

# YOUR BODY'S EMOTIONAL EXPRESSION

E very emotion travels throughout the body via the acupuncture
meridians. When your feelings aren't expressed, there's a
decreased flow of life force that results in symptoms. As
mentioned earlier, symptoms are a gift—the language your body
uses to get your attention. By listening to it, you awaken to the
subconscious emotions that you've disconnected from, and you're
able to respond to your body's needs.

Symptoms occur on three levels: emotional, structural, and
biochemical. The next few chapters will explain *why* there has been a
decreased flow of life force so that you can develop a comprehensive
understanding of the body's language.

There are five ways in which the body expresses itself
emotionally: *Thought Viruses, Emotional Cancer, Personal Invasion,
Shock,* and *Life/Death Mode.* Let me explain in detail how each of
these manifests itself.

## Thought Viruses

I first read about Thought Viruses in the book *Thought Viruses:
Powerful Ways to Change Your Thought Patterns and Get What You Want
in Life,* by Donald Lofland, Ph.D., a Neuro-Linguistic Programming

expert. Dr. Lofland wrote about four different types of Thought Viruses: *Trigger, Limiting, Killer,* and *Gemini.* A Thought Virus is no different from a virus that causes influenza or one that wreaks havoc on your computer—but it affects you emotionally rather than physically. By its very nature, a virus is weak until it has a host. As soon as it finds one, however, it replicates within that host and then spreads to another.

If you have antivirus software protection on your computer system, an inadvertently downloaded virus probably won't infect your computer. But let's say your computer exhibits the effects of a virus that's changed its program to make it react in a certain way. Is it the machine that's causing the malfunction or is it the virus? The same is true for your body. A virus doesn't naturally exist within it; in fact, it *can't* if the body is healthy. When the mind or body is in a state of lowered resistance, though, a virus can infiltrate your cells, penetrating their outer layer, burrowing in, and changing the DNA pattern. A cell or mind reprogrammed by a virus will begin to respond in the way that the virus has been designed.

Likewise, a Thought Virus can't live in your mind unless your system isn't protecting itself properly. So how do you shield yourself from Thought Viruses? You use Present Time Consciousness (PTC), which includes The Five Basics for Optimal Health of water, food, rest, exercise, and owning your power.

## Trigger-Thought Viruses

Trigger-Thought Viruses enter the mind via the sensory passages you use to perceive the world you live in. They're triggered by things you see, hear, smell, taste, feel, or intuit. Say that you're invited to a friend's house for a spaghetti dinner, and as soon as you walk in the door and smell the sauce, you begin to feel fear. Or maybe you enter a music store: Mozart's Symphony no. 39 is playing, and you're overwhelmed by anger and resentment. Or perhaps someone brushes against your arm, and suddenly you're feeling insecure.

Why does this happen? At some point during your life, you experienced a trauma or loss that was associated with a particular sense. When it occurred, spaghetti sauce was cooking, Symphony no. 39 was playing, or someone touched you in a certain way—and your feelings of fear, anger, resentment, or insecurity were internalized on a subconscious level.

The triggering of your senses caused your subconscious to forget about the present moment, and your body began to run the old pattern of trauma or loss. Your emotional and physical reactions go haywire—you feel as if you're spiraling out of control. However, it's not you . . . it's the Trigger-Thought Virus that has impregnated your DNA, causing you to react with emotions or feelings that have nothing to do with what you're actually experiencing.

Dysfunction is physiological as well as emotional, and thus it affects our behavior, depending upon the code of the virus. It can cause all types of aberrant reactions on an emotional, structural, or biochemical level—from headaches and muscle pain to indigestion and diabetes. Unless the Trigger-Thought Virus is recognized and then harmonized, the patterns will continue to run, affecting the body physiologically, emotionally, and behaviorally.

### Limiting-Thought Viruses

A Limiting-Thought Virus causes you to believe that your potential to succeed has limits. It restricts your ability to have good relationships, as well as to be healthy, financially stable, creative, and so forth. Limiting-Thought Viruses are often spread through your closest relationships—parents, teachers, co-workers, bosses, friends, and lovers—and they're implanted when you're feeling vulnerable. Here are a couple of examples of how a Limiting-Thought Virus works:

Joey is doing poorly in math. His teacher tells him, "Joey, you're never going to be good at math! You just don't get it." Joey, whose dad is an accountant, has dreams of going into the family business. That, however, involves math, and the Limiting-Thought Virus from his teacher infects Joey, who never pursues his aspiration.

David has his eye on a beautiful young woman. His friend says to him, "David, do you really think that girl would want to be with you? That kind of girl would never date you." Because David's emotional immune system is in a state of lowered resistance, he buys into his friend's point of view and allows the Limiting-Thought Virus to take over. Furthermore, whenever he sees a woman who he feels is "that kind of girl," he never even attempts to talk to her.

I once had a music teacher who told my mother, "Don't waste your money on Darren. He has no talent for playing guitar." I was crushed, since as a kid I was so psyched about the possibility of being in a band with my brother, who played the drums. Fortunately, I cleared that Limiting-Thought Virus and started playing guitar as an adult. I practice daily and am actually quite good. At my wedding, I played the instrument and serenaded my wife with a song I composed.

The most challenging Limiting-Thought Viruses that I've treated as a holistic physician are those that allopathic doctors spread to their patients: "Everyone in your family has diabetes and hypertension, so you're going to get it, too," "No matter what you do, because you have big bones, you'll always be overweight unless you take this pill or have this surgery," or "You only have three months to live." It's as if cancer or autoimmune diseases automatically come with expiration dates. Patients immediately buy into it—they take in the Limiting-Thought Virus that's based on their physicians' beliefs. Who gave the doctors the virus? They got it from their teachers, hospital training, colleagues, and the medical profession's Limiting-Thought Virus perspective on disease.

But bear in mind that there are infinite possibilities within every challenge. Although you may not be immediately aware of the solution, you should keep searching for the answer, no matter what the limiting beliefs of others are. When it comes to your health and making decisions about your treatments, you do have a choice. It's important not to assume that your doctor—or *any* doctor—is right or that he or she has all the answers. You'll find the solution to the health challenges that you're facing within you. With The LifeLine Technique, you'll be able to not only discover what the challenges are, but also to remove the limiting roadblocks that are inhibiting your body from achieving optimal health.

I don't treat viruses . . . I treat people. It doesn't matter what the diagnosis is—your body has the capability and the potential to heal itself.

## Killer-Thought Viruses

The Killer-Thought Virus is the most dangerous. It's a complex beast that challenges the mind in an extremely self-destructive way. Killer-Thought Viruses are a combination of multiple Trigger- and Limiting-Thought Viruses. They cause complete breakdowns, both subconsciously and consciously, and lead to incongruent function in the mind and body. They're the cause of suicide, both internal (through lifestyle and behavior) and external (self-induced death). They literally program the person for death.

For example, a woman in her early 40s came to see me after being diagnosed with a rare form of cancer. The condition was like a stealth plane, undetected by the immune system until it had progressed to an advanced stage. She had already undergone a bilateral radical mastectomy and a complete hysterectomy. During her first visit with me, I found and released three Killer-Thought Viruses having to do with anger, fear, and low self-esteem, which were associated with her being sexually molested at the age of three. The Killer-Thought Viruses were the root cause of the cancer. The patient identified the relationships in her life that increased the potential for Killer-Thought Viruses. She's now doing her best to own her power and has begun to create the appropriate boundaries in those relationships.

The great thing about discovering a Killer-Thought Virus through The LifeLine Technique is that when the frequency is balanced, there are amazing shifts in your perception. There's a level of clarity that wasn't there before. All of a sudden, you feel that your *reality* has returned, and you become aware, for the first time, of a *new* reality of hope and opportunity.

## Gemini-Thought Viruses

The Gemini-Thought Virus is the shadow side of a person's life based on polar opposites—that is, light/dark, yin/yang, and good/bad. It thrives on humiliation, shame, criticism, and judgment. It creates the feeling that you're an abandoned, vulnerable child and are unworthy of love. To overcome Gemini-Thought Viruses, you must learn to accept all sides of yourself, rather than just identify with the negative or the positive.

A rose, for example, is beautiful, powerful, fragile, and vibrant. It also has thorns that can cause injury—they are its shadow side. Gemini-Thought Viruses prevent you from having total self-acceptance. If you have a habit of procrastination, the shadow side will say, "You're always late, and you'll never be on time for anything." Instead of looking at your life as a work in progress or realizing that you have the potential to develop and improve your time-management skills, you only focus on what you're lacking. Another example is when something wonderful occurs in your life and your shadow side says, "You just got lucky," rather than celebrating your efforts or hard work.

You attract the people you need in your life in order to heal your shadow side. It's the pendulum effect: As far as it swings one way, it will swing back the same distance in the other direction. The Gemini-Thought Virus takes over when you don't own your power and live in PTC. The LifeLine Technique is a powerful tool for healing the shadow sides of yourself that limit you in countless ways.

### Emotional Cancer

Emotional Cancer is another category of the emotional expression of the Five Elements. It's very important to understand that Emotional Cancer isn't the same as cancer of the physical body. However, it can be a precursor and result in physical cancer if it isn't harmonized.

Cancer occurs when a normal cell mutates. The immune system is unable to recognize it, so it spreads, or *metastasizes*. Emotional

Cancer results when a feeling such as anger is trapped within the subconscious mind. The emotional immune system becomes confused and is unable to recognize it, causing the mind and body to have a maladaptive stress response. The result is a mutation of the emotions and an emotional metastasis of the anger. When the emotional immune system doesn't recognize self from nonself, emotions begin to spread like wildfire. A person who's unable to manage anger, fear, grief, or low self-esteem is expressing the symptoms of Emotional Cancer.

Fear mutated transforms into panic and anxiety. Anger will evolve into hate and rage. Low self-esteem will be converted into social phobias of seclusion and paranoia.

### *Personal Invasion*

You have your own space, including both your physical and energetic body. Boundaries are based on your experiences, and you use them to determine whether or not you feel safe. They're different for everyone, depending on how much you're able to let yourself go and surrender to the moment. Based on familiarity or desire, you allow certain people within your space. Personal Invasion occurs when you feel that your boundaries—emotional, physical, sexual, or spiritual—have been crossed without your permission.

How do you know when you're being personally invaded? You *feel* it as a level of discomfort when a certain person is around you. It's the tightness in your chest when you discover that someone has rearranged everything on your desk or rummaged through your dresser drawers. It's a twinge in your stomach when a person other than your lover or family member stands too close to you. It's the flash of anger you feel when someone breaks into your car or home, steals your wallet at the gym, or says or does something offensive.

An extreme level of Personal Invasion is rape. In many ways, the collective karma of our nation is Personal Invasion. The Pilgrims personally invaded the Native Americans . . . their space was everywhere; there were no boundaries or borders. They were a part of a collective, universal awareness that included sharing and living off the land, as well as being reciprocal and appreciative. The European settlers invaded their space, putting up boundaries and property lines, stealing land, and denying the humanity of the Native Americans.


*Shock*

Personal Invasion causes trauma to the body. The result is that both the emotions and the body lock up. Reacting in a fright, fight, or flight mode, the mind "walls off" the memory. Shock, therefore, is a walled-off area of emotion or energy. When this feeling has been internalized, it expresses itself in other ways.

One of its most prominent physical manifestations is allergies. A young boy survives a fall from a magnolia tree that's in full bloom. After a time, all of his broken bones heal. However, the Shock of the accident is still rumbling through his body, so aberrant reactions on a physical and/or emotional level begin to occur. It may take years for the subconscious memory to be triggered; however, once it's tapped, the child develops an allergy to flowers that begin to bloom in the exact month he fell from the tree.

While it's true that environmental sensitivities are more common these days, allergies occur at a root level, where Shock resides. Since September 11, 2001—and more recently, the complete devastation of Southeast Asia by a tsunami and New Orleans by Hurricane Katrina—I believe that the entire world has been in Shock. I've witnessed an increase in allergies, as well as other flu-like symptoms. It's not just the toxic environment that's causing this, it's the toxic level of emotions that have been sealed off and denied. Those feelings seep out and are expressed in many ways, such as through chronic pain or organ dysfunction and recurrent relationship challenges.

Internalized emotion can be balanced with the power of Infinite Love & Gratitude. However, you need to take personal responsibility by living in Present Time Consciousness and loving yourself unconditionally. Once Shock is identified, it takes one second to clear it and it's gone. Afterward, it's important to make the necessary lifestyle changes to ensure that your body continues the healing process.

If you continue down the same life path you've always trod, you'll keep getting the same results. Clearing the Shock is only the first step. It's not the magic silver bullet that kills the werewolf. If you find yourself in a situation where something reminds you of a loss or trauma, it's best to allow yourself to *feel* and observe the impact of that experience, and *express* your emotions right then. By maintaining The Five Basics for Optimal Health (water, food, rest, exercise, and owning your power), your body, mind, and spirit will have all the tools necessary to handle the challenges that you face.


### Life/Death Mode

The last area of emotional expression in the Five Elements category is the Life/Death Mode. To understand it, imagine a light switch in your body: When it's turned on, your body is functioning in the Life Mode; when it's turned off, your body is operating in the Death Mode. In the Life Mode, your body readily regenerates and heals. However, with certain losses or traumas, the switch can be turned off, causing your body to live in the Death Mode. At this point, your body begins a cycle that makes it susceptible to breakdown, which eventually will lead to degenerative disease and premature death. In the same sense, death is more apparent when life is diminished.

Disease isn't added to the body; rather, health is taken away. You can't add darkness to a room—you can only dim the lights. Because you're an electromagnetic being, you attract and repel experiences based on the conscious and subconscious polarity of your emotions. When you're in a Death Mode, you have a subconscious death wish that's draining your life force.

Let me give you an example. Something traumatic happens to you: You lose your job, your relationship ends, or you're in a car accident— or maybe you're hit by a Thought Virus while in a vulnerable state. All of a sudden, the proverbial switch of the subconscious mind turns off, and you're now living in a Death Mode. What does that mean?

Every time a traumatic experience is subconsciously triggered, the reptilian brain sends out signals as if it's actually happening. Your life and body literally begin to fall apart. As a result of the subconscious disconnection from past trauma, the experience lives on by creating a Death Mode. There's a part of you that subconsciously wants and needs to be released. Not until this happens will the body or your will to live change.

Autoimmune diseases occur when the body is in the Death Mode. Does this mean that it's attacking itself? If the body is naturally a self-healing organism, then that question doesn't make any sense. Instead, thanks to the field of psychoneuroimmunology, it's been proven that thoughts affect your nervous system, immune system, and hormonal regulation. Toxic thoughts trigger the body to switch to the Death Mode, propelling it to attack itself.

My experience with patients has taught me that when the Death Mode is switched to the Life Mode, people begin to heal. So if the body is talking via autoimmune issues, you have to ask why. Which belief systems, feelings, or thought patterns are being denied that are forcing the body to live in the Death Mode? It's a difficult reality . . . on the other hand, what an opportunity to *awaken!* Rather than looking for the elusive "cure" outside yourself, open up to the fact that the *cure is within you.* The greatest doctors in the world—lupus specialists or MS experts—haven't "cured" anybody. There's never been a pharmaceutical drug that's *cured* anyone of anything. The medications just get rid of the symptoms, which are the body's only way to communicate with you.

There are other options. The approach shouldn't be "one-size-fits-all," cookie-cutter health care. It must be multidimensional in order to take into account the broad and ever-widening spectrum of realities that each individual experiences, internalizes, and often manifests as illness. *Each journey to disease is different; therefore, each path back to health must be tailored to the individual.*

# CHAPTER 17

# YOUR BODY'S
# STRUCTURAL EXPRESSION

The acupuncture meridians are integrated with every structural component of the body. Your body actually has a structural language that it uses when you've subconsciously internalized, denied, or disconnected from your emotions. The specific meridian that has a decreased flow of life force will determine which structural aspect of the body will "speak."

For three months, I experienced midline back pain, which awakened me every morning at 6 A.M. In addition to running The LifeLine Technique, I received acupuncture, craniosacral treatments, massage, chiropractic adjustments, and applied kinesiology, and I took additional nutritional supplements in order to help my body heal. The symptom would decrease, but it always returned the next morning at 6 A.M.

During a massage on this area of my back, I had a memory of myself as an infant. I was born with bowed legs and was placed in a lower-body cast to correct the structural imbalance. The cast kept my feet, legs, and pelvis immobilized during the first year of my life. As my back was massaged, I realized how many dysfunctional emotional and physical patterns in my body were associated with this early life experience.

Even though I adapted to the cast and built upper-body strength by pulling myself around with my arms, the cast inhibited the development of my natural cross-crawl pattern, planting seeds of imbalance. It was also during the massage that I began to realize the subtle link between the pain in my back and other symptoms and traumas I'd experienced throughout my life. For example, I recalled being in junior high and high school, wondering "how" to walk. It was almost as if walking wasn't natural for me. I realized that rupturing my left Achilles tendon 15 years later was also related. At the time, I was going through major turmoil in my life, and I was internalizing anger. The anger triggered subconscious memories of the original trauma of being stuck in the cast.

The hours of five to seven in the morning are when the large intestine acupuncture meridian is at its highest function. This is the time I woke up every morning with excruciating pain. Based on applied kinesiology, the area of discomfort in my back correlated with the muscles of the large intestine—the quadratus lumborum and the hamstrings. The back pain I felt can be likened to a ripened fruit, grown from the seeds planted during my infancy in the cast, ready for harvest. After running The LifeLine Technique on the memory of being in a cast, the back pain is now completely healed, and I've been pain free ever since.

This experience is a great example of the interconnectedness of the Expression Channel on a structural level. When you find the boulder that's inhibited the natural flow of your river, it can be removed, allowing the body to do what it does best—heal.

Remember what Dr. Victor Frank says: "What you have is not what you've always got." "What you have" is a symptom, which is the result of multiple autonomic reflexes that your body has produced throughout your life to warn you of imbalance. When we internalize, deny, or disconnect from the emotions that are the result of challenging or painful experiences, the body expresses itself with symptoms.

There are all types of autonomic reflexes that exist in the body. One that most people are aware of is called the *psychosomatic reflex,* which relates to internalized emotions evolving into physical pain. For example, a woman came to see me who had been suffering for years from abdominal discomfort. No matter what she did, she wasn't able to alleviate the pain. Using The LifeLine Technique, her body released the internalized emotion of anger that she felt toward her mother. The harmonization of the negative feeling with Infinite Love & Gratitude enabled her body to heal.

There are other autonomic reflexes that travel and interconnect throughout the body. One is a *viscero-somatic reflex*. This reflex is stimulated when an organ is stressed, causing a signal to be sent to a specific part of the body, which results in pain. Poor food choices, dehydration, and toxicity will lead to a viscero-somatic reflex—for instance, sugar is a poison that has the potential to cause one. An example of a viscero-somatic reflex is gallbladder dysfunction inducing right-shoulder pain. An imbalance within the heart will result in referral pain down the left arm or into the jaw. Kidney stones lead to back pain. The *somato-somatic reflex* is caused by physical misalignment. This reflex is the result of overuse, direct trauma, and poor posture. Chiropractic adjustments are a great way to balance these reflexes.

Each organ has a connection to the physical body in every possible combination. Recognizing these reflexes gives the expression of a symptom a whole new meaning. These autonomic reflexes exist within the body as a survival mechanism. They're produced to warn you that something is throwing you off balance. Without them, you'd be unable to recognize that you've consumed too much sugar, are dehydrated, aren't getting enough exercise, are lacking sleep, or are in a bad relationship. They enable you to discern the complex matrix of the mind-body-spirit connection.

When we internalize, deny, or disconnect from challenging experiences, the emotions that we're suppressing become stuck in different structural components of our bodies. The body holds on to these emotions in the muscles, joints, organs, fascia, lymphatics, circulation, nerves, cartilage, scar tissue, fat tissue, integument, and bone. Any of these areas has the capacity to obstruct the body's ability to flow energetically. Treating the symptom won't heal the root cause of the pain. In fact, numbing yourself with a medication, such as an anti-inflammatory or a painkiller, will result in your inability to recognize that the imbalance still exists within a specific structure of the body.

The LifeLine Technique demonstrates a clear connection between the structural body and the acupuncture meridians of the Five Elements. When symptoms are expressed structurally, it's due to the subconscious internalization or denial of, or disconnection from, emotions, causing a decreased flow in the body's life force within its various structures. Let's take a closer look to see the specific ways the body expresses itself structurally:

— **Muscle** is the tissue of the body that primarily functions as a source of power. There are three types in the body: (1) The muscle responsible for moving extremities and external areas of the body is called *skeletal muscle;* (2) heart muscle is referred to as *cardiac muscle;* and (3) the muscle in the walls of the arteries and bowel is called *smooth muscle.* These are the areas where you store past memories; conflicts; experiences; feelings, including repressed anxieties, fear, and guilt; and your levels of self-worth, self-esteem, joy, and vibrancy.

— A **joint** is the area where two bones are attached for the purpose of allowing the motion of body parts. It's usually formed of fibrous connective tissue and cartilage. (An *articulation* or an *arthrosis* is the same as a joint.) The various types are grouped according to their motion, including a ball-and-socket, hinge, condyloid, pivot, gliding, and saddle joint. The joints are the connections between thoughts and feelings and movement and action. They're the source of stability and balance in the body.

— **Organs** are a grouping of tissues that are made up of specialized cells. Each has a specific function that's both independent of, and interdependent with, all the others. There are organs of digestion, respiration, elimination, reproduction, detoxification, and assimilation; and they're the storehouse of your thoughts, feelings, and beliefs. Every cell in the body is constantly in the process of regeneration and degeneration. There's a continuous balancing between these cycles that will either influence the body toward health or disease. Each of the organs has corresponding emotions based on the Five Elements.

— **Fascia** is the Latin word for "band" or "bandage." It's a flat band of connective tissue below the skin that covers underlying tissues and separates different layers from one another. Fascia encloses muscles and is where we express our need for protection.

— The **lymphatic system** presents a network of vessels, nodes, and lymph-producing organs crucial to the body's immune response. The immune system determines that which is "self" and "not self" and then fights off microscopic "intruders." Vital to locating and destroying them are the T lymphocytes, produced by the thymus gland, located near the heart. The spleen is also a source of lymphocytes. The lymph vessels collect the "drainage" of lymphocytes and macrophages (white blood cells) from the capillaries and then modify or return them to the blood system, draining into the veins near the heart. The new science of psychoneuroimmunology studies the interaction of psychological factors (such as stress) and the immune system. With The LifeLine Technique, we can see the link between various personality determinants and health. The lymphatic system is also the place in the body most closely linked to your identity and your ability to define your own thoughts and feelings, rather than having them defined by others.

— The **circulatory system** moves blood throughout the body and is composed of the heart, arteries, capillaries, and veins. This remarkable system transports oxygenated blood from the lungs and heart throughout the body via the arteries. It also carries nutrients and waste products through the capillaries, which are situated between the arteries and veins. The blood that's been depleted of oxygen by the body is then returned to the lungs and heart through the veins. The blood represents the circulation of feelings of love and life.

— The **nervous system** is composed of three parts: the central nervous system (CNS), the peripheral nervous system (PNS), and the autonomic nervous system (ANS). These three distinct parts integrate every function of every cell, organ, and system of the body. It's through the electrical conduction of the nervous system that you're able to walk, breathe, think, feel, and adapt to an array of extremes in many different environments.

The nervous system integrates all parts of an organism so that it's able to optimally function as a whole. It communicates via electrical currents that travel through synapses. Synapses form when electricity jumps from one synaptic cleft to the next. It's very similar to telephone-pole relay stations. When there's trouble with your phone, the first place to check is its connection to the wall outlet. If it's plugged in, the next step is to see whether there's a blockage along the phone lines entering your home. If they're okay, assess the ones that feed your local area. And if those are clear, officials evaluate the city or main area where all calls are generated (that is, the phone company). The final checkpoint would be the satellite sending the signal from outer space.

The same scenario is true in the body. The region expressing the symptom may be the location of the symptom's cause. Or it might be a communication breakdown from the symptom to another area in the body or mind. Finally, there could be an internal source that's causing the symptom to be expressed. There may be a relationship issue that's resulting in stored emotions, environmental pollution, or poor eating habits, leading to the symptom. It's usually a combination of all these scenarios.

Many symptoms can be associated with dysfunction in the nervous system. Numbness implies a withdrawal of feelings, perhaps because there's too much pain for you to absorb in a particular place. It's a way of denying the hurt, pushing it away, or forgetting that part of yourself. Nerve pain is a signpost showing you where you need to connect with psycho-emotional pain. It indicates that you're holding on tight, so you need to work at letting go.

— **Cartilage** is a nonvascular structure found in various parts of the body. In adults, it's chiefly found in the joints; the torso; and various tubes that are to be kept open permanently, such as air passages, nostrils, and ears. In the early period of fetal development, the greater part of the skeleton is cartilaginous. Breakdowns in the cartilage occur for the same reasons as in joints, usually implying a deep resistance to or fear of movement.

— **Scar tissue** is the end result of inflammation. *Itis* is the suffix that's used to describe an inflammatory disease process: *Gastritis* is inflammation of the stomach, and *arthritis* literally means "inflammation of the joints." Every area of the body can have an "itis" added to it, denoting inflammation there. When this condition persists, scar tissue is sure to form, creating an entirely new subset of challenges. The greatest of these is that scar tissue doesn't conduct energy—the healing power that potentiates health and balance. Scar tissue that crosses acupuncture meridians restricts the flow of chi (life force) through those meridians. So when it develops, there's a decrease in chi, which leads directly to a decrease in the circulation to that area. Remember that emotion is energy in motion. When scar tissue is present, all aspects of life force are inhibited, contributing to the internalized, denied, or disconnected emotions remaining locked in the body.

— The **adipose**, or **fat tissue**, of the body serves as an energy reserve. Subcutaneous fat provides an insulating layer that prevents heat loss. Fat is an important constituent of cell structure, forming an integral part of the cell membrane. It acts to support and protect certain senses and organs, such as the eyes and kidneys. Fat tissue stores both emotional and physical poisons and toxins. As a person breaks down and metabolizes fat tissue, these harmful materials are released. If the detoxification routes aren't open and there's dehydration in the system, the metabolism will slow the breakdown of fat.

Fat tissue is used to guard yourself from internalized, denied, or disconnected traumas. It's like a wall of protection against further hurt. At the same time, this blocks out feelings, which makes you numb to what's really being felt on the inside. If being overweight is an issue, the bigger you get, the more likely you are to reject yourself and feel ugly and unlovable. Losing weight occurs through a deep shift in attitude, starting with an acceptance of yourself just as you are—you need to give yourself the love you long for, and then you can start working on the layers of fear that lie beneath the excess weight.

— **Integument,** or **skin,** is the largest organ of the body. Debbie Shapiro's book, *Your Body Speaks Your Mind,* describes it as "waterproof, washable, elastic, self-mending and tactile." It protects you against water loss and intake, while allowing you to perspire; defends you against infection and exposure to foreign substances; and regulates your temperature. Shapiro writes: "The skin is the outermost expression of [your] innermost being." Derived from the same primordial tissue as the nervous system, the skin registers every feeling, emotion, belief, and experience. The acupuncture meridians and points are areas where energy is channeled reciprocally from the universe through the skin and into the depths of your being. Symptoms of the skin are often connected with difficulties with communication and respecting boundaries.

— **Bone** is the hardest structure of the body. It also possesses a certain degree of elasticity. The skeleton is created from bone, and it provides the supportive inner framework of the body. Bone is the innermost core of yourself. The outside is hard and dense, while the inside is porous and soft, filled with marrow. Along with producing vital immune cells, bone marrow nourishes you with minerals, salts, and nutrients; and the hard outer shell forms a strong, resilient framework upon which your whole being is built. Debbie Shapiro describes bones as the densest form of energy within the physical body. Like the rocks in the earth, they support and sustain. They hold up your physical being and give life to the muscles and fluids. The same is true about your core beliefs lending you constant inner strength and support, while finding expression in your lifestyle, behavior, and relationships. Imbalances or disease in the bones, therefore, represent conflict with the deepest part of your being.

The functional aspects of the human body's structural integrity are quite complex. The structural body begins to break down when it's forced to exhibit the emotions that we've subconsciously compartmentalized. Knowing this, we discover the gift in the structural expression of pain or discomfort. We now can choose to use the power of Infinite Love & Gratitude to release the emotions that are inhibiting the body from healing and functioning optimally.

As technical as it may seem, for each of these individual structural expressions, the treatment is simple—Infinite Love & Gratitude. Physical changes will occur instantaneously on a structural level within the mind, body, and spirit when The LifeLine Technique is performed.

# CHAPTER 18

# YOUR BODY'S
# BIOCHEMICAL EXPRESSION

Nothing is ever wasted in life. Just as in the law of conservation (energy can neither be created nor destroyed; it just changes form), the same is true within the body. It's constantly keeping checks and balances of both its external and internal environment. This process enables it to maintain harmony in every moment.

When the body is deficient, it will automatically start to feed itself. When it's in an excessive state, it will automatically begin to drain. Every cell, organ, region, and system is keeping tabs to maintain optimal health from a micro to macro perspective. For example, an ankle will lose energy when it's sprained. The body instantly responds to the deficiency by swelling, which is its way of channeling energy to that area. Blood rapidly rushes down, along with other fluids that contain minerals, nutrients, and white blood cells to fight infection and help the ankle heal. Western medicine says to "rest, ice, compress, and elevate" a swollen ankle, and it will then hopefully be better in 72 hours. The LifeLine Technique, on the other hand, expedites the healing and enables the body to release and recover from an injury. On a root level, even twisting your ankle is caused by subconscious internalized, denied, or disconnected emotions.

Let me give you an example. I was having lunch in a restaurant with my office manager when our waiter came limping up to our table. We asked him why he was limping, and he told us that he'd severely sprained his ankle one week before. He said that the pain, swelling, and bruising had persisted and that he was very frustrated.

"Would you like to heal your ankle right now?" I asked him.

"Sure," he replied. "What would we need to do?"

"I'd be gently pressing down on your arm and saying to your body, 'Infinite Love & Gratitude.'"

"Okay, let's do it," he said. "As strange as it sounds, that couldn't hurt me."

In the middle of the restaurant, I began to run The LifeLine Technique on him. It took me less than ten minutes. When I finished, I asked him to stand up, walk, and check out his ankle. He noticed the difference immediately.

"Oh my God, this is amazing!" he cried out as he walked around the restaurant without a limp.

I then checked The Five Basics for Optimal Health. I recommended that he increase his water intake and be sure to consume a gallon per day to satisfy his body's need for proper hydration. I also told him to follow a healthy eating plan, taking care to restrict his sugar intake over the next week in order to decrease any inflammatory response his body might be having. Last, I encouraged him to embrace this experience as an opportunity to learn and stay connected to the present moment.

Not only did The LifeLine Technique immediately enhance the self-healing mechanism that allowed him to recover, it also helped him understand the emotions that he was disconnecting from that led him to sprain his ankle in the first place.

The body's capacity to heal itself is infinite, so stay in the moment and deal with the situation that you're in. The frequency of Infinite Love & Gratitude will harmonize and balance your body. The LifeLine Flow Chart will reveal where and why the energy in your body is imbalanced, as well as what's keeping it from healing instantly. The longer you stay disconnected, the longer it takes for the body to heal.

One of the major characteristics differentiating Western medicine from The LifeLine treatment approach is the view of symptoms and disease. In Western medicine, 50 people who are all diagnosed with the same ailment will be given the identical medication or surgical advice. For example, with diabetes, there are certain medications used to control blood-sugar levels. As the condition progresses and the patients develop retinopathies in the eyes or neuropathies in the extremities, there are specific surgical procedures that are then performed. People will undergo multiple laser surgeries on their eyes for the retinopathies, and when the disease has progressed to the point of gangrene in the extremities, they'll undergo amputation.

In The LifeLine approach, people who have been diagnosed with diabetes will be evaluated individually. The treatment plan will focus on where the primary imbalances are within the body. They will all be educated about the need to maintain The Five Basics for Optimal Health to allow their bodies to heal. The LifeLine practitioner will use muscle testing to assess regions, organs, glands, pathogens, and systems; and balance them on an emotional, biochemical, structural, and spiritual level.

No two people who are treated with The LifeLine Technique receive the exact same care, because no two people are identical. No one has the same family, eating habits, lifestyle, trauma, or losses. Every experience you've had in your life has shaped you to be where you are at this very moment. There's a subtle balance being maintained within your body at all times. Sometimes there's excess in one area and a deficiency in another.

For example, when you have an excess of emotional stress due to insecurity, the feeling of fear within the body is elevated. This emotion will automatically begin to drain the kidney acupuncture meridian, causing the symptom of back pain. By masking the discomfort with medication, you're doing nothing to alleviate the fear, the root cause of the symptom.

The LifeLine Technique will guide you through the Flow Chart like a laser, pinpointing the deficiency in the kidney acupuncture meridian. Through different layers of the original symptom of low-back pain, the Flow Chart will help you recognize the insecurity and fear that's being internalized. Once identified, the emotional experience is harmonized with Infinite Love & Gratitude. As a result, the body will have no need to express itself with low-back pain.

Excess or deficiency can both lead to imbalance. The regulatory systems of the body are in a constant symphony of adaptation. When the energy is running high, the mechanisms of the metabolism speed up to balance any excess. The opposite is also true: When it's running low, the metabolism slows down to store up energy and feed the body in its deficient state.

I have a friend who's trained in using The LifeLine Technique. While at a coffee shop with his wife, a woman spilled a scalding cup of coffee on his leg. He instantly began sending Infinite Love & Gratitude to the area of the burn. The next day, the only sign of the accident was a small red dot. By draining the excess energy that was flowing because of the burn, his body was able to heal itself quickly.

The biochemical expression of the Five Elements is associated with the creative (Shen), destructive (Ko), or connecting (Luo) cycles of the acupuncture meridians. These cycles are inhibited when the acupuncture meridian is *hypo*functioning or *hyper*functioning. When the acupuncture meridian is hypofunctioning, it needs to be fed. When it's hyperfunctioning, it has to be drained. These actions allow the cycles to continue in a harmonious fashion, and they're accomplished easily using the power of Infinite Love & Gratitude.

Everything in the body happens for a reason. When you awaken to the subtle balance that it's maintaining in every moment, you're empowered by the natural laws of the universe. There's a flow that exists within the universe, as well as within your physical being, that enables the body to maintain homeostasis. It's when you disconnect from your natural flow that the body begins to express symptoms—which can be the result of an excess or deficiency. Regardless, though, The LifeLine Technique brings the body back to balance.

# CHAPTER 19

# BREAKING OUT OF THE HOLDING PATTERN

I had an eye-opening experience with a new patient. Melanie, age 39, was referred to me by her medical doctor for consultation and treatment. She was suffering from severe allergies and searching for another means to heal.

"I've had my allergies since birth," she explained to me during our first session. The list included several food and environmental sensitivities that limited her ability to eat and work. In addition to the allergies, she had chronic numbness along her spine and into her extremities, which debilitated her both physically and emotionally. Melanie had sought the aid of dozens of doctors over the years, but none of them were able to help her find relief.

As I listened to Melanie discuss the effects of the allergies on her life, I noticed a common theme of ownership that's shared by many people when it comes to illness. She took complete possession of the allergies and the chronic pain as if they were threads of tissue connecting her skin. She wore them like badges. The symptoms and diseases that Melanie's body used to express itself had become her identity. I wondered if she was aware that so many relationships in her life were defined by this identity.

I began to run The LifeLine Flow Chart, and within 15 minutes of our session, the numbness disappeared. By the time we finished, 90 percent of the symptoms had completely abated. For the first time in

Melanie's life, she experienced a sense of inner health and well-being. Despite this new feeling of hope, she was afraid.

"I don't know what to think of myself anymore," Melanie said.

I immediately realized that she was talking about her identity, which had been stuck in a holding pattern of limiting beliefs and suffering. We created a treatment plan to detoxify Melanie's mind and body of the poisonous emotions and chemicals that were preventing her from achieving her optimal potential. The mind and body must be purged before a person is able to heal.

Sometimes symptoms can become locked, like a tornado, in a continuous loop of imbalance. These are called *holding patterns,* the places where symptoms (disconnections from our emotions) are so deeply rooted in our lives that they become part of our being. And like airplanes in a holding pattern, the symptoms are stuck, waiting for air-traffic control to give the green light for landing. The LifeLine Technique provides the means to land, to take the first step in breaking this loop by locating where the denial of our power is rooted. When the holding pattern is released, the body is able to restore balance.

Let's take a closer look at the various aspects of holding patterns. We've already discussed how our beliefs affect our health. I'll now focus on other aspects of the mind, including limiting beliefs and their origin, along with the chakras.

~

As a result of The LifeLine Technique, I awakened to the connection between the universe and the body. The energy of nature enters our bodies via the microcosmic orbit, otherwise known as the superconscious (or the Power Center in The LifeLine Flow Chart), which is the main driver of our biocomputer. It's the *mind* of the body. The microcosmic orbit acts as an attractor field for emotions that are stored in the subconscious mind. It's the connection or liaison between the universe and the physical and emotional symptoms we experience.

The microcosmic orbit travels along two pathways:

1.  On the anterior of the body along the Ren (Conception Vessel) acupuncture meridian—beginning at the perineum, moving up the midline of the body, and ending at the inner aspect of the lower lip

2.  On the posterior of the body along the Du (Governing Vessel) acupuncture meridian, which begins at the tip of the tailbone, runs up the spine at the midline, continues over the head, and ends on the inner aspect of the upper lip

These two vessels intersect in the soft palate, located at the roof of the mouth. When you use your tongue to touch the soft palate, it's like touching two wires together: The two energies ignite, instantaneously strengthening your entire system. This is why in meditation, tai chi, and yoga, it's recommended that the tongue is kept pressed against the soft palate while breathing.

The microcosmic orbit produces an attractor field, an identifiable pattern, which emerges from our subconscious emotions. The microcosmic orbit is composed of seven chakras. The Sanskrit word *chakra* means "wheel" or "disk," and each one moves with a spinning motion, forming a vortex. The vortices are the specific portals throughout the body by which energy enters and exits.

Each chakra is associated with the acupuncture meridians, various physiological functions of the body, and certain beliefs. They correspond to a specific vibratory frequency, ranging from lower to higher along the spectrum of the rainbow. Think of the mnemonic "ROY G BIV" (red, orange, yellow, green, blue, indigo, and violet) as a way to remember which chakra corresponds to each color. The shades of the rainbow are created from the bending of light. Lower vibratory frequencies are observed at the end of the spectrum of red. As the frequencies increase in rate, the colors change sequentially into orange, yellow, green, blue, indigo, and violet.

The chakras are like jellyfish—they have tendrils that simultaneously reach inward to the body and outward to the universe. They serve as magnets, attracting and repelling experiences that represent the subconscious mind. When you've internalized, denied, or disconnected from an experience, the energy that's attracted is of an aberrant frequency that affects the associated chakra. For example, limiting beliefs about your own worth or value have a vibrational frequency that's channeled into the third chakra. This chakra is yellow and is our connection to self-empowerment, and the limiting beliefs associated with it will attract experiences such as abusive relationships or self-destructive behavior.

The assemblage point is a hole formed in the body's microcosmic orbit when the chakras are leaking energy. Our experiences are drawn to us through this point. By balancing the chakras with Infinite Love & Gratitude, the attractor field is harmonized, closing off the assemblage point and securing the microcosmic orbit. When the microcosmic orbit is intact, you'll no longer attract limiting situations on all levels, enhancing your health, finances, relationships, and spiritual growth. However, you can't idly sit by after these fields have been harmonized. You have to take responsibility for the choices you've made and learn from the consequences.

The following is a breakdown of the chakras and their association with the body.

## First Chakra: Root—Color Is Red

**Physical Issues:** Lower back, sciatica, tailbone, rectum, colon, adrenals, feet, hands, and immune system.

**Emotional Issues:** Physical security; group safety; feeling at home; ability to stand up for oneself; stability with family, relationships, work, and money.

**Energy:** All is one—ground the spirit with the body; accept oneself, and work on the physical plane in a loving way.

**Root Chakra's Energy Will Leak:** When you subscribe to family or social beliefs that no longer serve you; when you consider your religion, political beliefs, social class, and so on to be better than others; when you hold on to negative experiences in your family.

**Root Chakra's Energy Will Be Reinforced:** When you maintain a sense of pride in your ancestry and family traditions; when you draw upon your family for love and support.

## Second Chakra: Sacral—Color Is Orange

**Physical Issues:** Genitals, reproductive organs, pelvic cavity, large intestine, lower vertebrae, appendix, bladder, hip area, wrists, and ankles.

**Emotional Issues:** Self versus other; moving away from the tribe; pleasure surrounding sex, recreation, and eating; physical and mental enjoyment; power and control; blame and guilt; ethics and honor in relationships.

**Energy:** Respect one another; use your creative forces; be devoted to the self; show integrity and honor within all relationships.

**Sacral Chakra's Energy Will Leak:** When you attempt to control others in relationships; when you fuel fears about making or losing money; when you harbor unresolved conflicts about your sexuality.

**Sacral Chakra's Energy Will Be Reinforced:** When you go with the flow in relationships; when you release the power of money as a motivating factor; when you authentically express your sexuality.

## Third Chakra: Solar Plexus—Color Is Yellow

**Physical Issues:** Abdominal cavity, digestive organs, kidney, pancreas, liver, gallbladder, spleen, endocrine glands, calves, forearms, middle part of back and spine, and upper intestines.

**Emotional Issues:** Individual power and self-esteem; responsibility for making decisions; self-mastery and personal honor; sensitivity to criticism; intuitive voice.

**Energy:** Honor oneself; take responsibility for your choices and decisions; learn to maintain strong personal boundaries, along with your tribal ones.

**Solar-Plexus Chakra's Energy Will Leak:** When you break your commitments to yourself; when you manipulate others to gain their approval; when you fail to maintain clear personal boundaries.

**Solar-Plexus Chakra's Energy Will Be Reinforced:** When you take pride in your work; when you trust your intuition; when you keep your word.

## FOURTH CHAKRA: HEART—COLOR IS GREEN

**Physical Issues:** Heart center, circulatory system, chest, breasts, rib cage, lungs, diaphragm, thymus gland, knees, and elbows.

**Emotional Issues:** Love, failure, and loneliness; disorientation and alienation; hatred, grief, and anger; resentment and bitterness; forgiveness and compassion; hope and trust.

**Energy:** Love is Divine power; cherish yourself first and then others; express caring in actions; release emotionally suppressed trauma; be nonjudgmental of others.

**Heart Chakra's Energy Will Leak:** When you allow past negative experiences to limit your choices; when you hold on to resentments; when you don't allow others to love you.

**Heart Chakra's Energy Will Be Reinforced:** When you forgive others unconditionally; when you love yourself; when you care about others enough to let them experience the world in their own way.

## FIFTH CHAKRA: THROAT—COLOR IS BLUE

**Physical Issues:** Throat, vocal cords, thyroid, parathyroid, and mouth.

**Emotional Issues:** Power of the will; judgment and criticism; outward expression and inward acceptance.

**Energy:** Surrender personal will to Divine will; express your truth—the power of the spoken word; have the ability to speak.

**Throat Chakra's Energy Will Leak:** When you let others define your needs and wants; when you tell lies; when you experience shame.

**Throat Chakra's Energy Will Be Reinforced:** When you exercise self-control; when you empower others; when you speak honestly.

## SIXTH CHAKRA: THIRD EYE—COLOR IS INDIGO

**Physical Issues:** Nervous system, pituitary gland, higher brain centers, eyes, ears, and nose.

**Emotional Issues:** Intuition and emotional intelligence; intellectual abilities; openness to new ideas.

**Energy:** Seek only the truth; have a balanced state of mind; see the truth and Divine perfection in all things; clear the subconscious in preparation for intuition.

**Third-Eye Chakra's Energy Will Leak:** When you hold on to old grief; when you close your mind to nonrational possibilities; when you insist on logical explanations for your internal experience.

**Third-Eye Chakra's Energy Will Be Reinforced:** When you take emotional risks; when you open your mind to extravagant possibilities; when you follow your hunches.

## Seventh Chakra: Crown—Color Is Violet

**Physical Issues:** Top of head, highest brain centers, and pineal gland.

**Emotional Issues:** Faith, wisdom, and spirituality; selflessness; power to view situations from an expanded perspective; ability to trust life; sense of oneness with all creation.

**Energy:** Live in the present moment; allow the spiritual doorway to remain open; experience a connection with the Divine.

**Crown Chakra's Energy Will Leak:** When you live a life without faith; when you put conditions on your spiritual experience; when you reject guidance unless it comes in a form you approve.

**Crown Chakra's Energy Will Be Reinforced:** When you pray consciously; when you express gratitude; when you regard your life as a vehicle for spiritual development.

~

Earlier we explored the ways in which your beliefs are influenced by your relationships with your parents, siblings, partners, teachers, religion, gender, race, age, media, and so on. These relationships are at the core of what creates the infrastructure of your values. In addition, your senses—vision, smell, hearing, taste, touch, and intuition—affect your perception.

Your impressions of your external surroundings send signals via the nervous system to every cell in your body, which enables the internal environment of your body to know what's going on in the outside world. This communication between the external and the internal environment provides your body with the greatest opportunity to optimally adapt to any experience it's confronted with. When you've internalized, denied, or disconnected from an emotion, your mind or chakras will attract experiences that are associated with the suppressed feeling. Instead of seeing what you're actually experiencing, on a subconscious level you perceive the original experience that you've disconnected from.

You know that something is happening because you have uncomfortable feelings. However, on a conscious level, you don't make the mental link to the original traumatic experience. Your subconscious is keeping you stuck in a holding pattern of denial and disconnection because it perceives the experience as the original traumatic event. Not until the subconscious holding pattern is broken and you have conscious awareness of the limiting belief can you authentically respond to what you're actually experiencing.

For example, a child grows up with a critical parent who never gave any praise and for whom nothing ever seemed to be good enough. As a result, she developed a limiting belief associated with self-worth or self-esteem. Or a kid may have grown up with a mother or father who survived the Great Depression and whose fears were forged by a lack of money or food. As a result, that child acquired a limiting belief about the need to hoard beyond what's needed for survival.

Both of these individuals hold the energy of limiting beliefs within their subconscious minds and will continue to attract experiences that reinforce them. The child with the negative perception of her self-worth will come to question her value in her work, marriage, and each of her relationships. The one with the limiting beliefs about hoarding beyond what's needed for survival will attract experiences associated with never having enough money, food, clothes, and so forth.

With Infinite Love & Gratitude and The LifeLine Technique, these people can create a conscious connection to their subconscious limiting beliefs, breaking the holding pattern of suffering and victimization. Once it's overcome, they're able to embrace their greatness and the infinite potential that exists in each moment.

# Chapter 20

# Interrupting Your Spirit's Journey

re you connected to your feelings? Are you expressing them, either through words or actions? For many of us, the answer is no. We've been conditioned *not* to feel, not to be authentic . . . we've disconnected. We've blocked the pain and are comfortably numb. The journey to awakening our spirit has been interrupted by limiting beliefs, imbalanced lifestyles, loss, or trauma.

I believe the primary reason for numbness (besides habit) is the fear of change or of falling out of balance, which often makes the fall harder. We've learned to operate on autopilot, shielding ourselves from discomfort in any way we can in order to block our feelings or keep ourselves numb. Emotional eating, excessive alcohol, overworking, shopping, sex, smoking, and substance abuse are all ways in which we remove ourselves from our emotions.

When you deny pain, you deny your free will. Over a period of time, you disconnect from your ability to handle challenging experiences because you're unaware of what you're truly feeling. The more you shield yourself, the more you have to reconcile with anger, fear, guilt, shame, blame, or low self-esteem that accumulates when you don't acknowledge your thoughts, feelings, and beliefs. While the goal isn't to wallow in painful emotions, I encourage you to acknowledge, experience, and confront them—no matter how challenging.

*The Tibetan Book of Living and Dying* says: "Problems can be transformed into an opportunity for growth." You don't really have "problems"; you only think you do by the way you interpret your circumstances. A "problem" is a situation that creates an opportunity to react or respond in either a productive or destructive manner . . . in other words, the "problem" is an illusion. It's a limiting perception of an experience—it's the perception of an experience *without gratitude.* Breaking the pattern of disconnection by staying in tune with challenging situations enables you to learn from them. Unless you do, you'll continue to make the same mistakes over and over again.

When you were in high school, if you didn't pass algebra, you were unable to move on to trigonometry. You were required to retake the same class over and over again until you understood the material well enough to make it through the exams. Life is the same way: It provides multiple tests that you need to pass to move on. You'll marry the same person, with a different face and name, over and over again until you learn the lessons of your previous relationship. You'll continue to confront identical financial challenges in business until you learn from the mistakes that you've made. You'll be faced with the same health issues repeatedly until you take responsibility for the unhealthy lifestyle choices that you've made.

Once you embrace an experience that you've internalized, denied, or disconnected from, you'll move forward to the next one. In this way of flowing through life, there's no failure. Every problem, challenge, and difficulty becomes an opportunity to learn, transform, and create a new skill to awaken the spirit within you.

Just as water, sound, and light travel in waves and particles, so does life. Sometimes the wave is traveling up, while other times it's traveling down. Particles are the specific moments we live, such as the one you're experiencing while reading this book. They're the opportunity to feel and stay connected to Present Time Consciousness. Your thoughts, feelings, and beliefs will create emotions and sensations within your body that guide you to the next moment, and the next . . . either carrying those particular thoughts, feelings, and beliefs or creating whole new ones. The culmination of your moments form a wave in either an upward or downward motion. An infinite number of external factors can influence the flow of your life. Health issues, financial troubles, and relationship turmoil all can lead to stress that causes disconnection. This does nothing for the situation you're in— in fact, it leads to further challenges down the road.

Let's say that you're traveling down your stream of life and instead of a "particle" coming your way, you get hit by a boulder. That "boulder" or traumatic experience goes beyond the scope of your ability to maintain balance, and it sends you spinning beneath the surface of the water. You get caught in a whirlpool, which plunges you deeper. When you feel this current drawing you below, a natural reaction is to fight against its pull—but it's best to let yourself go with the flow. If you do, it will shoot you back to the surface, headed in a safe direction once again. However, if you choose to struggle against it, you may get sucked under and never come up again. Or you may return to the surface and be moving on a new course that has even greater dangers in store for you. . . . Instead of the boulder and the whirlpool, now you're heading in a direction that's leading to a 50-foot waterfall!

The boulder has changed and redefined your reality. You're no longer living in PTC—you're continually reacting to the trauma. You may suddenly feel depressed, anxious, angry, or fearful; or you might have chronic conditions such as constipation, sinus congestion, headaches, or back pain. Your body will keep communicating these symptoms as long as necessary until the boulder is removed and you're reconnected to your spiritual path.

### The "Pavlovian Bell"

Ivan Pavlov was a physiology professor in Russia in the late 1800s and early 1900s. However, he's best known for the contributions he made to the field of psychology in a study that uncovered the effects of "classical conditioning" on behavior.

Pavlov was observing the digestive process of dogs, doing his best to understand the connection between salivation and the action of the stomach. His hypothesis was that they were closely linked by reflexes in the autonomic nervous system, but he wasn't sure exactly how. He set out to determine whether external stimuli affected the process. Initially, he starved the dogs to get them in a lower state of resistance. The animals salivated when they saw and ate their food, and Pavlov began to ring a bell at the same time that he fed them. After a while, the dogs started to salivate when they heard the bell, even if no food was present. In addition, Pavlov discovered that they responded to what's called "differentiation of stimuli." He found that ringing bells with different tones would also trigger the dogs to salivate.

In 1903, Pavlov published his results, calling this response a "conditioned reflex," meaning a behavior that has to be learned. Although the focus of his award-winning life's work would remain physiology, Pavlov recognized that the discovery of conditioning could explain the actions of psychotic people, especially those who withdraw from the world because they associate all stimuli with possible injury or threat.

Dr. Scott Walker, developer of the Neuro Emotional Technique (NET), realized that the same principles of classical conditioning affect us as a result of an initial trauma. Building upon the work of Dr. Jennifer LaMonica, Dr. Walker demonstrated that we store the emotions of such an event in our bodies in what's called a neuro-emotional complex (NEC). When we see or hear something that recalls the trauma, even on a subconscious level, our reaction is similar to that of Pavlov's dogs and the bell: We return to the original occurrence in a classical-conditioning response. Trauma lowers the resistance of the body and creates an internal environment that's more susceptible to this type of reflex.

Addiction is an example of a conditioned response. It's a holding pattern in the spirit where we've been conditioned to numb ourselves to pain. Whenever a situation triggers the feeling associated with an original trauma, the body yearns for an opiate release in order to numb the pain. The manifestation of addiction is different for everyone, but the interesting aspect of the molecules of emotion in the body—neuropeptides—is that they bind to the same receptor sites as heroin. With this in mind, we're better able to appreciate the body's biochemical dependency on emotions.

Addiction is a symptom of longing to know one's truth but being afraid to do so. It inhibits the journey to awakening your spirit, because it represents the internalized fears of facing painful experiences that you've been conditioned to block out. Consciously or subconsciously, you hear the "Pavlovian bell" and instantaneously yearn to be numb. You tell yourself that you aren't addicted and that you have control. However, the subconscious mind feels discomfort and pain, and the rest is history . . . you'll then do whatever is necessary to dull the pain.

We all have addictions and long to know our truth, but when the original trauma is triggered consciously—or more commonly, subconsciously—fear sets in. The bottom line is the loss, denial, and manipulation of love, along with the lack of self-love. The initial trauma creates a limiting belief that filters our sensory perception and propels us into a cycle of addiction.

~

Linda, who is 47, came to see me with a primary complaint of being addicted to sugar. She was stuck in a cycle that disempowered her. Once she began to eat something sweet, she lost all control. I told Linda that before she got to where she was going, she had to be okay with where she was at. She needed to accept, both consciously and subconsciously, that she was a sugar addict.

I asked her to state: "My name is Linda, and I'm okay that I'm a sugar addict." Her muscle was strong when she spoke her name; however, it went weak when she said, "I'm okay that I'm a sugar addict." We must accept where we are presently before we move forward.

As I ran The LifeLine Flow Chart to this declarative statement, Linda's body began to tell the story of what had been keeping her locked into the addictive response to sugar. It revealed that she was internalizing fear from an emotional loss that had caused shock. The trauma was being held by a limiting belief associated with her crown chakra that had begun when she was three and a half. Due to the shocking experience, at that time Linda first developed a perception of being disconnected from a higher power or purpose. When her muscle went weak, the age of the initial trauma was revealed to be three years and six months.

I could see from the expression on her face that she knew exactly what the original shocking experience was. Her arm went weak as she recalled the incident when her father had died in a tragic car accident. She had taken on her mother's fear of moving on in the wake of her husband's death. This internalized shock created an attractor field. Until Linda dealt with her dad's death, she was trapped in a holding pattern of numbing internalized grief. Being addicted to sugar was the external experience that was drawn to the inner emotional trauma. She dulled the pain of grief and fear by disconnecting through sugar.

The death of her father masqueraded as a sugar addiction in Linda's limbic brain for 43 years. Every time an experience was somewhat similar to the original occurrence, the limbic structures of her brain would be triggered. This stimulation caused them to attempt to send a signal to her neocortex. However, because Linda had subconsciously disconnected from the experience, the signal was rerouted to the reptilian brain, which kept her autonomically in a state of obsession, compulsion, and ritualistic behaviors, expressed as sugar addiction.

Whenever there's trauma, the direction a person is looking at the time locks the memory in the subconscious mind. The specific eye direction is inhibited from processing the event during sleep. Rapid eye movements (REMs) process experiences from the short-term memory banks into the long-term ones. When trauma occurs, REMs are blocked as a safety mechanism or a circuit breaker to protect the person from being emotionally overloaded. The memory becomes locked in the eye movements, in a purgatory-like state.

Dr. Francine Shapiro awakened to a technique that uses eye movement and other forms of rhythmic stimulation to help trauma victims. With Eye Movement Desensitization and Reprocessing (EMDR), she demonstrated how the brain can unlock painful memories and heal trauma. The LifeLine Technique expands upon EMDR by determining the specific eye gazes locked out of REMs. By having a person follow my hand through different eye patterns, I re-create the exact number of REMs necessary to process the trauma into the long-term memory banks of the brain. The method of healing is fast, noninvasive, and reproducible.

The LifeLine Technique is content free, which means that it isn't necessary to talk about the traumatic experience to heal. Sometimes people share their memories, and sometimes they don't. Nonetheless, the release is clear in their eyes. The healing takes place with Infinite Love & Gratitude.

When a patient comes in with a specific symptom that The LifeLine Flow Chart indicates is being held in the electromagnetic field, it's released from the spiritual body through synthetic REMs. This frees the traumatic memory that's been locked away, allowing it to be processed by the brain's cortex. The synthetic REMs reconnect the spirit's flow to the will of the person, while at the same time reconnecting his or her mind and body. Once this is accomplished, that person will release the shocking incident without having to reexperience the pain of the trauma.

During the second stage of Linda's treatment, I discovered the direction of her gaze at the time she learned of her father's death. She was looking down and to the right, which kept her brain in a holding pattern and inhibited the REMs in that direction. The lack of REMs prevented the conscious processing of the grief and fear related to the traumatic childhood experience. Finding and processing the specific eye movement made it possible to create a conscious connection to this subconscious experience, helping Linda release the addiction to sugar.

The sugar addiction was a gift that enabled Linda to embrace the emotions she'd disconnected from. Using muscle testing, I discovered which of The Five Basics for Optimal Health Linda needed to focus on: By maintaining a healthy eating program, exercising regularly, and owning her power, she would be equipped to reconnect to her feelings of grief and fear that *caused* the sugar addiction. Linda left the office smiling, feeling lighter and empowered to embrace her truth.

Emotions that are buried alive never die. Every challenge provides us with an opportunity to heal and achieve our highest potential.

# CHAPTER 21

# DISCOVERING THE
# PEARL IN THE OYSTER

In the beginning was the Word, and the Word was *Love.* The vibratory frequency of this emotion is infinite . . . it's the interconnection of everything. When I speak of the collective conscious or universe, I'm referring to Infinite Love, to which we're always linked. But when we choose to view life in a limited way, we're disconnecting from this power.

Thanks to modern science, we understand the human body in a detailed way, both anatomically and functionally. The same is now true of the electromagnetic field, which surrounds the body and vibrates with varying frequencies of light and energy.

Kirlian photography and other scientific means enable us to view and understand the human electromagnetic field. Emotions begin as an energetic frequency originating from the collective conscious or universe. When we have a particular experience, that frequency is filtered into the body through the microcosmic orbit, creating specific thoughts, feelings, and beliefs that the brain categorizes and integrates. It translates these electromagnetic frequencies into images, voices, pictures, and memories that connect them to the physical realm . . . the spirit to the body.

When these impressions are painful or uncomfortable, we'll sometimes subconsciously dissociate from them. We know that the cause of symptoms is the disconnection from our emotions. This begins in the microcosmic orbit and is called the assemblage point. As mentioned earlier, the microcosmic orbit consists of seven chakras, appearing as spirals or vortices that trace vertically through the spinal column. Although it seldom appears visible to the untrained eye, it's as real as the light from the sun, radio waves, or x-rays.

Life begins as energy and then potentially manifests into the physical realm. The assemblage point is the anatomical location in the energetic field where we've initially disconnected from our emotions. It's like a pearl in an oyster—it's the treasure that's bestowed upon us when we embrace the original painful or challenging experience from which we've disconnected. Pearls aren't formed by a natural process inside an oyster, but rather when an accidental intruder (such as a grain of sand) enters a mollusk's shell. To defend itself, layer after layer of a substance called nacre grows and forms like onion skins around the particle. These layers are semi-opaque and consist of calcium carbonate, which makes up the pearl and becomes a coating for the particle.

Inevitably, natural pearls vary depending on the shape being coated. A process was developed to imitate natural-pearl formation, creating "cultured" pearls. Like natural ones, cultured pearls grow inside a mollusk, but with human intervention. Shells are carefully opened and different shapes of beads are inserted. Over time the inserted beads become coated with nacre, which makes the pearls appear to glow inside and gives them a beautiful shine.

This same process occurs with experiences that are painful and challenging to human beings, except that we don't have a pearl to show for it—we have a symptom. When we disconnect from, internalize, or deny something, a mechanism is set into motion. The painful experience (the particle of sand) is the disconnection or assemblage point. It creates a layering around that moment, which grows in its own unique fashion, depending on the nature of the experience itself. The longer it's been denied, the more layers form around that original event, just like in the pearl. At the same time, the more there are, the greater the opportunity to heal—the greater the gift.

The symptom starts to grow, like a pearl, when it's ignored. It begins subtly in the microcosmic orbit as an uncomfortable thought, feeling, or belief that keeps creating layer after layer until it's removed. If the pearl stayed within the oyster and continued to grow for too long, the oyster would die. The same holds true for symptoms: By internalizing, denying, or disconnecting from a symptom, it has the potential to develop so many layers that it destroys the body. Embracing uncomfortable emotions—your pearls—enhances the health of your spirit and body and opens your life to Infinite Love.

As we now know from Dr. Emoto's work, living your life with the attitude of gratitude literally changes the molecular structure of the water that makes up your body. Being grateful is an act of courage and trust that the universe is perfect. Considering that you're a manifestation of the universe, there's a reason for every experience you encounter. Your challenge in life is to embrace whatever comes your way. From your first breath to your very last, life is painful and challenging. It's by opening up to the pain and challenges with gratitude that you choose not to suffer.

The meaning and purpose of life is discovered in the process of overcoming difficulties with dignity, courage, and faith. We all have the choice to discover the "pearl" in the oyster of life. Grab it with both hands, and embrace the beauty of the experiences that are being offered to you.

*Let my life force be linked to my heart.*
*Let my heart be linked to the truth in me.*
*Let that truth be linked to the eternal,*
*that eternal, which is unending bliss.*

— Laghn Nyasa Upanishads

# PART II

## OWNING YOUR POWER

# CHAPTER 22

# THE POWER TO
# CREATE A HEALTHY LIFE

What is health? The word *health* is a derivative of *wholeness* and *healing*. It means "a state of complete balance and harmony." The source of true health is maintaining balance on an emotional, structural, biochemical, and spiritual level. Our bodies are miraculous self-healing organisms built to monitor anything that happens.

For example, when we cut ourselves, white corpuscles instantly rush to that spot to fight infection, while the platelets congeal the blood and seal up the wound. It all happens automatically—we don't have to think about it. Our body already knows exactly how to repair itself, just as it understands how to extract nutrients from food and dispense it as energy to various parts of the body.

In order to create the ideal conditions for your body to take care of itself, you must be proactive in your efforts. You must accept *complete responsibility* for your well-being. The LifeLine Technique provides the tools necessary to restore the body's balance and facilitate optimal health.

Taking care of yourself entails more than watching your weight. It means becoming intuitively attuned to the subtle and sophisticated ways in which your body works so that you're aware and can respond when it's out of balance. It involves recognizing how the internalization or denial of, or disconnection from, your emotions creates the conditions for lack of health. It means understanding that feeling sick isn't a bad thing, but rather is the body's way of saying that it's time to take responsibility and heal. It requires that you consciously drink pure water, eat wholesome foods, get enough rest, exercise, and own your power.

The LifeLine Technique is the best possible tool for rebalancing the body so that it will regenerate itself. However, to facilitate the healing process, you must maintain a healthy lifestyle.

The Five Basics for Optimal Health are:

1.  Water
2.  Food
3.  Rest
4.  Exercise
5.  Owning your power

For each of these components, there are three aspects:

1.  Quantity
2.  Quality
3.  Frequency

Each of The Five Basics for Optimal Health is explained in depth in the following pages, including some guidelines on how best to use them. You don't have to be a doctor to understand your body, nor do you have to comprehend every aspect of holistic health care. The most important things you can do to develop optimal health are to stay in Present Time Consciousness, pay attention to what your body is telling you, set goals, and take steps to achieve them.

According to the science of Psycho-Cybernetics, you have the power to program yourself for success. Dr. Maxwell Maltz, a plastic surgeon, is credited with discovering Psycho-Cybernetics, which is the application of the science of cybernetics (goal-oriented functions of mechanical systems) to human behavior. Dr. Maltz contends that "positive thinking" only works when it's consistent with your self-image—which is based on your experience, rather than on intellectual knowledge. Consequently, in order for The Five Basics for Optimal Health to effectively help you improve the quality of your well-being, you'll have to go beyond reading this book—you'll have to take action!

In his book *Psycho-Cybernetics,* Dr. Maltz writes that it usually requires a minimum of 19 days to effect any perceptible change in your mental image. And to make it happen, he says, you have to have a plan. Dr. Maltz recommends five steps to achieve success, which he defines as the ongoing *process* of achieving a goal:

1.  "Your built-in 'Success Mechanism' must have a goal" that you conceive of as "already in existence—now." (For example, during the process of writing this book, I maintained a vision of it as a bestseller.)

2.  "The automatic mechanism is teleological"—it must be "oriented to 'end results.'" The means to achieving the goal will become clear in the process.

3.  You should embrace mistakes or temporary failures with the attitude of gratitude. By valuing pain, fear, and challenges, you'll find the hidden meaning—the opportunity within an experience—and achieve your life's purpose and goals. Just remember to stay present and pay attention to both positive and negative feedback.

4.  "Skill learning of any kind is accomplished by trial and error, mentally correcting your aim after an error until a 'successful' motion, movement or performance has been achieved." After that, forgetting past mistakes and remembering positive responses are the keys to ensure that continued success is replicated.

5.  "You must learn to trust your creative mechanism to do its work and not 'jam it' by becoming too concerned or too anxious as to whether it will work or not." Go with the flow . . . *let it work,* rather than *make it work.*

The key to activating your "Success Mechanism" as it relates to your health is visioning. When you close your eyes and think about yourself as a healthy person, what do you see? What do you look like? How do you feel? What's the qualitative difference between now and the "new self" that you're creating?

Take a moment and write down your vision of wellness. As you integrate The Five Basics for Optimal Health into your daily life, use your written vision as a source of motivation to stay on track. If you need more than just words on paper, I recommend the techniques outlined by noted art therapist Lucia Capacchione, Ph.D., in her book *Visioning*. Because "life is a work of art, designed by the one who lives it," Dr. Capacchione recommends creating a collage of images, symbols, and words to support your vision of what you want your life to be.

No matter which path you choose, be courageous, follow your heart and intuition, and keep moving. Julia Cameron, the author of *The Artist's Way,* uses the mantra "Leap, and the net will appear." The only mistake you can make is not doing anything at all.

# CHAPTER 23

# WATER:
# THE ESSENTIAL COMPONENT
# OF OPTIMAL HEALTH

Visualize a constantly flowing stream. Notice how the water is moving, pushing any obstructions out of the way. Now think about a retention pond filled with stagnant water. Observe the debris, scum, algae, and mold rising to the surface. Look at the pathogenic life beginning to form. The more water you drink, the stronger the flow of your internal stream, making it difficult for harmful organisms and disease to take root in your system. I'm sure you've heard before that you can live an extended period without food, but not without water, which is why it's an essential component of optimal health. Water plays a role in nearly every bodily function—from regulating temperature and cushioning joints to bringing oxygen to cells and removing waste.

Your body is composed of 75 percent water and 25 percent solid matter. Brain tissue is 85 percent water; blood is 82 percent; and the lungs are nearly 90 percent. The body is like a sponge: It's made up of trillions of cells that absorb and hold water. According to the late Dr. F. Batmanghelidj, a medical doctor and the author of the book *Your Body's Many Cries For Water* (**www.watercure.com**), the need for water is an essential part of human evolution:

When the human body developed from the species that were given life in water, the same dependence on the life-giving properties of water was inherited. The role of water itself in the body of living species, mankind included, has not changed since the first creation of life from salt water and its subsequent adaptation to fresh water.

Because water conducts electricity, it isn't safe to hold a hair dryer or radio while standing in a bathtub or to swim during a lightning storm. However, as an electrical being, you need conductivity to facilitate the operation of all of your body's major functions—thinking, circulation, breathing, and elimination. And as the primary conductor of electricity, water carries the necessary electrical charges (information) to every cell in the body. Each one is dependent upon water to function optimally . . . if the channel is blocked in any way, the body won't function properly.

Dehydration is a condition in which the body's ability to operate as a self-healing organism is blocked. It affects blood pressure, blood-sugar metabolism, digestion, and kidney function. Thirst means the body is already in this state, and dry mouth is the last symptom of chronic dehydration.

What causes dehydration? Besides the fact that many people don't drink enough water, they also consume excessive amounts of coffee, sugar-filled coffee drinks, regular and diet soda, herbal and black tea, sports drinks, and concentrated juices.

Sugar dehydrates the body. Caffeine is a diuretic that causes the body to eliminate fluids. Have you ever felt as if your mind still wasn't clear even after drinking a cup of coffee or tea? It's likely that the mental fog was initially caused by dehydration, and the caffeinated beverage made it worse.

Most of us think of thirst as the common signal that our bodies need water. However, because we've ignored it or responded with fluids that make the situation worse, we've become desensitized. Consequently, as we grow older, we gradually lose our perception of thirst, compounding the challenge and actually speeding up the aging process. Fatigue is the first symptom of dehydration. By the time we feel thirsty, we're already dehydrated. In addition to fatigue, pain is another sign the body sends that it needs more water.

Dr. Batmanghelidj's extensive research on the effects of dehydration (which are detailed in his book) has determined that many common ailments are actually the result of not drinking enough water, including:

- Morning sickness in pregnant women
- Allergic sensitivities
- Heartburn
- Colitis
- Rheumatoid arthritis
- Fibromyalgia
- Back and angina pain
- Migraines and other headaches
- Depression
- Leg pain when walking
- Obesity
- High blood pressure and cholesterol

The FDA's healthy-eating guidelines recommend a minimum of eight glasses of water (64 ounces) a day. However, Dr. Batmanghelidj recommends that most of us drink a lot more than that—half of our body weight in ounces of water. For example, a 180-pound person would drink 90 ounces of water. My experience has shown that optimal health will best be achieved and maintained when we drink one quart (32 ounces) of water for every 50 pounds of body weight, rounding up to the highest quart. For example, a 180-pound person would need to drink four quarts, or 128 ounces, of water on a daily basis.

Hot weather or exercise increases the body's required needs for water. If you drink coffee, tea (herbal, black, or green), or juice, be sure to also take in an equal additional amount of water for every ounce you consume of these other beverages so that your body will be fully hydrated. There's no nutritional value gained from drinking soda or any other sugary or artificially sweetened beverage. Even water with a slice of lemon is a diuretic and therefore increases your daily requirement.

Water is best consumed at room temperature and sipped all day long. It should also be free of chemicals, bacteria, and heavy metals. Because of this, bottled or filtered water is preferable to tap water. The challenge I encounter with bottled water is that it's "dead"—there's actually an expiration date on the outside. By the time it's consumed, the water has lost oxygen and vitality from its source.

The bottled water that I've personally evaluated with pH strips reveals acidity, which leads to inflammation in the body. Chronic inflammation—either localized or systemic—will result in some form of degenerative disease. In addition to the cost factor, researchers have found that certain plastics leech chemicals into the water, causing other health challenges. In fact, some have been found to bind to the same receptor sites as hormones, thus creating hormonal imbalances.

As cited in the April 1, 2003, issue of *Current Biology* (13:546–553), researchers discovered that even extremely low levels of the compound called bisphenol A (BPA) produced genetic abnormalities. The journal reported that BPA exhibits hormonelike properties and imitates the effects of naturally occurring estrogens.

Dr. Joe Mercola, a noted holistic physician, recommends purchasing water in either clear, polyethylene, five-gallon containers or the transparent (polyethylene) bottles that are sold at the grocery store, because they don't transfer chemicals into the water (the cause of that awful "plastic" taste of the water in many cloudy-bottled varieties).

The filtration system that I personally use utilizes PiMag water-filtration technology. I've found through muscle testing that PiMag water consistently increases the strength of everyone I evaluate. This water has a stable pH of 7.4; therefore, it's alkaline. An alkaline environment is essential for maintaining balance and optimal health, since disease such as cancer thrives in an acidic setting.

PiMag water was discovered in 1964 by Japanese botanists. They noticed a narrow stream flowing between two hills near a small town in Japan. One hill was largely magnetite, and the other contained calcium compounds, which produced ions with a net positive charge. The stream between them coursed over a bed of silicates—the material that forms natural crystal—and the combination produced negative ions. The scientists observed that the water in this stream had remarkable effects on the surrounding plant life. They set out to reproduce this natural water in a laboratory. As a result, an enhanced system of filtration was developed, which is known as PiMag water technology. This system adds several components to the water, including the benefits of magnetic and far-infrared energy.

The primary stages of PiMag filtration include a stainless-steel screen and carbon filters. Carbon has been used for decades in scientific labs to remove impurities. Porous coral sand chips make up another layer of natural, nonchemical filters to remove contaminants and improve taste. Particles as small as one-tenth of a micron are trapped during an ultrafiltration stage, which is based on the technology used in kidney dialysis—the pore size is the smallest in the industry. A third process filters water through clay ceramics and stones, reflecting far-infrared energy and several minerals, including calcium, to the water. In addition to all the microfiltration, the water is energized and enhanced as it flows through powerful magnets and ceramic magnetite, oxidative, and pH-stabilizing stones.

As mentioned earlier, the work of Dr. Masaru Emoto demonstrates that water has consciousness, as well as other *life-giving* qualities. Dr. Emoto, whose work is documented in volumes I, II, and III of the book *Messages from Water,* began by studying the crystallization process of water as it passed from a liquid into a freezing state. He extracted crystals from various vials of water and studied them under a dark-field microscope that had photographic capabilities. He soon realized that the nature of the crystals was based on the source of the water—that is, natural springs, city water systems, snowflakes, and stagnant ponds. This discovery made Dr. Emoto curious to see whether the frequency of words or sounds would have any impact. Through repeated experiments exposing vials of water to spoken and written words, as well as music, he demonstrated how thoughts and words alter the molecular structure of water.

One of the most profound of Dr. Emoto's experiments involved a group of instructors from all over Japan. He told them that he'd be placing a cup of ordinary tap water on his desk at a specific date and time, and he asked them to transmit their feelings to that water—to send "chi and soul" of love and wish for the water to become clean.

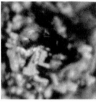 

Tap Water Before
Positive Intention

Positive Thoughts of
Chi, Soul, and Spirit

He extracted crystals of water before and after the cup was placed on his desk. The transformation was astonishing, confirming the power of thought on water.

On January 17, 1995, the Great Hanshin-Awaji Earthquake occurred in Kobe, Japan. Three days later, Dr. Emoto took photographs of the crystals found in the city's tap water. It was as if the water captured the fear, panic, and deep sorrow of the people immediately after the quake—the crystals were completely destroyed.

People from around the world helped with the reconstruction of the city. The citizens of Kobe received praise and blessings for coming together in a time of crisis. They transformed the tragedy of the natural disaster into an opportunity to unite their efforts for restoring their home. The crystal shown here, extracted three months after the earthquake, seems to have collected those feelings.

Immediately
After Earthquake

Three Months
After Earthquake

We live on a planet that's more than 70 percent covered in water, and our bodies are composed of 75 to 90 percent water. The implications of Dr. Emoto's work are astonishing, not only for health, but for the well-being of the entire planet. We have the power to transform the structure of water through our thoughts, words, and actions, which means that we have the ability to change the course of our health in the same way. The efficacy of The LifeLine Technique is based on the premise that Infinite Love & Gratitude, whether written, spoken, or reflected in someone's actions, has tremendous power to heal.

As we now know from Dr. Emoto's research, not all water is created equal. The energy of the fluid you drink determines the health-giving properties it has for the body. It's now understood that water can be damaged by several factors, including the environment, the emotions of the surrounding people, music, the pressure in pipes and from water pumps, straight-line pipes or conduits (in nature, water curves and spirals), as well as exposure to negatively charged chemicals, heavy metals, or other contaminants. The combination of these factors results in the loss of water's charge, or vibratory rate.

For optimal health, don't drink unfiltered tap water! The chlorine and fluoride used to "purify" it are toxic chemicals and have been known to cause severe health challenges. Many houses have lead or copper pipes, and the heavy metals immediately go into the water. Tap water can also contain many toxins, pesticides, and bacteria.

The bottom line is to do the best you can with what you have. No matter what type of water you're drinking, writing "Infinite Love & Gratitude" on the container increases its energetic quality. Structure is directly related to function: Infinite Love & Gratitude enhances the pure, crystalline structure of water, thus increasing its functional healing potential.

# CHAPTER 24

# KICKING THE SUGAR HABIT

Sugar is the biggest "drug" scandal in the world today. Used for its taste and/or as a preservative, sugar is extremely addictive, has no nutritional value, is high in calories, is poisonous to the system, and prompts the body to enter a degenerative state because it leads to insulin sensitivity. Sugar abuse is epidemic and catastrophic—instances of diabetes and obesity, especially in children, are out of control.

### Symptoms and Illnesses Related to Eating Too Much Sugar

| | | |
|---|---|---|
| Mood swings | PMS | Learning disabilities |
| Poor concentration | Memory loss | Chronic fatigue |
| Headaches | Spaciness | Arthritis |
| Sugar cravings | Vaginitis | Irritability |
| Menstrual problems | High cholesterol | High triglycerides |
| Obesity | Fibromyalgia | Frequent colds |
| Diabetes mellitus | Yeast infections | Running ear |
| Depression | Low libido | Joint and muscle pain |
| Allergies | Rashes | Epilepsy |
| High blood pressure | Migraines | Cardiovascular disease |
| Hyperactivity | ADD | |

(Courtesy of Dr. Jacqueline Paltis, author, *The Sugar Control Bible and Cookbook*)

If you don't add refined, cane sugar to your coffee, tea, or cereal—or if you're a vegetarian or vegan—you may think this doesn't apply to you, but it's time to take off the blinders: Sugar reactions can be triggered by *any* food that breaks down in the body the same way. When we talk about sugar, the list includes white *and* wheat bread; whole-grain *and* white flour; brown *and* white rice; along with pasta, crackers, cereals, all potatoes, popcorn, and tofu. *All* simple carbohydrates, refined or processed foods, and starches result in a massive insulin secretion that processes these foods so that your body can use them.

Most eating programs today are too high in simple carbohydrates: enriched and whole-grain refined flour (bread and crackers), pastry, pasta, rice, concentrated sweeteners (sugar, fructose, and honey), ice cream—even ketchup. Carbohydrates, simple and complex (especially potatoes, dried beans, and grains), ultimately break down into simple sugars. Digested and assimilated rapidly by the body, they can provide quick, short-term energy, raise the blood-sugar level, and stimulate the production of insulin. Carbohydrates are beneficial when eaten in the form of whole fresh fruits and vegetables with all of the fiber intact. Fruits and vegetables contain vitamins, minerals, enzymes, and antioxidants. They're also alkaline and help neutralize the acidity of animal protein.

If we eat too many carbohydrates or not enough protein, our body becomes imbalanced. Sugar cravings are a symptom, just like a headache, and are a sign of imbalance in your sugar metabolism. They're a sign of a breakdown in communication between the systems responsible for maintaining the equilibrium of your sugar metabolism. Almost every person who enters my office is struggling with some aspect of insulin sensitivity and sugar imbalance. That means one or all of the three organs that are partners in the process—the liver, pancreas, and adrenal glands—are very likely in crisis. Although we've been taught that blood-sugar-metabolism challenges are the result of the improper functioning of the pancreas, this isn't true, except in the case of type 1 diabetes.

The liver communicates with, and serves as the modulator between, the pancreas and the adrenal glands. It's the organ that's responsible for telling the pancreas how much insulin to secrete in order to handle the meal you have just eaten. Your liver continues to monitor the situation to ensure that the blood-glucose levels have decreased. Then it sends a message to the adrenal cortex to secrete enough glucocorticoids to raise your blood glucose and maintain an even feeding of nourishment to the brain.

According to Dr. Jacqueline Paltis in *The Sugar Control Bible and Cookbook,* Johns Hopkins University conducted a study in which the cadavers of 5,000 diabetics were autopsied. Only 2 percent of the bodies examined had a degenerated pancreas—however, 98 percent had liver disease. What does that say about diabetes? . . . It's a liver disease. How does the liver play out its role?

Let's look at a typical person whose eating habits primarily consist of sugar and carbohydrates. This individual, on average, eats two meals per day. After lunch, he's feeling a bit sluggish, so he eats a candy bar and drinks a can of diet (or regular) soda. Inside his body, all the communication channels are shut down until he eats, and an alert goes out that there's glucose in the system. The liver has been asleep, and the infusion of glucose startles it awake.

*Wow!* thinks the liver. *Look at all this glucose!* The liver immediately says to the pancreas, "Why aren't you secreting insulin?"

"You never sent me the message to do that," the pancreas responds.

"Well, just do it now!" the liver exclaims.

"Okay!" the pancreas yells back. It opens all the channels, and the system is flooded with insulin.

"Red alert!" the liver screams. "Mayday! Mayday!"

The gush of insulin causes the blood glucose to plummet. Meanwhile, the liver falls asleep again. The man whose body is experiencing all these changes goes into a hypoglycemic reaction and is more fatigued than ever. The liver is startled awake again, and it begins yelling at the adrenals.

"What's the matter with you?" the liver demands. "Why haven't you secreted any glucocorticoids?"

"I never got the message from you," the adrenals protest.

"Well, I'm telling you now!" the liver snaps back.

The man has a burst of anger as the adrenals open all the channels, flooding the body with an outpouring of glucocorticoids. This leads to a raising of blood-glucose levels, and the man is now in a hyperglycemic (too much blood sugar) roar. It's an endless cycle until the liver, pancreas, or adrenals shut down in exhaustion, waving a white flag!

Dr. Paltis writes that blood-sugar malfunctions are the result of a communication breakdown:

> The liver cannot maintain the feedback loop (a kind of running dialogue) that lets the pancreas and adrenals know the blood glucose status. Methionine (an amino acid) is the chemical messenger in this communication, but the liver does not have enough of the right kind of methionine . . . to do the job. . . . In addition, methionine is the limiting amino acid (kind of a smallest common denominator) for the liver to process both sugar and protein.

The amino acid L-methionine is most highly prevalent in red meat, essential in Western eating programs to maintain a healthy sugar metabolism. Why? As a result of generational patterns and lifestyle, our bodies don't have the enzymes to break down protein from nonmeat sources such as legumes or tofu in order to extract and use the L-methionine. There is an exception—certain religious groups and cultures in India that are indigenously vegetarian have adapted over time to extract L-methionine from nonanimal sources. Our bodies, over several more generations, probably will do so as well.

However, the survival of the fittest, based on genetic adaptation and blood types, is also a factor. In the interim, we'll continue to perpetuate a degenerative process in the body if we don't eat red meat. Tuna contains L-methionine, but you'd have to eat 9 to 12 cans of it per day to obtain the same amount that you'd get from nine ounces of red meat per week.

If L-methionine is present and we're consuming it on a frequent basis, the communication between the liver, pancreas, and adrenals is more efficient and better facilitated. That's the key to blood-sugar metabolism—eating red meat to ensure that these pathways are turned on and in proper working order.

There's a lot of controversy about eating red meat. However, it shouldn't be about the meat, but rather about the farming standards used in raising cows. According to a recent analysis by the Union of Concerned Scientists, 70 percent of the antibiotics produced in the U.S. each year—nearly 25 million pounds—are fed to *healthy* pigs, chickens, and cattle to prevent disease or speed growth. The excessive use of antibiotics in livestock is contributing to the mounting concerns about antibiotic resistance in humans. The majority of the red meat purchased in supermarkets contains massive amounts of antibiotics and hormones unless the packaging specifies that the animals have been organically raised without these substances. And if that isn't enough, most cows are grain fed, which is creating the same sugar-metabolism imbalances that *we* develop from eating grains.

The best meat is organic and grass fed, free of antibiotics and hormones. Grass-fed meat has an optimal balance of essential fatty acids, which are important for many of the body's functions, including the immune system, hormonal balance, and the nervous system.

Our brains are very specific in the nutrition they need in order to function: They use glucose, the simplest form of sugar. There's something called the blood-brain barrier, a protective shield that guards the brain from toxicity, and glucose is the only nutrient that crosses it into the brain. When we eat refined sugars and processed carbohydrates, the body breaks them down immediately, causing a spike in our blood sugar and a rush of insulin into our systems. It takes a lot of energy for the body to deal with this instant source of glucose. However, when we eat proteins or fats, the metabolic process is slower, because not as much insulin is needed for digestion. The body maintains an even flow of glucose to the brain, rather than the spike reaction that occurs when we eat sugars or anything that breaks down similarly, such as carbohydrates.

The key to creating that balance is controlling the eicosanoid reactions within the body. Eicosanoids are a hormonelike substance manufactured by every cell in the body. They're divided into series 1 and series 2:

| Series 1 | Series 2 |
|---|---|
| Dilates blood vessels | Constricts blood vessels |
| Strengthens immune system | Weakens immune system |
| Reduces inflammation | Creates inflammation |
| Relieves pain | Increases pain |
| Increases oxygen | Decreases oxygen |
| Increases endurance | Decreases endurance |
| Prevents blood clotting | Promotes blood clotting |
| Dilates bronchial tubes | Constricts bronchial tubes |
| Fights cancer cell growth | Supports cancer cell growth |

(From: *The Sugar Control Bible and Cookbook*)

The only way to control the balance of eicosanoid production is through food selection—choosing substances that are high in protein, low in carbohydrates, and contain good fat. If you unlock a door with a key, whatever is inside is now at your disposal. When you eat sugar, the key opens the lock that secures the floodgates of insulin. When this hormone is secreted, it causes a series-2 eicosanoid reaction. On the other hand, when we eat protein such as eggs, steak, cheese, plain yogurt, or raw cashews, the key unlocks a valve for glucagon, which unleashes a series-1 eicosanoid reaction, enabling the body to heal.

It's important to eat protein often throughout the day and on a regular basis. Because protein is metabolized slowly, frequent eating will allow a consistent and even flow of glucose to the body. We're all aware that infants need to be fed every two hours. Even if we forget, the baby will let us know by crying or throwing a tantrum. As we age, our bodies also alert us if we aren't eating frequently enough. The message will come as fatigue, headache, concentration difficulties, irritability, or bursts of anger. The LifeLine Technique enables the practitioner to assess the functional balance of sugar metabolism without the invasiveness of needles. Through the use of a kinesiological reflex and semantic testing, functional blood-sugar metabolism and utilization can be assessed and balanced immediately.

This may surprise you, but tests that require fasting are an ineffective way to assess blood-sugar metabolism. The normal range of blood sugar is 80 to 120 mg/dL—yours may get up to 119 or 120, or it might go down to 80. The question is: How quickly does it drop, and how quickly does it rise? Conducting the fasting blood-glucose test every half hour ignores the fact that levels can change within *five minutes.* If the test were conducted every 10 or 15 minutes, rather than every 30, it could show more easily how rapidly the blood sugar spikes, and an assessment would be more functional. Still, that's a pain: Who wants to be pricked with needles, drink a horrible sugar solution, and feel terrible when it's very simple to do a muscle test? Muscle testing has been conducted effectively on hundreds of thousands of people throughout the world . . . it works.

Blood-glucose numbers aren't the only issue. What's critical is the body's adaptogenic property—its ability to return to balance. Whether the blood glucose is too high or too low, it's just a matter of turning the system back on so that it can maintain its own equilibrium. The traditional paradigm of blood-glucose treatment determines whether it's too high (diabetes) or too low (hypoglycemia) and medicates accordingly. However, on any given day, your blood sugar can fluctuate up or down, depending on whether your system is maintaining balance. That balance is based on water consumption, eating habits, rest, exercise, and how you manage stressful situations.

The essence of holistic and energy medicine is balance. It lets the body find *its own* "normal," which is *different* for everyone. By having six to eight small meals daily, drinking water, and eating high-quality foods, your body will balance itself.

I recommend that you use *The Sugar Control Bible and Cookbook* by Dr. Jacqueline Paltis. The program emphasizes frequent eating—every two hours—and requires some form of protein at that time. In addition, the program recommends:

- Eating a minimum of nine ounces of red meat per week.

- Drinking a quart of water per 50 pounds of body weight

or any fraction thereof. (For example, a 153-pound person needs four quarts of water per day.)

- Avoidance of all sweeteners, natural and artificial.

- Elimination or severe restriction of caffeine and nicotine.

The Chicago area (where I practice) was recently designated as one of the most overweight cities in the U.S. Obesity has become a chronic disease and the second leading cause of preventable death. Like its successful "Smokeout" campaign urging people to stop smoking, the American Cancer Society recently launched the "Great American Weigh In" in an effort to increase awareness of the risks of obesity, which is about to edge out smoking as the number one *preventable* public-health crisis in the country.

Obesity is the most neglected public-health challenge in the U.S., and I believe that the greatest culprit is sugar addiction and internalized, denied, and disconnected emotions. Unlike other high-protein regimens, the primary goal of the Sugar Control Program is *health gain* instead of weight loss, although shedding weight is a by-product. Rather than concentrating on dieting and the latest nutrition craze, it's important that we shift our focus to improving the quality of our health by developing a lifestyle that nourishes the body, rather than destroys it.

# CHAPTER 25

# FOOD:
# A HEALTHY EATING PROGRAM

*D*iet is a four-letter word, and the first three letters are "d-i-e." That says a lot. Fad diets may result in quick weight loss, but ultimately they create a yo-yo cycle that often leads to dis-ease and/or illness. That's why The Five Basics for Optimal Health incorporate a *healthy eating program,* rather than a diet.

Carbohydrate-metabolism imbalances and subclinical (that is, clinically undetectable) dehydration are the leading culprits behind most chronic, degenerative diseases. The eating guidelines contained in this book will help your body heal.

Before I outline the program, let me give you a few tips that I recommend to my patients. They'll assist you in successfully integrating these beneficial changes into your life. The more organized you are, the easier it will be to incorporate healthful eating into your daily routine. Here's what I suggest:

- Read Dr. Paltis's book before beginning the program. It will help you understand how the quantity, quality, and frequency of your food choices affect your health.

- Follow the recipes in *The Sugar Control Bible and Cookbook,* or modify your own favorites using permitted foods.

- Make a grocery list before you go shopping. You'll be more likely to purchase foods on the program, rather than ones that aren't on the permitted list.

- Whenever possible, prepare your staple foods in advance at least twice a week—roasted rice, raw vegetables, cheese, hard-boiled eggs, and plain yogurt with fresh fruit.

- Set the timer in your electronic organizer, watch, or computer as a conscious reminder to eat every two hours. Keep a food log in a small notebook (or in your organizer). Write down the time of your meal or snack, along with what you ate.

- Review your food log weekly to keep track of your progress. Note how you feel after each meal so that you become aware of any food sensitivities.

- If you find that you have to eat out or are invited to a dinner party, snack before you go. If you do, it's easier to resist the temptation of bread or sweets on the table.

- Keep apples and a bag of cashews and/or Brazil nuts in your car in case of an emergency.

The Sugar Control Program is based on meals of fresh vegetables and fruits; antibiotic- and hormone-free, grass-fed meats; organic dairy products; and a limited amount of sprouted grains. The following information outlines the foods permitted, as well as the ones that should be avoided, when following the plan.

*Permitted Foods for Healthy Eating*
*(All Foods Preferably Organic)*

## Fruits and Vegetables

- Fresh fruits and green vegetables (unlimited)
- Yellow vegetables (no more than 4–6 servings per week)
- Freshly juiced vegetables (1 cup per day)
- No fruit juices unless freshly juiced (carrot juice is allowed in limited amounts)

## Meat and Dairy

- Beef, venison, and buffalo (at least 9 ounces per week required)
- Lamb, poultry, and pork (unlimited)
- Liver or other organ meats
- Fish and shellfish
- Eggs
- Yellow/white aged cheese
- Whole milk (only if there isn't an allergy, skin condition, or weight challenge)
- Yogurt or cottage cheese using plain, whole milk

## Protein Snacks
### (Eat Some Protein Every Two Hours of Your Waking Day)

- Raw cashews and Brazil nuts
- Yellow/white aged cheese
- Raw cashew butter (made at home)

## Beverages

- Water (1 quart for every 50 pounds of body weight, rounded up to the next quart)

- Coffee and tea (1–3 cups per day). Whole milk or cream may be added—*no sweeteners permitted.* (Drink 1 additional cup of water for every cup of coffee/tea consumed.)

- Although coffee is permitted on the Sugar Control Program, I recommend removing it from your eating program because it leads to a cortisol release from your adrenal glands, which causes inflammatory reactions throughout the body. In addition, coffee (even organic varieties) contains carboxylic acid, which can destroy the intestinal wall, leading to a dysbiosis—a "leaky gut."

## Whole Grains

- Roasted whole-grain rice (unlimited—use any variety)

- *Toasting directions:* Wash the rice, and then toast it in a dry non-Teflon skillet over low to medium heat for about 15 minutes, stirring as you go, until the rice is golden brown. If the kernels begin to crackle and pop, lower the heat. Cool and store, or cook immediately.

- *Cooking directions:* Bring liquid to a boil (1 cup rice to 3 cups water). Cook covered over low heat for 45 minutes, stirring one or two times. Homemade broth may replace some or all of the water, and herbs may be used for flavor.

- You're allowed to have as much of this rice as you like. Toasting the whole-grain rice first helps the body use it as a protein instead of as a carbohydrate, so serve it hot as a side dish to replace starches. It also makes excellent fried rice (see recipes in Dr. Paltis's book). Eat any leftover plain rice in the morning, mixed with plain, whole-milk yogurt and fruit—it makes a delicious and satisfying breakfast. (You can add cinnamon for extra flavor!)

### Bread

- 100 percent sprouted-grain bread (no more than 2 slices per day)

- You'll find this bread in the freezer section of some health-food and better grocery stores. My favorite brand is Food For Life's Ezekiel 4:9® Sprouted Grain Bread. Food For Life also makes sprouted-grain tortillas, as well as hamburger and hot-dog buns. Just read the label, and make sure that the grains are 100 percent sprouted. There are many "sprouted grain breads" that contain *both* sprouted and unsprouted flour—they're to be avoided.

### Miscellaneous

- Vinegar, herbs, spices, mustard, Bragg Liquid Aminos, and condiments. Be a label reader: As long as a prepared food or condiment contains no sugar (or dextrose, sucrose, corn syrup, or fructose), it's permitted. All commercial and health-food mayonnaise contains either sugar or honey, and the health-food variety is made with canola oil. There's a great recipe for mayonnaise in *The Sugar Control Bible and Cookbook.*

- Cold-pressed vegetable oils, including olive, sesame, walnut, and rice bran—*avoid peanut and canola oil.* Cook only with olive oil or butter (ghee).

- All sprouts, including bean and alfalfa sprouts, sprouted lentils, sprouted grains, and sprouted seeds

- Cooked wine in prepared foods

## Prohibited Foods

The following foods are not permitted while you're following the Sugar Control Program. Strictly avoid them during that time. Follow the plan for two to six weeks by listening to your body (after that period, follow the 80/20 plan, which is explained in the next section). Regaining a balanced blood-sugar metabolism is the key to finding your way back to optimal health.

| | |
|---|---|
| **Sugar:** | White and brown sugar, dextrose, malt, fructose, sucrose, corn syrup, rice syrup, etc. |
| **Natural Sweeteners:** | Honey, stevia, Sucanat, molasses, maple syrup, barley malt, and MSG |
| **Artificial Sweeteners:** | Aspartame, saccharin, sorbitol, Equal, NutraSweet, Sweet'n Low, and Splenda |
| **Wheat Products:** | Bread, pasta, cereal, crackers, etc. |
| **Seeds:** | Pumpkin, sunflower, etc. |
| **Grains:** | Barley, oats, corn, millet, spelt, amaranth, rye, etc. |
| **White Rice:** | Rice crackers, cakes, syrup, and milk; Rice Dream |

| | |
|---|---|
| **Vegetables:** | Cauliflower, parsnips, beets, and rutabagas; all canned and frozen vegetables |
| **Fruits:** | Dried, canned, and frozen fruit; fruit juices; jelly, preserves, and fruit spread (sugar added) |
| **Potatoes:** | White and sweet potatoes; yams, potato chips, and French fries |
| **Sweets:** | Ice cream, frozen yogurt, cookies, cake, candy, chewing gum, and carob |
| **Beverages:** | Beer, wine, and liquor; soda pop (diet or regular) and tonic water |
| **Nuts:** | Peanuts, peanut butter, roasted nut butters, pecans, walnuts, etc. |
| **Soy:** | Soy milk and tofu |
| **Legumes:** | Beans, lentils, peas, and soy |
| **Starch:** | Rice and potato starch; cornstarch |
| **Cooking Spray:** | Any and all |
| **Condiments:** | Ketchup, barbecue and soy sauce, MSG, and margarine |

### The 80/20 Eating Plan

The 80/20 Eating Plan should be employed after strictly following the Sugar Control Program for a minimal of two to six weeks. Eighty percent of the time you should follow this eating program fully. For example:

- Make sure that you eat a serving of protein every two hours.
- Eat a minimum of nine ounces of red meat per week.
- Consume unlimited amounts of fresh fruits and green vegetables.
- Avoid the prohibited foods previously listed.

The other 20 percent of the time, you should live life to the fullest—life is to be celebrated. That means on holidays, vacations, anniversaries, birthdays, or days you declare to be special for you, have fun! Just be in tune with how you're feeling in the moment. If you're enjoying yourself, it usually means that your mind, body, and spirit are in balance. Your body metabolizes the foods on the prohibited list more efficiently when you're feeling on top of your game.

If for whatever reason, you aren't feeling balanced, make sure to strictly follow the program to enable your body to heal from the physical or emotional challenges that you're facing. Most people will eat sugary foods when they're under a lot of stress, but that's the time when your body needs to focus on the situation at hand rather than on foods that are difficult to digest and metabolize. Otherwise, enjoy a piece of birthday cake, have a glass of wine, sink your teeth into a baked potato, or even add some ketchup to your favorite hamburger.

What's most important is that you do your best to follow the 80/20 Eating Plan and authentically live in the moment.

# CHAPTER 26

# REST:
# YOU HEAL WHEN YOU SLEEP

There's a direct link between the quality of your sleep and the quality of your health. How well you rest is determined by whether you drink enough water, eat healthy foods, exercise daily, and own your power. Far too many people suffer from insomnia, which can have an emotional, biochemical, structural, or spiritual root. Causes include an eating program that's too high in sugar and refined carbohydrates, dehydration, physical or emotional trauma or stress, and not getting enough exercise.

Sleep deprivation not only affects the body's immune system, it can speed up the aging process and the onset of metabolic or hormonal imbalances. According to an October 1999 issue of the British medical journal *Lancet,* chronic sleep loss can speed the onset of type 2 diabetes, high blood pressure, obesity, and memory loss. It also can affect your mental and emotional state. Ever wonder why children and many adults are cranky when they don't get enough rest? In addition to fatigue, some of the effects of lack of sleep include irritability, blurred vision, slurring of speech, short-term-memory lapses, an inability to concentrate, and hallucinations. Keep in mind that the amount of rest you need is impacted by the state of your health, your level of stress, and your age.

The parasympathetic nervous system is the part of the nervous system that's activated for healing. When you're recovering from an injury, illness, or emotional trauma—or when you're depressed—it's quite common to feel fatigued. Your body is telling you that it needs more rest. When you're asleep, the parasympathetic nervous system is functioning at its highest level. This allows the body to slow down, regenerate, and focus on problematic areas . . . in other words, when you sleep, you heal.

Dreams increase during your body's healing/detoxification phase. They're a fantastic tool for understanding and facilitating your regenerative process. Since they're usually metaphorical rather than literal, it's helpful to write down your dreams as soon as you awaken. Using The LifeLine Technique, you can release their subconscious patterns, which helps you gain clarity about their meaning and, in turn, expedites the healing process.

Posture and the quantity and quality of rest all play a major role in your overall well-being. The healthiest posture for sleeping is on either side or your back. Use pillows to support the natural curves in your spine. One beneath the knees, while lying on your back, will support the lumbar spine. A single cushion under your neck will cradle the natural curve in your cervical spine. Hugging a pillow or keeping one under your head will help maintain proper alignment between your cervical and thoracic spine. Or, if you sleep on your side, it's best to keep a pillow between your knees in order to maintain proper alignment within your pelvis.

Good posture is imperative for proper health of the spinal column. The same applies when you're sleeping. Lying on your stomach will result in the compression of nerves in your cervical and lumbar spine and the flattening of your thoracic spine.

Common symptoms associated with sleeping on your stomach include spinal misalignments, headaches, numbness in the arms and hands, as well as a number of other neuromusculoskeletal challenges. Any posture held for an extended period of time—such as hunching over a computer keyboard or bending the neck to read—will impact your ability to sleep. These symptoms will be magnified if your posture is already poor.

When it comes to rest, there are a couple of things you should remember. On average, you should get between seven and nine hours of sleep per night. (Children need more.) Because the amount of sleep necessary is different for everyone, use muscle testing to discover the specific number of hours your body needs for optimal health.

Making sure you receive quality rest and relaxation is the most significant step you can take to reduce the stress of modern living so that you can be healthier and happier. Just as you prepare to start your day, you should also ready yourself for sleep. Follow these tips to get a good, restful night of sleep:

- Spend 15 to 30 minutes winding down before going to bed by taking the time to be quiet, meditate, read, journal, or listen to soft music.

- Perform deep-breathing exercises to facilitate relaxation.

- Don't watch TV right before you go to bed or fall asleep with it turned on.

- Eat a high-protein snack and a small piece of fruit several hours before you go to sleep.

- Take a hot bath or shower, or go to the sauna before going to bed.

- Avoid caffeine, medications (if possible), and alcohol just before retiring.

- Reserve your bed for sleeping, rather than using it as an alternative site for work.

The act of sleeping not only allows your body to heal, it also enables your mind to process and integrate your life experiences. Sleep is a wonderful tool to increase the potential of the body's natural healing capacity, especially when you're overwhelmed by stress. In many countries throughout the world, it's commonplace to have a time of day when everyone takes a nap. Make time to take a 15-minute siesta and give your body and mind the ability to regenerate and relax.

~ ~ ~

# CHAPTER 27

# CREATING A NEW VISION FOR YOUR LIFE

W
e breathe in order to bring oxygen into the body in a cycle that nourishes us and purifies the blood. *How* we do so is very important in determining the way we feel and think. For example, when we're sad or anxious, we breathe in short gasps. Normal, unconscious respiration is regulated through the autonomic nervous system. Focused breathing is an act of self-awareness, a way of staying in the moment and a reminder that we're alive. By switching our breathing to a deliberate, controlled action, we form a link between the conscious mind, deeper emotional states, and spiritual fulfillment.

Take a moment to pay attention to your breath, and breathe as you normally do. Most likely your chest rises and falls. Become aware of this area of your body and the muscles that move. Repeat this exercise a few times. Remember the feeling . . . this is shallow breathing. You may have noticed that if you breathe hard in this way for long periods, your chest begins to hurt.

The breath is the vehicle through which you maintain Present Time Consciousness. It's the link between the mind, body, and spirit; and when you're in tune with your breathing, you're connected to your inner being. In yoga, the asanas (postures) are a great way to prepare the body to sit for pranayama (breathing exercises) and meditation. The main target of attention should be on the connection between the breath and the movement of the spine. The focus of the *inhale* is on the expansion of the upper chest, rib cage, and abdominal areas, creating extension of the spine and flattening of the upper back. The focus of the *exhale* is on the contraction of the abdominal muscles from the pubic bone to navel, stabilizing the pelvis to help flatten the curve in the low back.

The following breathing exercises were recommended by my yoga instructor, Erin Walsh Rodriguez. Create time to either start or finish your day with them.

### Ujjayi Breath

In Ujjayi breath, there's a slight contraction in the back of the throat (at the glottis) that makes a whisperlike sound. Start by making an *"hhhaaaaa"* sound as you exhale, first with the mouth open and then closing it halfway through the breath as you continue to breathe out. Next, keep the mouth closed as you inhale and exhale, listening for the whisperlike sound. Cover your ears with the palm of your hands to internalize it. This is a heating breathing technique.

1.  Focus on the inhale and exhale equally.

2.  Concentrate on the inhalation, gradually lengthening it (that is, start with a four-second inhale, then progress to five seconds, six, seven, eight, and so on). Let the exhalation be free (no counting, but equal to or longer than the inhale). This has an energizing, stimulating effect.

3.  Focus on the exhalation, progressively lengthening it (same as in the previous step), letting the inhalation be free (no counting). This has a calming, grounding effect.

4.  After the breathing, sit and feel the effects.

## Ratio

There are four parts to the breath: the inhale; the pause afterward, known as "retention"; the exhale; and the pause following it, which is called "suspension." Working with retention and suspension adds a deeper dimension to the breath.

1.  Be aware of the four parts of the breath.

2.  Bring the inhale and exhale to an equal count and the pauses (retention and suspension) to an equal count. (For example, inhale eight seconds and pause for two seconds; exhale eight seconds and pause for two seconds. That's one round.)

3.  Practice *Samavrtti,* which means "same." The inhale, retention, exhale, and suspension are all equal. (For example, inhale six seconds and retain six seconds; exhale six seconds and suspend six seconds.) This is quite advanced.

## Guidelines

*Never* force the breath. The exhalation is always equal to or longer than the inhalation and the retention (hold after inhalation). Let the focus be on the smooth flow of the breath. Do at least 12 rounds of breathing.

After the breathing technique of your choice, sit and feel the effects physically in the spine, hips, and legs and in the capacity of the lungs. Sense the effects emotionally—do you feel stable, nurtured, and calm? Experience them mentally through clarity of mind and focus. Become aware of the impact spiritually—do you feel connected to something higher? Also, notice any feelings of discomfort, instability, irritability, confusion, or disconnection; and use The LifeLine Technique to find out what's causing them.

Even if it's only ten minutes each day, giving yourself time alone creates awareness that your mind is always filled with thoughts. Taking a few moments to be conscious of those thoughts, accepting them while continuing to breathe, is a way to reconnect with your inner self. I like to visualize a flame inside my mind. The more thoughts I have, the brighter it flickers. As I let the thoughts float through me, I enter a space described by Deepak Chopra as the "space between thoughts."

When you get to that place, the flame is bright and fills the mind. Achieving solitude in the "space between thoughts" opens the window to your feelings. It helps you develop a deeper awareness of who you are and the unlimited potential you possess. It's the moment in which you're *be-ing,* rather than *do-ing*—it's the "being" part of your humanness, which Ram Dass defined as "be here now." We're called human beings, instead of human doers, because we need to be . . . just to sit and to be.

### *Visualization and Focused Breathing*

Visualization combined with focused breathing is another way to harness your energy. The integration of the two will help you understand and know the "right now." While this is different for everyone, each moment is an opportunity to be aware of your truth and refill your spirit with passion, excitement, and joy.

Use the following exercises to explore the effects of visualization and focused breathing.

## Visualizing Your Light

Using Ujjayi breathing, you can visualize by simply lighting a candle and sitting comfortably on the floor or in a chair. If you like, use very soft instrumental music and incense. Breathe gently and deeply by slowly inhaling through your nose and exhaling through your mouth. Focus your breath, and let your mind flow, paying attention to whatever color emerges. Now, with each inhale, visualize this hue as a beam of light that starts at your toes and moves up and through your body. The goal is to focus your mind on this beam of light and to control its ascent as you breathe more and more deeply, filling your body with illumination.

### Creating a Magical Haven

Using Ujjayi breathing, gradually allow your mind to enter a place, real or imagined, that's quite special to you. Let your mind drift to this pleasant, peaceful refuge. It's a location that you know, one where you always can relax completely because you feel secure and safe—a setting where no person or thing can bother you. It can be a room, a house in the country, or a beach. . . . It's your magical haven. Now imagine this place in detail. Notice the light: Is it bright or dim, natural or artificial? Is it hot, warm, or cool? What's the source of heat? What are the colors, sounds, and smells that surround you? How about the shapes and textures? Are there any familiar objects that make this place special? Breathe in and out slowly, relaxing more deeply in your magical haven.

### Balancing Stress with Infinite Love & Gratitude

Take some time to focus on a stressful experience in your life. As you begin to zoom in on this picture and see it more clearly, pay attention to the emotions that are evoked within you. With your intention, send that part of you Infinite Love & Gratitude. Now, be in tune with the thoughts, images, or memories that emerge as your mind focuses on the difficult situation. As you do, send them Infinite Love & Gratitude. Next, concentrate on your body, and pay attention to how it feels to focus on the stressful situation. Does your body feel heavy or tight? How does your breath feel? Is your balance affected in any way? Whatever sensations arise within your body, send Infinite Love & Gratitude to that area and to those feelings. Now, bring your focus to the voice inside of your mind as you concentrate on the challenging experience. Pay attention to the beliefs that you have about yourself in this situation, and send Infinite Love & Gratitude to them. After you finish this exercise, notice how it feels to focus on the stressful situation. You'll find that you no longer have a negative charge toward it.

~

With visualization we can proactively use The LifeLine Law of Transformation and Creation to create the life we desire: *Emotions transform energy; energy creates movement; movement is change; and change is the essence of life.* When we utilize positive visualization, we turn energy into an attractor field of success, inner peace, and health.

Remember Arlene, the woman mentioned in the Preface who had been diagnosed with macular degeneration? As part of taking responsibility for her health, she used positive visualization to enhance her body's ability to heal. Through this technique and deep breathing, Arlene imagined her eyes 100 percent healed. She consistently thought the words *Infinite Love & Gratitude* as she focused on this idea. She acknowledged the feelings of anger that she'd internalized, denied, and disconnected from, using visualization to transform that anger into appreciation for her experience and what she learned as a result. Arlene released the limiting belief she held about the macular degeneration being permanent. Prior to seeing her ophthalmologist, she was already aware that her eyes had healed. Her doctor just confirmed what she'd already visualized within her mind.

You must imagine yourself healthy or already having overcome the challenge in order to succeed. Take the time daily to visualize difficult situations. Picture the successful resolution in your mind, and then observe its appearance in your life. By taking the time to imagine a positive result while being present with your breath, you're focusing your intention on creating a new vision for your life. Positive thoughts and focused breathing transform the energy of any challenging situation, thus enabling you to move in your desired direction.

~~~

# CHAPTER 28

# LIVING LIFE ONE
# MOMENT AT A TIME

D o you ever feel drained because your intention, focus, and energy are pulling you in multiple directions? Does it affect your ability to accomplish even the simplest tasks? Why does this happen? When you aren't connected to Present Time Consciousness (PTC), you're as unfocused as diffused light.

PTC opens the mind and heart to truly experience a moment. It's that minute perception of the distinction between comfort and discomfort. For example, when shaking hands, how tightly do you squeeze? Or while walking, are you conscious of your posture? The subtle awareness that's gained by living in PTC provides you with the opportunity to make the appropriate adaptations that allow for the optimal flow possible.

While sailing, it's imperative to be in touch with the wind. Let it guide you from moment to moment. When it picks up, pull in your sail and go for it. When it loses its power, loosen your hold on the sail and be patient. This will enable you to flow effortlessly . . . this is PTC.

Nature is a beautiful example of PTC—it follows the law of least effort. A tree doesn't expend any more energy than it needs to when the wind blows. In fact, it has specific enzymes that are secreted every time there's a breeze that help it adapt to the stress of the wind. You also have enzymes and hormones that are released when you're under stress. Just like the tree, you become stronger with every challenging situation you endure. However, when you don't practice PTC, you lose your ability to adapt and are at risk for injury and breakdown.

Every single instant provides you with an opportunity to maintain Present Time Consciousness. PTC is staying connected to your senses—what you see, hear, smell, touch, and taste and how your intuition is guiding you in the moment. The more you're aware, the more you feel, think, and react on the subtlest of levels . . . that is PTC.

A poem that beautifully expresses the potential we all have when living in PTC is called "Autobiography in Five Short Chapters." It was written by the late author and actress Portia Nelson:

CHAPTER ONE
I walk down the street.
There is a deep hole in the sidewalk.
I fall in.
I am lost. . . . I am helpless.
It isn't my fault.
It takes forever to find a way out.

CHAPTER TWO
I walk down the same street.
There is a deep hole in the sidewalk.
I pretend I don't see it.
I fall in again.
I can't believe I am in this same place.
But, it isn't my fault.
It still takes a long time to get out.

CHAPTER THREE
I walk down the same street.
There is a deep hole in the sidewalk.
I *see* it is there.
I still fall in . . . it's a habit . . . but,
my eyes are open.
I know where I am.
It is *my* fault.
I get out immediately.

CHAPTER FOUR
I walk down the same street.
There is a deep hole in the sidewalk.
I walk around it.

CHAPTER FIVE
I walk down another street.

Knowing what you need and when you need it is the essence of PTC. When you're focusing on things of the past, or when you're worried about the future, the anxiety gets in the way of living in the moment.

I had a patient named Gary whose chief complaint was abdominal pain whenever he walked. He couldn't move 20 feet without feeling discomfort. Gary had a history of severe cardiovascular disease. He'd been given multiple prescription medications to alleviate the symptoms, but instead of getting better, they became worse. By the time Gary came to see me for treatment, he and his family were desperate.

During the initial evaluation, I took an x-ray of his spine. I was trying to see whether there was some aspect of referral pain radiating from this area. I discovered that his abdominal aorta had completely calcified. Whenever Gary walked, the increase in blood flow caused the calcified arteries to expand beyond their capacity, and the result was intense pain. Gary was severely dehydrated and had a profound imbalance in his blood-sugar metabolism. I used The LifeLine Technique to harmonize his body to the medications that he was taking, and I had a discussion with his cardiologist about what I found.

During Gary's third visit, our work with The LifeLine Flow Chart revealed that he was internalizing feelings of grief that were causing a decreased flow of life force through his lung meridian. Gary informed me that he was mourning the death of his wife. I realized that his internalized sorrow was at the root of why he was experiencing such extreme abdominal pain. I told him that it was imperative he stay connected to his feelings of sadness. I expressed to him that the tears he shed were a tribute to the love he had for his wife and the beautiful impact she had on his life. Gary owned his power by confronting the challenge of grief, expressing his feelings whenever he experienced them.

A month later, he began to notice that the abdominal pain was lessening and even disappearing for much longer periods of time than ever before. During a follow-up visit, Gary reported that for the first time in more than a year, he'd been pain free for five days. When there was discomfort, its severity had decreased tremendously. Gary continues to take supportive nutritional supplements and drainage formulas to help his body heal, and he observes The Five Basics for Optimal Health to support and facilitate the beneficial changes within his body.

Life can be challenging, and at times we feel as if there's no hope. What an honor and gift it was to help this beautiful man realize the inherent power he possessed as a human being! By learning to express his feelings and live in PTC, Gary profoundly changed his own life.

When you stay in the moment and focus on what's at hand, you not only feel more fulfilled, but you also preserve and enhance your body's unlimited potential for healing. While working on this book, there were times when I felt very focused and rooted in PTC. Then, all of a sudden, the moment would disappear. What pulled me out of it? Without warning, I'd be filled with doubt about whether I could clearly communicate what I needed to share as a holistic physician and teacher. Whatever the origin of the insecurities I was feeling, staying in the moment clarified the lesson that I needed to learn and allowed me to manifest my authentic self to write this book.

Uncomfortable emotions oftentimes cause us to disconnect from PTC. Instead of experiencing pain, fear, or challenges as an opportunity, we run, hide, and numb ourselves. By staying in touch with these aspects of life, we're able to learn from the experience and move on.

Denying pain or discomfort doesn't make it go away—it just escalates the damage and turns a painful moment into suffering.

The body is more susceptible to breaking down when we disconnect from it. Imagine that you're driving your car and your brake light starts blinking red, warning you of a potential hazard. Would you ever go into your glove compartment, pull out a hammer, and smash the brake light . . . then continue driving as if nothing ever happened? That would be pretty silly, because soon the brakes would fail, with or without the warning.

Think of a challenging situation, and visualize your conscious awareness of it as a continuously flowing river. Observe how your emotions about this issue simultaneously pull you in myriad directions. Notice how it's much more difficult to deal with it when you're at the mercy of the river's current.

Now, imagine stepping onto the river's bank. You'll begin to appreciate the experience from an entirely new perspective. Pay attention to the emotions that have surfaced. From this vantage point, you're able to own your power and make a clearer, more rational decision about the situation. When you're in PTC, you're aware of your senses and emotions and have the ability to act or react authentically.

To the observer, the fight movements of martial artists seem to be happening at warp speed. But to the individual engaged in the combat, they occur in slow motion. These warriors are so used to being in PTC that every punch, block, and flinch is split into "nano" pieces. In PTC, movement becomes the law of least effort—which was a motto of an extraordinary martial artist, the late Bruce Lee. Lee was able to break bricks and boards only one inch away from his hand. He could throw a person across the room with a one-inch punch because he used the least amount of effort within that single concentrated moment. Was it because he was superstrong? No . . . Bruce Lee was the master of PTC.

It's your God-given right to have unlimited joy, love, and passion; and if it isn't happening, you have the power to *make* it happen. Right now is the time—it's not at the *end* of the journey; it *is* the journey itself. You don't have to wait until you make a million dollars, meet Mr./Ms. Right, obtain the "perfect" body weight, or live in your dream house. None of these factors change who you are on the inside. The only thing that alters what you feel inside is PTC. This is the right time to work on your life.

By learning about the basics of a healthy lifestyle (the quantity, quality, and frequency of water, food, rest, exercise, and owning your power), you'll take responsibility for yourself and make the changes that your life is telling you are necessary.

Everyone has their own PTC. No one can tell you when or how to begin . . . the time is always right now.

~~~

# CHAPTER 29

# EXERCISING YOUR PASSION

Most of us are obsessed with our weight instead of being focused on our health. We believe that we could be "fit and fabulous" if only there were a pill to take, as opposed to exercising and eating healthfully. Unfortunately, despite the millions of dollars earned by the makers of lose-weight-quick supplements, there isn't a single item on the market that's been found to be the silver bullet—the product that turns an obese body into a *healthy* one. Some of them are even dangerous.

The only way to become truly healthy is by embracing The Five Basics for Optimal Health. Fitness is multifaceted, so you need a program that addresses the issue from all angles. Give yourself the gift of exercise every day and it will dramatically change—and add years to—your life. Recent studies have shown that 60 minutes of daily exercise improves your body's ability to use insulin and metabolize food; helps you maintain a healthy weight; increases your energy levels and mental clarity; contributes to healthy bones, muscles, and joints; makes you stronger; improves your balance; reduces feelings of depression and anxiety; and heightens your self-esteem. If you don't have 60 minutes to spare, you can begin with 15.

Here's a simple breathing exercise that has no physical or age restrictions . . . anyone can do it. Lie on your back or sit in a chair. Focus on contracting and relaxing each part of your body. While maintaining a rhythmic, diaphragmatic breathing pattern, hold each contraction for ten seconds, and then relax for ten seconds. Begin with your feet, contracting and relaxing them. Next, proceed to your legs. Continue this process of contracting for ten seconds and then relaxing for ten seconds as you move up to your buttocks, low back, abdomen, chest, shoulders, arms, hands, and face. Finally, contract all the muscles of your entire body for five seconds, and then relax them for five seconds. Continue this exercise for a total of 15 minutes. Feel the stress that you hold in your body just melt away. This is a great way to jump-start your day—it will enhance your circulation, improve lymphatic drainage, and increase your vitality.

Beyond this, depending upon what your goals are, adding walking, weight training, cardiovascular workouts, Pilates, or Nia (Neuromuscular Integrative Action) will help you build confidence, become stronger and more flexible, and gain endurance, both physically and mentally. Two of my favorite forms of exercise are tai chi and qigong.

Tai chi is the ancient Chinese art of moving meditation based on the Taoist understanding that all things comprise the harmony of two complementary forces—yin and yang. Through the study and practice of tai chi, you learn to apply the principles of the yielding overcoming the unyielding and the soft overcoming the hard. As the body learns to yield and soften through this practice, the mind becomes more open and flexible, allowing you to focus your attention in a spontaneous manner and have a deeper connection with the moment.

My tai chi master utilizes exercise and meditation to help his students gain awareness of the infinite power of chi. I'm in awe of his wisdom, strength, and gentle way of living. He explains, "Every experience is an opportunity to flow or be stuck. Use tai chi practices and meditations, and apply them to the challenges you face in life."

Qigong is used for healing and increasing vitality. It's an integration of physical postures, breathing techniques, and focused intention. The effect of both ancient arts is the reconnection of the mind and body to the spirit. Try the following qigong exercise called "Stand Like a Tree":

Stand with your feet about hip width apart. Position your spine on top of your hips, imagining a string of pearls stacking one on top of the other. Verify your alignment in front of a mirror. Rest your head at the center of the gravity that runs through your spine. Drop your chin, and free the back of your neck. You may notice that you feel like falling forward, but you won't. Make sure that your palms are parallel to the ground.

As you stand, breathe deeply, expanding your stomach as you inhale and pulling your navel to your spine as you exhale. The goal is to connect to an open state of awareness while doing nothing else. Do this for one minute, and work on extending the time to ten. This may sound simple, but it can be extremely challenging at first. In the beginning, after just a few seconds, you'll begin to feel the resistance—blockages and stagnation—in your body, and your mind will get very noisy. Embrace the discomfort. It allows you to become acutely aware of what's going on in your mind and body and expand your ability to use PTC, which will help heal your body at a much quicker rate. The longer you hold the tree posture, the more grounded and stronger your mind-body-spirit connection.

~

There are several key factors that are very important if you want to get the most benefit from exercise. First and foremost, each fitness program depends upon the individual. Yours should be customized for your individual structural, emotional, biochemical, and spiritual needs. Seek out the assistance of a trained and certified professional in order to create a program that best suits you.

Make exercise one of your passions. The beauty of passion is that it evolves. Continue to explore new ways of strengthening your mind and body through your daily exercise program. Remember that it takes a minimal of 19 days for a change in behavior to become a habit.

Here are some steps you can take to develop the healthy habit of fitness:

1. Set goals and write them down, including the amount of time you'll spend and the types of exercise you'll perform on each day.

2.  Every single day, mentally commit yourself to achieving your minimum of 15 minutes of exercise. Dr. Lucia Capacchione, the author of *Lighten Up Your Body—Lighten Up Your Life*, says that the key to any lasting change is "to experience your physical body as it is." She recommends a relaxation and meditation exercise in which you take an inner journey through your body. The goal is to get to know it, become sensitive to its changes, and feel at home so that you're aware when physical and emotional changes take place.

3.  Remain in PTC while exercising. Stay in touch with your breathing and your body. The saying "No pain, no gain," will get you in trouble. If any exercise is causing major discomfort, stop—your body is sending a warning signal to slow down.

4.  Reward yourself. Celebrate the fact that you're taking such good care of yourself.

5.  If you're having a hard time working out by yourself, give the gift of exercise to a family member or friend by asking him or her to join you.

Exercise is one of the most crucial components of healing. Research has found that *everyone* can benefit from regular physical activity, and physical decline associated with aging can even be *reversed* through exercise.

When was the last time you rode a bike, went on a hike, put on a pair of Rollerblades or ice skates, or danced? When was the last time you took a walk that wasn't in a parking lot or a grocery store? One session of aerobic exercise has been found to help people with diabetes drop their blood-glucose levels by as much as 50 to 70 points. Just imagine what a regular regime of exercise, combined with the other healthy-lifestyle components, will do for your well-being and vitality!

There's an old adage: "What the mind conceives and believes, it will achieve." Use the power of Infinite Love & Gratitude and The LifeLine Technique to release limiting beliefs, attitudes, self-destructive behaviors, and addictions that are preventing you from achieving your health and fitness goals.

# CHAPTER 30

# OWN YOUR POWER: RECLAIMING YOUR AUTHENTIC SELF

There's so much pain in life in the form of fear, death, failure, and shame. Without question, there will be times when life is overwhelming and you may not feel equipped to handle the hurt. It's important to remember that you weren't put on this magnificent planet to suffer—rather, you're here to learn and awaken to the infinite potential that exists within you.

Owning your power is living with Infinite Love & Gratitude. It means embracing all aspects of life with passion, purpose, and courage. Owning your power—reconnecting to the emotions that lie dormant in your subconscious mind—is the key to reclaiming your authentic self.

Over the past several years, many books have been written about the "authentic self." *Authentic* is defined as "genuine" and "real." It's different for everyone. It means being true to yourself in a way that only you know, because you can *feel* it . . . it feels easy, harmonious, and congruent. The same holds true when you aren't being authentic with yourself. You get that uncomfortable sensation inside, and it feels heavy somewhere in your body. You also know when other people aren't being authentic with you—it's a gut reaction that you sense immediately.

No matter what situation you're experiencing, it's vital to view it through the authenticity of your heart. This part of you speaks without judgment. Your emotions are a pure reflection of what you're going through. By embracing life with an open heart—your authentic self— you're able to transform chaos into harmony. It's been said, "Life isn't about finding yourself. Life is about creating yourself." By choosing to own your power and embracing the moment, the burdens of your past will no longer hinder you from seeing your future.

Many of us have a long history of being disconnected from our emotions, dating back to childhood. Our parents, as a result of their own disconnections, warned us against displaying our emotions. They often said: "Children should be seen and not heard," or "Be a big boy [girl]—don't cry." Consequently, we weren't encouraged to express the emotions associated with our experiences. The best way to reconnect to your feelings is to pay attention to what your body is telling you. Remember that it speaks with symptoms that are the consequence of emotions being triggered in the subconscious mind. Every feeling and resulting emotion is the body talking loud and clear. Notice, for example, that when you find someone difficult to deal with, that person literally becomes a "pain in the neck." Or think about the times when you have a "gut reaction" to a person or an event. Denying your intuitive feelings causes the body to speak out—the longer you internalize your feelings, the louder it will yell.

If you have an uncomfortable feeling but you're unable to immediately pinpoint it, take some time to be still and quiet. Focus on your body and scan it: What sensations are you aware of? What emotion emerges? After you've identified the feeling, the next step is to own your power and authentically express it. In terms of health, the *real* self is the person who speaks his or her mind, shares feelings, shows emotion, and is comfortable saying no when it's appropriate. For most of us, doing so is difficult. The word *emotion* can be broken down into two parts: "e" and "motion." *E* stands for "energy," and *motion* means "movement," which signifies that *all emotions must stay in motion.*

When you repress your emotions internally and don't express them authentically, it forces your body to find another language to communicate them. This "body language" can be a pain, organ dysfunction, imbalanced sugar metabolism, or reveal itself as numerous other symptoms associated with the mind-body-spirit connection. Open expression of emotion—owning your power—is a key component of healing. There's scientific research to substantiate this.

Dr. Candace Pert, researcher, neurobiologist, and author of *Molecules of Emotion,* has demonstrated the connection between our emotions and our health. She discovered neuropeptides, which are the chemicals in the body triggered by emotions:

> My research has shown me that when emotions are expressed—which is to say that the biochemicals that are the substrate of emotion are flowing freely—all systems are united and made whole. When emotions are repressed, denied, not allowed to be whatever they may be, our network pathways get blocked, stopping the flow of the vital feel-good, unifying chemicals that run both our biology and behavior.

The LifeLine Flow Chart guides us through the emotional maze of the Five Elements, demonstrating how life force, or chi, becomes blocked within the acupuncture meridians of the body. Grief, for example, is associated with the metal element and travels in the lung/large-intestine acupuncture meridian. Fear is connected with water and moves through the bladder/kidney meridian. When we internalize, deny, or disconnect from an emotion, it leads to a decreased flow of our life force through the acupuncture meridians, triggering our body to speak with symptoms. For example, internalized grief can cause the body to respond with sinus blockages or bronchitis. When we ignore symptoms—the voice of the body—it leads to pathology or a complete breakdown.

According to ancient Buddhist teachings, change is a process of opening and training the mind. Most of us have learned to disconnect from pain, and this denial prevents authentic healing from occurring. However, by embracing the hurt, we're able to let go of it, facilitating healing on its deepest levels. Just as a wound needs to be cleaned of dirt and debris so it will repair itself, internalized emotions also need to be released. The LifeLine Technique removes the true causes of symptoms and disease, thereby helping you feel. *Remember that you must learn to feel if you want to heal.*

I have a friend who lives in Europe. Last spring, she sent me an e-mail about a breakthrough she had with allergies:

> I figured out that most of the allergies were psychological. I was having a "wild" relationship at that time, and anytime anything went wrong, it was hard for me to breathe. I was unable to figure out what the problem was. There did not seem to be a specific allergy component. As soon as I got out of the relationship, the symptoms began to improve.

The asthma symptoms my friend was experiencing went away.

A commonly experienced emotion is anger, which generally is a result of hurt—a by-product of denied feelings and not speaking one's mind in the first place. It's a cycle of pain that only you have the power to break. Unexpressed anger causes a decreased flow in the liver/gallbladder acupuncture meridians, resulting in difficulty with neutralizing poisons and toxins.

I once had a patient with breast cancer. When we began to work together, she was making amazing strides, and her oncologist was extremely happy with the way she was healing. Everything seemed to be progressing well. One day she told me that she believed she'd developed cancer so that her husband would pay attention to her and treat her with more respect. Well, he *did* do these things once she received the diagnosis, but as soon as she began to heal, he went back to his old ways—and lo and behold, the cancer began to spread. She told me that she "hated him"; however, she was afraid of hurting his feelings and upsetting her children. She chose not to speak her truth, and she died a short while later.

The chemicals the body produces that accompany anger are so extremely toxic that, left internalized, they'll fester into disease. Unless anger is expressed, the body won't heal.

Dr. Deepak Chopra says, "There is no purpose in suffering except as a guide to your truth." In other words, pain can provide a road map to reclaiming your authentic self, but to follow it, you must acknowledge and release the hurt as soon as it occurs. You have to pay attention to your feelings. So stay in Present Time Consciousness, and speak your truth!

You can reconnect with your feelings through:

- Exercise
- Meditation
- Maintaining Present Time Consciousness
- Journaling
- Writing poetry, stories, or songs
- Listening to yourself and others
- Forgiveness
- Any aspect of creative expression, including music, dancing, and painting
- Treatments with The LifeLine Technique

One of the great benefits of The LifeLine Flow Chart is that it helps us pinpoint where and how we've internalized, denied, or disconnected from our emotions. It points to the effect these feelings are having on us and releases them from the subconscious mind.

With The LifeLine treatments, you begin to witness and experience the connection between your feelings and the pain or dysfunction in your body. You soon develop a deeper sense of awareness about yourself and your environment, learning to trust your intuition and feelings. You begin to *create* authenticity for yourself. In other words, you respond when your body speaks with a symptom, telling you that you aren't being true to yourself. The beautiful thing about this process is that there's no such thing as failure. Life will continually challenge you, presenting you with situations to test how authentic you are. Each moment will push, pull, lead, or drag you—or block your way—to the next moment. And you'll *feel* that motion somewhere in your body. The more you practice owning your power, the better you'll be at moving with the flow of life.

# CHAPTER 31

# CHILDREN:
# THE BRIDGE TO THE FUTURE

C hildhood is a sacred time—a period of wonder, innocence, and authenticity. Children hungrily and attentively see, touch, taste, hear, feel, seek, and reach, absorbing the world around them through all of their senses. They're unabashed about expressing their feelings: When they're happy and joyful, they smile, giggle, or laugh; when they're upset, they yell, scream, or cry. The beauty of a child's spirit is his or her ability to live in PTC and be authentic in the moment.

As kids mature, they begin to learn patterns of self-expression based on interactions with their families, neighbors, teachers, religious leaders, and other adults in their environment. They imprint and mirror their surroundings . . . they're a reflection of the internalized or denied thoughts, feelings, and beliefs of their mother and father. Therefore, there's a subtle but necessary balance between guiding, protecting, and parenting children and inhibiting them with the fears and taboos of family, society, race, religion, or humankind in general. That's why it's so important that parents maintain PTC in all their interactions with their kids. Raising a child is a *conscious* behavior, just as love is a learned behavior—and people who accept the responsibility for molding and shaping another human being's life must do so with conscientious and tender care.

Teach your children to own their power, believe in themselves, be optimistic, and have faith in the infinite power and capacity that we all have as human beings to love, heal, succeed, and achieve any goals that we're willing to work hard enough to make happen. Most important, give your kids the gift of health by introducing them to The LifeLine Technique treatments and philosophy. Help them maintain The Five Basics for Optimal Health: quantity, quality, and frequency of water, food, rest, exercise, and owning their power.

According to the World Health Organization (WHO), the American Academy of Pediatrics (AAP), and the journal *Pediatrics,* along with the impact of watching too much television, today's children are suffering the ravaging effects of nutrient-poor eating choices based on junk food, soda, caffeine, and sugar. The result: Obesity, tooth decay, allergies, asthma, nervous-system disorders, depression, anxiety, lethargy, learning disabilities, sensory-integration difficulties, social-skills dysfunction, hyperactivity, and violent behavior are at crisis levels among children. The allopathic medical community's response is to say that these kids suffer from attention deficit disorder (ADD) and attention deficit hyperactivity disorder (ADHD), and to prescribe stimulants and antidepressants—as well as a slew of other drugs—for every symptom that they encounter.

Dr. Fred Baughman, Jr., who has more than 35 years of experience as an adult and pediatric neurologist, is one of the nation's most vocal opponents of the use of pharmacological drugs to deal with ADHD. He says that the drugging of millions of normal children is "the single, biggest health care fraud in the U.S." According to Dr. Baughman, 500,000 children were diagnosed with ADHD in 1985. Today, that number has risen to between five and seven million, and WHO has condemned the "dangerous proportions" of kids on drugs.

A recent study by the University of Michigan, reported to the Pediatric Academic Societies in May of 2000, found that the latest trend among physicians is to prescribe both stimulant drugs *and* antidepressants at the same time. The lead author of the study, Jerry Rushton, himself a medical doctor, stated: "One of the biggest questions this study raises is whether the children who are prescribed both types of medication have both types of disorders, or whether their physicians are recommending these medications for other reasons."

I've successfully treated thousands of children who have been diagnosed with ADD and ADHD—conditions that are a result of many factors, including blood-sugar-metabolism imbalances; dehydration; overexposure to electromagnetic energy from cell phones, computers, and TV; overmedication; lack of communication within the family; and the child's yearning for attention.

Alec, a nine-year-old patient, was diagnosed with ADD. His teacher was putting pressure on his parents to have him placed on medication, but Alec's parents were resistant and looking for a healthier route than taking pills to control his behavior. They realized that there must be more to his behavioral challenges—after all, Alec had exhibited the ability to follow instructions and excel in the martial arts. So, did he have ADD, or was something else going on?

Fortunately, Alec's mother—who was already a patient—decided to bring him in for an evaluation. Through The LifeLine Technique, I found that Alec had a major sugar-metabolism imbalance and was sensitive to wheat and dairy products. We balanced his blood sugar by changing his eating program and harmonized him to the allergies. Within a few weeks, Alec had made great strides at home and at school. His teachers and mother noticed enormous improvements in his behavior and health. Now aware of foods that impact him in a negative way, Alec is making much wiser choices and feeling better about himself.

Jake, age seven, had been prescribed five medications—lithium, Adderall, Celexa, clonidine, and Strattera. His mother contacted me because he was having trouble with constipation, which she believed was the cause of his difficulties. She thought that the behavioral challenges were a result of the poisons and toxins trapped in his body due to the constipation.

Using The LifeLine Technique, I harmonized Jake to the medications he was taking because I knew that they were harming him. However, as I've said earlier, it isn't within my licensure to recommend that someone stop taking medication. It's important that the doctor who prescribed the drugs be the one to wean the child off of them. Going off medications too quickly can be disastrous.

Jake's parents took responsibility and helped their son to understand and follow The Five Basics for Optimal Health. Within a month, there were major improvements in his attitude, health, and behavior. His bowels began moving multiple times a day, and there was a dramatic change in his self-esteem. Unfortunately, Jake's medical doctor was initially resistant to taking the boy off the medications. However, his parents have owned their power and have been insistent. As I write this book, Jake now only takes one of the five medications, and the process of weaning him off the last one is about to begin.

How can we possibly justify giving stimulants and antidepressants to children because they're *acting like* children—especially when they're actually suffering from the effects of sugar-filled, unbalanced, and unhealthy food choices? Unless we as parents and health-care practitioners step forward to take charge of our children's health, we'll be mortgaging our future to the fast-food, soda, and pharmaceutical industries. The only return on our investment will be a generation of kids who are poisoned and lethargic . . . candidates for addiction, chronic illness, and pathological disease.

The LifeLine Technique successfully works for children who are too young to understand or actively take part in the treatment. I use a surrogate when they're unable to consciously participate or are in a weakened state. As I discussed in Chapter 4, surrogate muscle testing involves the use of someone else's indicator muscle to assess a patient who is unable to do it for him- or herself. This method is based on the principle that we're all electromagnetic beings. Thus, by touching another person anywhere on his or her body, you're able to connect to that individual through your intent. The same is true of using a surrogate's arm to assess your own system. I often use my wife, Sara, as my surrogate to evaluate myself with The LifeLine Technique. Let me share several examples of the application of this method with you.

After seeing scores of doctors and undergoing every conceivable medical diagnostic test, including blood work, stool samples, urinalysis, and allergy tests, a mother brought her infant son to see me. Brian suffered from severe allergies, skin rashes, and eczema.

His mom was breast-feeding him, and I asked her to bring in foods that she'd been eating. Using her as a surrogate, I held those foods next to her body and to Brian's. Whenever I found a weak muscle, I harmonized his body to the substance using The LifeLine Technique. As a result, I cleared the food sensitivities and released the internalized emotion that had triggered the allergic reaction.

Brian's mother was placed on omega-3 essential fatty acid and probiotics, which she passed on to him. Within a month, Brian was 95 percent improved. After his mother's long odyssey seeking relief from doctor after doctor, she found it with The LifeLine Technique. Brian is now only seen for checkups to help maintain his optimal health.

In another case, I received an emergency call on my day off from a patient whose son, Jared, age five, was confined to bed, unable to move his neck. Any attempt to move Jared resulted in severe pain and crying. His mother had to put "pull-up" diapers on him because the excruciating pain made a trip to the bathroom extremely difficult. When I arrived at their home, I realized that Jared was experiencing a severe case of acute torticollis, a spasm of the sternocleidomastoid muscle, located in the neck. I began by running The LifeLine Technique's Conscious Mind Portal, using Jared's mother as a surrogate. When I touched his neck, his mom's arm went weak, allowing me to access the subconscious patterns that were creating this very painful symptom. After running The LifeLine Flow Chart through twice, Jared was able to get out of the bed and move his neck.

As we continued to work, the emotion of resentment came up. I soon discovered that Jared developed the symptoms on his baby brother's first birthday. We used the Conscious Mind Portal to tap in to the internalized stress that was eating away at him, resulting in torticollis. By the time I finished, Jared was feeling much better. I advised his mother to use arnica gel (a homeopathic) to assist with the relaxation of the muscles in his neck. I also communicated to both of them how important it was to drink water and own their power.

I reiterated to Jake's mother how sensitive her son was and how important it was for her to express her unconditional love to him. I said to Jared: "You're so lucky to be a big brother and to be able to celebrate this great day with your baby brother." He obviously made no conscious connection between the resentment over the birthday party and the neck pain. However, by creating the awareness for Jared and his mother, the emotion was released on a subconscious level, allowing his body to heal instantly.

Symptoms are like the cover of a book. If you're walking around a bookstore, the book cover is usually what catches your eye . . . it intrigues you. You're drawn to open the book and look at its chapters in order to learn what the story is all about. Don't judge a book by its cover. This is how The LifeLine Technique works: It reveals the "story" underlying the symptom to help you appreciate why your body is expressing itself. By exploring the symptom with The LifeLine Technique, you'll learn from its story (which sometimes has many chapters) why it's occurred in the first place. The more you examine the symptom using The LifeLine Technique, the quicker you'll find the solution.

Take the case of Elena, age 11, who was experiencing severe pain and muscle spasm in both of her legs, making it very difficult for her to walk. Unable to determine what was wrong, Elena's pediatrician recommended that she take an over-the-counter, anti-inflammatory drug, which did nothing to relieve the symptoms. The true root cause, however, was unknown until she came in for a treatment.

As I worked on Elena, running the symptom through The LifeLine Flow Chart, it became apparent that a major blockage was occurring in her root chakra. (This chakra relates to feeling grounded and secure, and is tied in with limiting beliefs associated with family.) The emotion of grief came up multiple times while running the Flow Chart. I discovered that both of her great-grandparents had recently died within a month of each other, and that a close family member was also very ill and in the hospital.

After about 20 minutes of running The LifeLine Flow Chart, the pain in Elena's body decreased by about 90 percent. I discussed the importance of a healthy lifestyle with her and her mother, which included drinking two quarts of water daily, avoiding sugar and carbohydrates, getting rest, and owning her power. I explained to

Elena that it was okay for her to express her emotions of sadness or grief. I encouraged her to allow her tears to flow if she felt like crying.

The next day when I called to check on Elena, her mother reported that it truly was a miracle: Elena was doing amazingly well. But it really *wasn't* a miracle . . . it was The LifeLine Technique that allowed me to help Elena and her mom understand the true meaning of the symptoms she was feeling in her legs. By harmonizing the internalized emotions associated with the grief over her great-grandparents' deaths, her body healed itself.

Just like the title of the Crosby, Stills, Nash & Young song, "teach your children" to value their health. I believe that the first step is to educate parents so they understand the importance of The Five Basics for Optimal Health and how to prevent the patterns of dis-ease and pathology from developing. Even before you have a child, you can optimize *your* health. As a matter of fact, I've helped dozens of couples who'd been medically diagnosed infertile to become pregnant and deliver healthy babies by having them follow The LifeLine program.

At the same time, I want to make sure that parents are aware of the resources, alternatives, and options available to help their children evolve and develop into happy, healthy, and fulfilled human beings. Wellness is a lifelong practice, but it begins with a first step: parents—both mothers *and* fathers—owning their power and taking responsibility for their children's health.

The LifeLine Technique in no way replaces the need for a pediatrician. However, in this day and age, it's important that parents are empowered with information about the true nature of symptoms. By understanding The LifeLine Technique and philosophy, they'll be doing everything possible to provide safe, effective, and natural ways to help maintain the optimal health of their children.

Parents have two choices about how to approach their kids' health: (1) to use medications to deal with the symptoms that their children are facing, or (2) to understand the natural expression of symptoms that the body uses to communicate. The latter, proactive choice will empower parents and children alike to heal in an authentic way.

Parents have the ultimate responsibility to protect their kids' well-being by giving them love, embracing healthy lifestyles, creating appropriate boundaries, and teaching them to own their power. The time to act for children is now!

~ ~ ~

# CHAPTER 32

# MASTERING THE GAME OF LIFE

L ife is so complex and chaotic at times—and yet there seems to be a sense of order and simplicity to the randomness. Depending upon your chosen view, you either align yourself with the order and simplicity or get lost and disconnect from the complexity and chaos. But what if life were a game? How would you play? What would the rules be? Most important, how would you master the game of life?

Let's begin with the rules:

**1. The universe is infinite.** Plato was speaking of the first rule of life when he said, "Mathematical objects, such as infinity, are real in their own right, and the mind has the power to grasp them directly in some way." From the concept of time and the cosmos to the cycle of the seasons and life itself, the universe is infinite—it's forever expanding and undefined. Therefore, as a being of the universe, your mind possesses the nature and potential of the infinite. The universe and mind are the great frontier, the unending entity of boundless mystery. Acknowledging your connection to them is fundamental to understanding the unlimited potential that you possess. This view is magnified infinitely by the core truth that you're a spiritual being having a human-being experience. By *be-ing*, you experience the infinite essence and wonder of life.

**2. You have free will, a choice with every experience.** "To be or not to be—that is the question." Shakespeare taught the second rule of life when he wrote the play *Hamlet.* The act of "being" is a choice to stay connected to the moment, no matter how difficult it may be. This is living in Present Time Consciousness. When you practice this, you awaken to the stream of consciousness and flow of thoughts that are always present within your mind. In PTC, your feelings are heightened, and you tune in to the subtleties of comfort and discomfort. You have the option to stay in touch with this awareness or to disconnect from it. You have a choice "to be or not to be." Living in PTC enables you to trust your intuition and use your internal guides to help you flow from moment to moment. Even when it appears that you don't have a choice, you always do. Every instant is a mini-lifetime, a ripple in the ocean that manifests as the experience itself.

**3. Everything is interconnected. For every choice that you make, there will be a consequence.** Everything is interconnected in the infinite universe of energy. The LifeLine Law of Transformation and Creation states: "Emotions transform energy; energy creates movement; movement is change; and change is the essence of life." As a result of change, you experience life. From the fast or slow beat of a heart to the shallowness or depth of a breath, life moves forward through the action of duality, transformation, and creation. It's by taking responsibility for your choices that you experience the flow of life and the greatest opportunities for growth.

The consequences of your decisions occur internally, within the body; as well as externally, in the universe of which you're a part. Every thought, feeling, and belief motivates you to choose to act either out of fear or faith. The question that you should ask yourself before you act is: *Am I making this choice out of fear or out of faith?* To be a master in the game of life, always choose faith. Be courageous, and embrace the fear. Remember that movement and change are the essence of life and are the consequences of the decisions that you make. Because 98 percent of your reality is subconscious, you may not always be aware of the repercussions of your choices. However, for every one that you make, there will always be a consequence.

**4. Judgment is prohibited.** Judgment is the lack of Present Time Consciousness. It's a reaction based on preconceived notions about a person, race, religion, gender, nationality, and so forth. Living in PTC—embracing your intuition, feelings, and beliefs—facilitates your ability to transcend judgment and make the best choices. Judgment is prohibited if you want to master the game of life. No matter what decisions you've made in the past or what consequences you're now experiencing, stay in the moment and rediscover the lessons that your life has been teaching you. Remember, life isn't about suffering and victimization—it's about learning from your past and present so that you can experience your full potential. Every moment provides you with the opportunity to be in touch with your emotions and react authentically. Do your best not to deny your intuition or feelings about an experience. Stay connected, and trust your senses . . . you'll then break the bonds of judgment.

**5. The greatest power is self-love.** Unconditional acceptance, forgiveness, and letting go are essential to unleashing the infinite power of self-love. Self-love acknowledges that the universe is perfect, and therefore so are you. Accepting your perfection is fundamental to exercising your limitless potential, empowering you with the courage and determination to face the pain, fear, and challenges of life. Self-love is the process of self-discovery—acknowledging, honoring, and releasing the parts of yourself that you've subconsciously internalized, denied, and disconnected from.

The greatest adversary to self-love is fear. Resisting change because you're afraid of losing your identity keeps this emotion alive. Ralph Waldo Emerson once stated, "Self-trust is the essence of heroism." When you accept and own your power of self-love in a nonjudgmental way, you embrace the fear that's kept you stuck in a cycle of self-denial and self-destruction. Caring for yourself is the fuel—the passion—that motivates faith-based decisions. Being courageous in and of itself is an act of self-love.

**6. You'll experience pain, fear, and challenges.** Throughout history, the greatest accomplishments have been achieved through determination, persistence, blood, sweat, and tears. Everyone experiences pain, fear, and challenges. It's the choices you make when faced with difficult situations that empower you to transform them into an opportunity for growth. Embracing this rule is vital to living a life without judgment.

When you think about it, life would lack its quintessential beauty and meaning without pain, fear, and challenges. By learning to confront life with courage and passion, you appreciate the power you've always possessed to overcome its greatest obstacles. These stumbling blocks function innately as a self-defense mechanism to protect you from harm. By awakening to their inherent function, you continue to move, adapt, and transcend life's most difficult experiences and transform them into triumph, abundance, and peace. Embracing your power awakens you to the lessons and gifts that these challenges bestow. Learning the lesson and accepting the gift provides you with awareness, insight, and power that you would have never achieved without them.

**7. Embrace life with the attitude of gratitude.** The attitude that you have toward any experience is a choice. You can always view the cup as being half full or half empty, but the most courageous way to move through life is by choosing to find the good in every instant. Rather than surrendering to emotions of negativity and despair, consciously and creatively embrace life with the attitude of gratitude. Accepting challenges as opportunities immediately transforms the situation into a chance to develop your higher self. The act of expressing appreciation, such as saying thank you, symbolizes the value an experience has had for you. Without this acknowledgment, it lacks meaning, and your trials and tribulations appear as if they'd occurred by coincidence. However, nothing in life is accidental. The attitude of gratitude expands your view of an experience beyond the "self" to an infinite perspective of possibilities and potential, thereby breaking the bond of suffering and victimization. By embracing pain, fear, and challenges with gratitude, you'll discover the real value and meaning of your life.

**8. Take responsibility for your life.** As you've learned from reading this book, symptoms or challenges are your life's way of telling you to take responsibility. Think of living as the process of painting a masterpiece: Every breath, experience, and intention adds to the beauty of your blank canvas. The vibrancy of the colors of life are felt when you cherish yourself unconditionally. It's with self-love that you're able to embrace the pain, fear, and challenges, as well as the infinite potential within you to transcend the most monumental of obstacles.

Taking responsibility means that you'll make the choice to maintain Present Time Consciousness, despite the circumstances. It signifies that you won't judge the consequences of your choices, but rather learn from them. By opting to take responsibility for your life, you'll be inclined to embrace your experiences with the attitude of gratitude. Through gratitude you'll find fortune in misfortune and reconnect step-by-step to the infinite potential of life. You are Michelangelo, and the uncarved block awaits you . . . so create your *David.* Each moment is an opportunity to release the artist within.

**9. Life has meaning.** Turn on the news and you'll hear about war, genocide, political upheaval, scandals, poverty, starvation, racism, pollution, suicide, bankruptcy, death, hatred, violence, serial rapists, cancer, HIV/AIDS, children shooting each other, catastrophic floods and other natural disasters, gang violence, biological warfare, pedophiles, terrorism, financial coups, rampant obesity, domestic violence, spiraling divorce rates, resistant bacteria, increasing numbers of high-school dropouts, infertility, declines in literacy, depression, road rage, drug overdoses, carjackings, train bombings, assassinations, child molestation, pornography, addiction, ADD, celebrity court trials, homophobia, sexism, conflicting values between generations, technological breakdowns, nuclear weapons, international standoffs, overmedicating, rises in hospital death rates, malpractice . . . fear . . . fear . . . fear . . . fear. . . .

Can you imagine if life didn't have meaning and all these crises were occurring just "because"? This is our wake-up call! Life is painful, yet there's value in pain. Life is scary, yet there's meaning in fear. Life is challenging, yet every challenge is an opportunity. We need to ask the question *Why?* and be willing to hear the answer. We must own our power by embracing the infinite truth of a moment without judgment and with compassion and love. It's so easy to judge these experiences; however, we risk our future if we miss the chance to learn from our past and present.

Take a deep breath and reflect on the awesomeness of life. Have you ever seen the northern lights, a coral reef, or a baby being born? There's a rhythm and harmony that's an intricate part of every life process. Through science, humankind has revealed and unleashed some of the greatest mysteries of the universe. However, as much as it's taught us, it appears as if we're light-years away from living at one with the universe. It's through meaning that we discover the preciousness of life—our own as well as those of others. In the midst of horrific news and other challenges, we often internalize, deny, or disconnect from life's meaning. We succumb to illness, cynicism, and hopelessness. But we have a choice . . . a choice to own our power, embrace life with passion, and reconnect to Infinite Love & Gratitude.

A single moment truly lived is the same as living a thousand lifetimes. The wisdom of the universe teaches us that each moment is genuinely experienced when we awaken to the power of Infinite Love & Gratitude—the key to mastering the game of life.

# CHAPTER 33

# IMAGINE YOURSELF HEALED

There's a power whose magnificence is everywhere. We see it in every moment: in the sun, the rain, and children playing. We hear it all around us, from the depths of silence to the crescendo of a symphony. From a fragrant field of flowers to the freshness of a newborn baby, its scent transforms our very souls. Every experience with this power brings us closer to our authentic selves, to the source of God—the Divine or collective conscious that's within all of us. It's the essence of every moment . . . it's Infinite Love & Gratitude.

We're always aware of this power, even though we've numbed ourselves with food, alcohol, drugs, sex, work, or relationships to make it easier to deny. In so doing, we're fearful, lonely, angry, and judgmental. In our denial, we're bogged down on a dead-end, painful journey.

Allowing yourself to fully experience everything that you see, hear, smell, touch, taste, and create while acknowledging and accepting each resulting emotion, is an opportunity to own *your* power.

I implore you to begin your healing journey now. Reading this book has given you the tools—guidelines for healthy lifestyles, coupled with a revolutionary healing technique that harmonizes the greatest adversary, your subconscious mind. Take the first step! Break out of your comfort zone. Let go of the belief that the state of your health—discomfort, dis-ease, and dysfunction—is just "the nature of life." Surrender the guilty conviction that chronic illness is the price you must pay for sowing "wild oats" when in your youth. Release the thought, feeling, or belief that health is reserved only for the young, and that aches and pains are a sign you're "getting old." Popping pills, receiving injections, or submitting to unnecessary surgeries are only temporary stopgaps. You may poke your fingers in a dam that's sprung multiple leaks, but eventually there will be an overflow, and the health that you were fighting so hard to preserve will be lost.

Because your body is a self-healing organism, those aches, pains, and chronic illnesses are actually a gift—a sign that you *can* have vibrant health if you're willing to claim it and do the necessary work. Living in Present Time Consciousness, owning your power, embracing life with passion, and following healthy lifestyles that support harmony and balance in the body will help it release the imbalances that lead to dysfunction and dis-ease.

Is it challenging? Yes! The years of internalizing, denying, and disconnecting from your emotions have molded a pattern that's easier to maintain than to change. However, you can break that pattern and use your newly acquired knowledge to enhance the quality of your own life. It starts with making a choice—a choice to imagine yourself healed.

Everything is possible! Your current state of health, heredity, genetic predisposition, ethnicity, or medical history *doesn't matter!* The LifeLine Technique is the bridge over troubled waters, the path from the world of dysfunction and disease to the realm of freedom and passion. The choice is yours, and the journey toward optimal health is simple: It begins with Infinite Love & Gratitude.

Rest assured, there will be internal doubts, obstacles, and detractors lurking about. Change may not occur as fast as you want. There will be allopathic doctors who challenge you by saying, "You're incurable. You'll have irritable bowel syndrome [or acid reflux, fibromyalgia, diabetes, hypertension, and so on] for the rest of your life." The process of change, however, requires determination and constant practice. All symptoms are an opportunity for healing. Every feeling of discomfort opens the door to health, growth, and power. Each limiting belief, feeling, or thought is a wall that's ready to be scaled.

Thomas Edison, the great American innovator, inventor, and creative thinker, once said, "Many of life's failures are people who did not realize how close they were to success when they gave up." There's no failure in life when you do your best and own your power—just the opportunity to learn lessons that will keep you on a course to achieve your highest goals: optimal health, dignity, happiness, and peace of mind.

As Marianne Williamson has written in her book *A Return to Love: Reflections on the Principles of <u>A Course in Miracles</u>*: "We were born to make manifest the glory of God that is within us. It's not just in some of us; it's in everyone. As we're liberated from our own fears, our presence automatically liberates others."

The process of healing is a spiritual journey—the evolutionary path to awakening your spirit. Make it fun! Just remember: At the moment you choose to own your power and to *feel,* you've already succeeded. . . . *Imagine yourself healed.*

# The LifeLine Technique
## Glossary of Terms

**Assemblage Point:** The continuum of energy orbiting the midline of the body and moving along the microcosmic orbit that represents the specific point in our superconscious where the internalization or denial of, or disconnection from, our emotions originally occurred; the energetic disconnection within the subconscious mind.

**Biochemical Expression:** There are two forms of biochemical expression: (1) meridian drainage (detoxifying the meridian by opening the routes of elimination and discharging the toxic accumulations); and (2) meridian feeding (which refers to hypofunction, or less-than-optimal function, of a corresponding meridian and the need for this area to be fed with life force).

**Body:** The body is a mirror of the energy that feeds its potential. Every thought, action, and reaction is a reflection of the patterns that have programmed our bodies. This programming begins the moment the sperm meets the egg.

**Chakras:** A Sanskrit word, *chakra* means "wheel" or "disk." Chakras are the energy centers of the body. Each one moves with a spinning motion, forming a vortex. It's these vortices that filter the energy of the environment around us and disperse it through the seven chakras of the body. The chakras connect the body to the collective consciousness. They're the active component of the subconscious mind.

**Chi:** In Chinese medicine, *chi* refers to life force or electromagnetic energy. Chi is emotion.

**Circadian Flow:** The rhythmic flow of life force. In the Five Element theory, it refers to the 2-hour period during the 24-hour daily cycle in which each acupuncture meridian functions at its peak.

**Collective Conscious:** If there's a question, the answer can be awakened by channeling the collective conscious, which is Infinite Love & Gratitude. Other names for this entity include the universe, the macrocosm, the Divine, the innate, or God.

**Conscious:** The conscious is what our senses perceive and bring to the awareness of our higher mind. Two percent of our reality is conscious. The conscious part of the human brain is the cortex. Not until something becomes conscious can we learn or change.

**Conscious Body Portal:** Represents the subconscious patterns that are creating physical pain or inhibiting the body from healing. The Conscious Body Portal uses physical discomfort as a way into the subconscious mind (for example, low-back pain, headaches, or stomach pain).

**Conscious Mind Portal:** Represents the subconscious patterns that are creating difficult situations in life or inhibiting us from releasing stress. The Conscious Mind Portal provides awareness of the emotional connection to physical symptoms or stressful experiences in life, such as addictions, phobias, traumatic memories, panic attacks, and so forth. It can be used to set goals through declarative statements about where we are presently in life or where we'd like to be.

**Disease:** A state of the physical body where there has been a pathological breakdown of at least 40 percent. When these pathological processes can be observed through diagnostics, such as blood and urine tests and radiographic procedures, a diagnosis can be given to them. The medical profession treats disease; The LifeLine Technique practitioners treat people.

**Dis-ease:** *Dis-ease* means "without ease," and relates to physical discomfort as a result of stress; poor eating habits; lack of water, exercise, and rest; as well as the internalization or denial of our emotions. It's the body's way of expressing imbalance.

**Emotions:** Any specific feeling; any of various complex reactions with both mental and physical manifestations, as love, hate, fear, anger, and so on. Emotions can be broken down into two parts: *E* stands for "energy," and *motion* implies "movement"—meaning *all emotions must stay in motion*. The subconscious internalization or denial of, or disconnection from, emotions results in the manifestation of symptoms in the physical body. To achieve balance within the mind and body, we must authentically express our emotions.

**Expression Channel:** The Expression Channel enables The LifeLine practitioner to know why an acupuncture meridian has a decreased flow in life force. It will always be either emotional, structural, or biochemical.

**The Five Basics for Optimal Health:** The quantity, quality, and frequency of water, food, rest, exercise, and owning one's power are the five components necessary for an optimally healthy lifestyle.

**The Five Element Theory:** The Five Elements—*Fire, Earth, Metal, Water,* and *Wood*—explain precisely where there's a decrease of life force in the body and in what way it's not flowing. The Five Elements help us understand that the natural flow of energy that takes place in nature also occurs within the body.

**Free Will:** Free will is choice, which is only possible when we're functioning in the conscious mind. The LifeLine Technique awakens the subconscious to the conscious, thereby creating a new perception of reality. Regardless of whether or not we think, feel, or believe we have a choice, we always do. If at some point we didn't have a choice, by becoming conscious, we create the opportunity for one. The choice in life is to pick fear or love . . . always choose love!

**Frequency:** A measure of electricity distinguished by the units of hertz. The body is electrical, and multiple frequencies make up and create it. The vibrational frequency of the mind will determine the vibration at which the body will function. Low vibrations have a greater attractor field to imbalance and disease. High ones enable the body to release the holding patterns of imbalance, empowering the body to heal. Infinite Love & Gratitude has the highest of frequencies.

**Frequency of Disease:** A low vibrational frequency of the mind leads to stagnation within the body. Stagnation results in an accumulation of toxicity, which will eventually lead to disease.

**Harmonize:** The restoration of balance between the mind, body, and spirit occurs with the healing frequency of Infinite Love & Gratitude.

**Holding Pattern:** The area in which a symptom is being held: the mind, body, or spirit. The holding pattern enables The LifeLine practitioner to know where and why a symptom is being harbored in the body. It represents subconscious addictions.

**Holographic Principle:** One part contains the whole of life—that is, a single cell represents an entire being. When there's a symptom in one area of the body, the rest is also holding it. The LifeLine Technique focuses on a single symptom (emotional or physical), therefore balancing the entire person.

**Ko:** Each of the Five Elements has a relationship to the others. The Ko is the destructive or controlling cycle.

**The LifeLine Law of Transformation and Creation:** Emotions transform energy; energy creates movement; movement is change; and change is the essence of life. It's the fear of change that keeps us stuck in a cycle of self-destruction.

**The LifeLine Technique:** The LifeLine Technique is an evolutionary way to release the root cause of symptoms and disease. It uses muscle testing, a Flow Chart, and the healing frequency of Infinite Love & Gratitude to harmonize the subconsciously internalized, denied, or disconnected emotions that have resulted in symptoms. It's a fast, safe, and powerful tool. The cornerstone of The LifeLine Technique is The Five Basics for Optimal Health—the quantity, quality, and frequency of water, food, rest, exercise, and owning your power. Anyone can be trained to use The LifeLine Technique.

**Luo:** The connection between the yin and yang acupuncture meridians of a particular element. The Luo cycle represents the interdependence of polar opposites.

**Microcosmic Orbit:** The microcosmic orbit is the circulating flow of energy that follows the Ren and Du acupuncture meridians along the midline of the body. This flow of energy has polarity and attracts and repels life experiences according to what we've subconsciously internalized, denied, or disconnected from. The chakras are individual channels along the microcosmic orbit that connect the macrocosm of the collective conscious to the microcosm of the body. The microcosmic orbit is the mind.

**Mind:** The mind is composed of four parts: the conscious, subconscious, superconscious, and collective conscious. It's the storehouse of our beliefs, which filter our perception of the environment and affect the autonomic function of the nervous system, triggering the sympathetic "fright, flight, or fight" survival mode or parasympathetic relaxation/healing mode. The energy of Infinite Love & Gratitude connects the subconscious to the collective conscious.

**Passion:** Intense emotional drive or excitement, as in "passion for life." It's the fuel for the will and is what gives life meaning.

**Pathology:** Pathology is diagnosable disease. For it to be present, the body needs to have broken down 40-plus percent.

**Power Center:** The Power Center is the area of The LifeLine Flow Chart that represents the subconscious mind. Also known as the superconscious or microcosmic orbit, it consists of the mind (beliefs), heart (feelings), and will (thoughts). When we subconsciously internalize, deny, or disconnect from our emotions, we're denying our power.

**Present Time Consciousness (PTC):** PTC is the act of staying connected to a moment, no matter how challenging, painful, or frightening. PTC enables us to acknowledge, honor, and embrace our feelings; stay in tune with our senses and intuition; and experience the world without judgment. By authentically responding to what we're experiencing, PTC empowers us to live life with courage and faith, rather than out of fear.

**Shen:** Each of the Five Elements has a relationship to the others. Shen is the creative cycle.

**Spirit:** Spirit is the body's electromagnetic field or life force. It's also known as *chi* or *prana*.

**Subconscious:** The subconscious mind is 98 percent of our reality. Pain, fear, and challenges are the language used to communicate that we've subconsciously internalized, denied, or disconnected from an emotion. It's through pain, fear, and challenges that we discover the subconscious mind. The subconscious aspects of the brain are located in the limbic and reptilian centers.

**Superconscious:** The superconscious is also known as the Power Center—mind (beliefs), heart (feelings), and will (thoughts)—which connects us externally through the chakras to the collective conscious, as well as internally to the conscious and subconscious. The superconscious is the microcosmic orbit.

**Symptoms:** The language the body uses to communicate imbalance. Whether a symptom is physical or emotional, it's an opportunity that the body gives us to heal on a deeper level. Symptoms are gifts that, when "unwrapped," lead to the most extraordinary truths of our lives. They are the body speaking the mind.

**Triad of Health:** The Triad of Health represents the body in The LifeLine Flow Chart. The body can be separated into four parts—emotional, biochemical, structural, and spiritual. It represents the specific location where an imbalance has occurred, leading to a decreased flow of life force.

**Vibration/Vibrational Frequency:** Vibrations are rapid, back-and-forth, oscillating movements. Movement is change, and change is the essence of life. High vibrational frequencies naturally repel low ones. The LifeLine Technique removes roadblocks in the mind, body, and spirit by harmonizing low vibrational frequencies with the healing frequency of Infinite Love & Gratitude.

**Yang:** The Chinese name given to represent *positive, hollow, white, sky, external, male, active, above, kinetic,* or *fire.* Depending upon the perspective, something may be yang or yin. The yang acupuncture meridians are the outer meridians along the Five Elements.

**Yin:** The Chinese name given to represent *negative, solid, black, earth, internal, female, passive, below, potential,* or *water.* Depending upon the perspective, something may be yin or yang. The yin acupuncture meridians are the inner meridians along the Five Elements.

# LIVE BLOOD CELL ANALYSIS

BEFORE

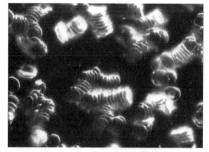

A 32-year-old woman with symptoms of stress and feeling overwhelmed.

AFTER

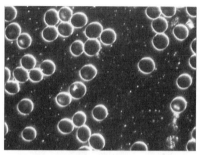

Using the power of Infinite Love & Gratitude, released subconscious feelings of yearning for stability, dating back to the age of 8 when her family moved frequently.

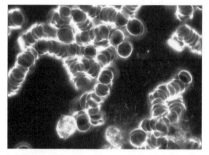

A 56-year-old man with symptoms of chronic chest cold and impatience because of lingering illness.

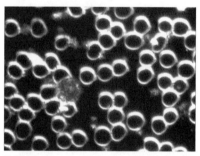

Using the power of Infinite Love & Gratitude, released subconscious emotion of depression.

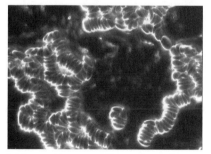

A 44-year-old woman with symptoms of a facial rash.

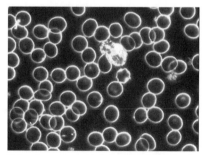

Using the power of Infinite Love & Gratitude, released subconscious feelings of sadness, impending doom, and yearning associated with missing her father when she was 8.

BEFORE

AFTER

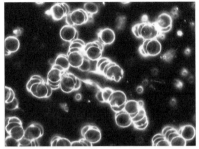

A 39-year-old man with symptoms of poison ivy on his arm.

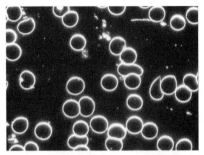

Using the power of Infinite Love & Gratitude, released limiting belief of being inefficient and the subconscious emotion of depression

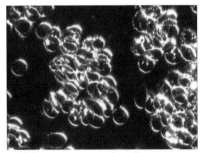

A 50-year-old woman with severe stress and frustration.

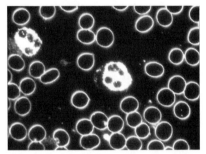

Using the power of Infinite Love & Gratitude, released the subconscious emotions of helplessness and vulnerability associated with the memory of a rape at the age of 19.

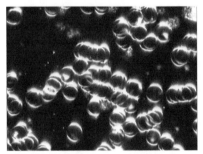

A 37-year-old woman with symptoms of asthma.

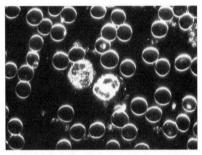

Using the power of Infinite Love & Gratitude, released subconscious feelings of impending doom.

BEFORE

AFTER

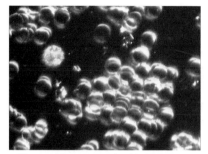

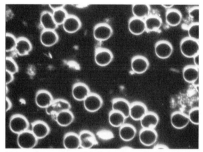

A 31-year-old woman with a bladder infection.

Using the power of Infinite Love & Gratitude, released the subconscious limiting belief associated with feelings of impending doom.

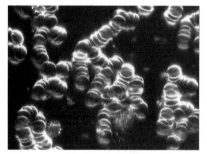

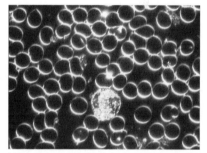

A 26-year-old woman with chronic back pain.

Using the power of Infinite Love & Gratitude, released the subconscious feeling of depression.

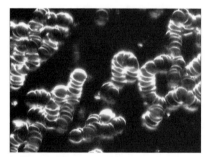

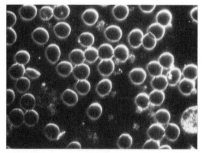

A 47-year-old woman with symptoms of confusion stemming from not feeling that her life is on track.

Using the power of Infinite Love & Gratitude, released the Gemini-Thought Virus holding the emotion of anguish stemming from a disagreement with her husband.

BEFORE

AFTER

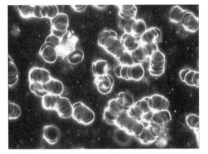

A 57-year-old woman with symptoms of pain in her thumb.

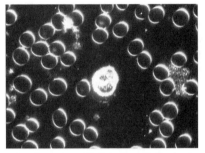

Using the power of Infinite Love & Gratitude, released the subconscious core limiting belief of paralyzed will and anger.

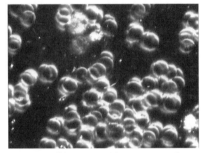

A 65-year-old woman with symptoms of shoulder pain.

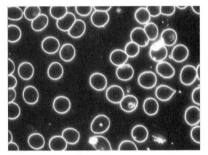

Using the power of Infinite Love & Gratitude, released the subconscious emotions of low self-esteem and anger stemming from an argument with a sibling.

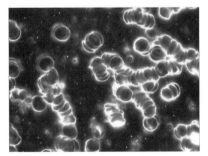

A 40-year-old man with symptoms of chronic indigestion.

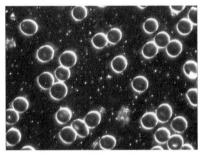

Using the power of Infinite Love & Gratitude, released subconscious emotion of paralyzed will stemming from a pending divorce.

BEFORE

AFTER

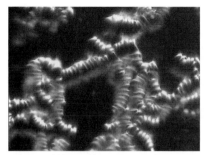

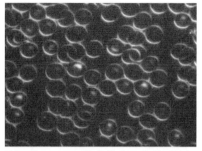

A 9-year-old boy with symptoms of severe migraine headaches.

Using the power of Infinite Love & Gratitude, released subconscious feelings of internalized anger toward his parents because of their divorce.

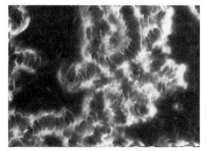

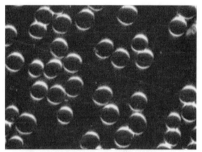

A 41-year-old woman diagnosed with breast cancer.

Using the power of Infinite Love & Gratitude, released subconscious feelings of depression associated with being emotionally and verbally abused by her husband.

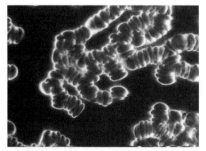

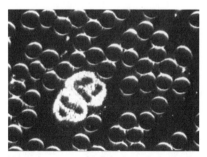

A 42-year-old man with symptoms of acid reflux.

Using the power of Infinite Love & Gratitude, released subconscious thoughts of shame related to a family situation.

BEFORE

AFTER

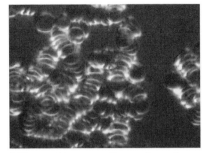

A 53-year-old woman with symptoms of insomnia.

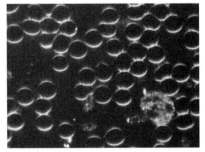

Using the power of Infinite Love & Gratitude, released subconscious fears about her future due to the reorganization of the company where she worked.

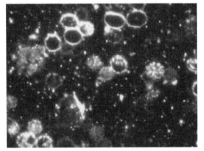

A 6-year-old boy with disruptive behavior; diagnosed with attention deficit disorder (ADD).

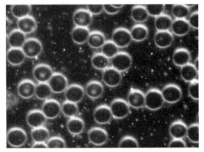

Using the power of Infinite Love & Gratitude, released subconscious feelings of frustration stemming from the birth of a sibling.

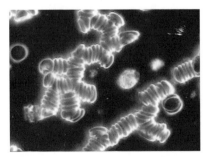

A 32-year-old woman diagnosed with fibromyalgia.

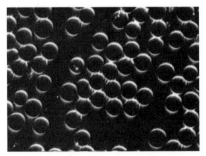

Using the power of Infinite Love & Gratitude, released subconscious feelings of grief she internalized for three years following the death of her mother.

BEFORE

AFTER

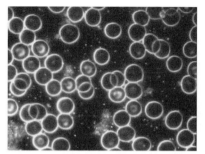

A 40-year-old woman whose attempts to get pregnant had been unsuccessful.

Using the power of Infinite Love & Gratitude, released subconscious beliefs that her age made it impossible to get pregnant. She had a baby 11 months later.

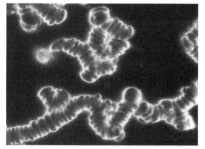

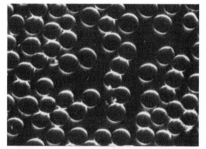

A 50-year-old woman plagued with environmental allergies.

Using the power of Infinite Love & Gratitude, released the subconscious thoughts and feelings of fear and shame stemming from childhood sexual abuse.

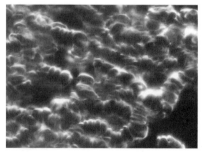

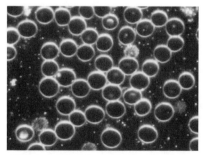

A 36-year-old woman suffering from severe neck pain.

Using the power of Infinite Love & Gratitude, released subconscious feelings of jealousy toward a co-worker who received a promotion.

BEFORE

AFTER

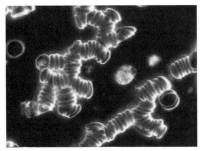

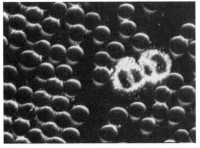

A 20-year-old college athlete with a pulled hamstring muscle.

Using the power of Infinite Love & Gratitude, released subconscious feelings of grief related to the death of his grandmother.

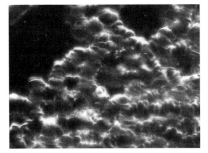

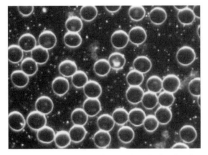

A 53-year-old woman with severe perimenopause symptoms, including mood swings and hot flashes.

Using the power of Infinite Love & Gratitude, released subconscious fears arising from suddenly being responsible for her elderly father.

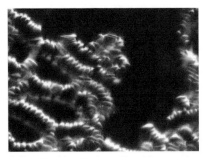

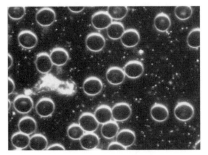

A 60-year-old man who suffered from panic attacks for 15 years.

Using the power of Infinite Love & Gratitude, released subconscious feelings of contempt resulting from an argument with his boss that occurred the week before the advent of the attacks.

BEFORE

AFTER

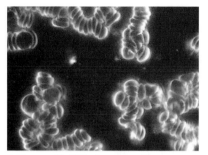

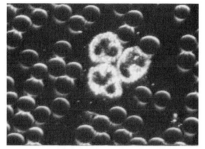

A 12-year-old child who suffered from severe fatigue.

Using the power of Infinite Love & Gratitude, released subconscious feelings of dread about going to middle school.

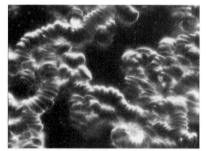

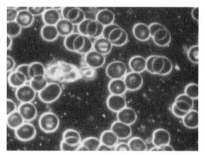

A 38-year-old woman who had severe symptoms of tingling and numbness but all of whose medical tests were negative.

Using the power of Infinite Love & Gratitude, released subconscious thoughts of self-dislike stemming from her childhood.

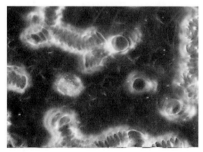

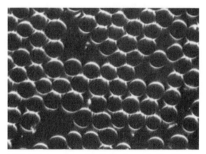

A 29-year-old man complaining of bursitis in his shoulder.

Using the power of Infinite Love & Gratitude, released subconscious feelings related to being smothered by his mother.

BEFORE

AFTER

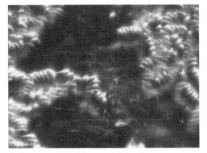

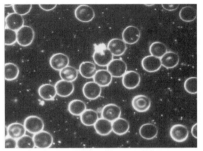

A 14-year-old with severe blood-sugar-metabolism imbalances.

Using the power of Infinite Love & Gratitude, released subconscious anger about being harassed by a bully at school.

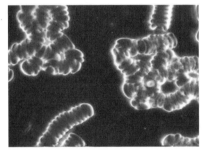

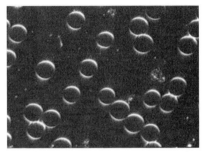

A 75-year-old recent widow with severe dizziness.

Using the power of Infinite Love & Gratitude, released subconscious anxieties about her future.

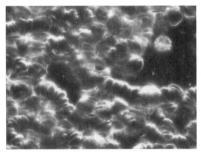

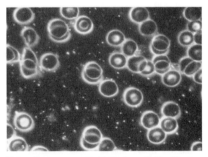

A 43-year-old woman with persistent upset stomach.

Using the power of Infinite Love & Gratitude, released subconscious beliefs that she should be perfect.

BEFORE

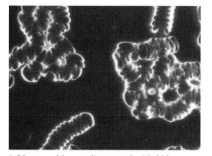

A 31-year-old man diagnosed with kidney stones.

AFTER

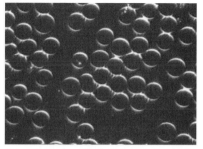

Using the power of Infinite Love & Gratitude, released subconscious feelings of powerlessness in the wake of cutbacks and decreased job security at work.

# Information and Resources

**The LifeLine Technique™**
Dr. Darren R. Weissman
*The Power of Infinite Love & Gratitude*
The LifeLine Technique™ Seminars
Certification for The LifeLine Technique™ Practitioners
The LifeLine Technique™ Products
www.infiniteloveandgratitude.com
(866) 398-9864

**Total Body Modification**
Dr. Victor Frank
www.tbmseminars.com

**Neuro Emotional Technique**
Dr. Scott Walker
www.netmindbody.com

**International College of Applied Kinesiology**
Dr. George Goodheart
www.icak.com

**The Hidden Messages in Water**
Dr. Masaru Emoto
www.hado.net

**The Biology of Belief**
Dr. Bruce Lipton
www.brucelipton.com

**Dr. Candace Pert**
*Molecules of Emotion*
www.candacepert.com

# RECOMMENDED READING

*Ageless Body, Timeless Mind,* by Deepak Chopra, M.D.

*Anatomy of the Spirit,* by Caroline Myss

*The Art of Happiness,* by His Holiness The Dalai Lama
and Howard C. Cutler, M.D.

*Ask and It Is Given: Learning to Manifest Your Desires,*
by Esther and Jerry Hicks (The Teachings of Abraham)

*A Better Way to Live,* by Og Mandino

*The Body Electric: Electromagnetism and the Foundation of Life,*
by Robert Becker, M.D.

*Chi Nei Tsang,* by Mantak Chia

*Conversations with God* (Books 1–3), by Neale Donald Walsch

*Cross Currents: The Perils of Electropollution, the Promise of Electromedicine,*
by Robert Becker, M.D.

*DMT: The Spirit Molecule,* by Rick Strassman, M.D.

*Embracing Our Selves,* by Hal Stone, Ph.D., and Sidra Stone, Ph.D.

*EMDR,* by Francine Shapiro, Ph.D., and Margot Silk Forrest

*The Four Agreements,* by Don Miguel Ruiz

*A Garden of Thoughts,* by Louise L. Hay

*Getting the Love You Want,* by Harville Hendrix, Ph.D.

*The Gift of Fear,* by Gavin de Becker

*Infinite Mind: Science of the Human Vibrations of Consciousness,*
by Valerie V. Hunt

*Inner Wisdom,* by Louise L. Hay

*The Love and Power Journal,* by Lynn V. Andrews

*Man's Search for Meaning,* by Viktor Frankl

*Many Lives, Many Masters,* by Brian Weiss, M.D.

*The Mastery of Love,* by Don Miguel Ruiz

*Molecules of Emotion,* by Candace B. Pert, Ph.D.

*The Power of Intention: Learning to Co-create Your World Your Way,*
by Dr. Wayne W. Dyer

*Power vs. Force: The Hidden Determinants of Human Behavior,*
by David R. Hawkins, M.D., Ph.D.

*Psycho-Cybernetics,* by Maxwell Maltz, M.D., F.I.C.S.

*A Return to Love: Reflections on the Principles of A Course in Miracles,*
by Marianne Williamson

*The Seven Spiritual Laws of Success,* by Deepak Chopra, M.D.

*The Story of Edgar Cayce: There Is a River,* by Thomas Sugrue

*The Sugar Control Bible and Cookbook,* by Jacqueline Paltis, D.C., N.D.

*There's a Hole in My Sidewalk,* by Portia Nelson

*There's a Spiritual Solution to Every Problem,* by Dr. Wayne W. Dyer

*The Tibetan Book of Living and Dying,* by Sogyal Rinpoche

*Traditional Acupuncture: The Law of the Five Elements,* by Dr. Dianne Connelly

*25 Things Every New Mother Should Know,* by Martha Sears, R.N.,
with William Sears, M.D.

*Unlocking the Mysteries of Birth & Death,* by Daisaku Ikeda

*Visioning: Ten Steps to Designing the Life of Your Dreams,*
by Lucia Capacchione, Ph.D., A.T.R

*The Way of Energy,* by Master Lam Kam Chuen

*Wheels of Life: A User's Guide to the Chakra System,* by Anodea Judith

*Why People Don't Heal and How They Can,* by Caroline Myss

*You Can Heal Your Life,* by Louise L. Hay

*You Can Heal Your Life Companion Book,* by Louise L. Hay

*Your Body's Many Cries for Water,* by F. Batmanghelidj, M.D.

*Your Body Speaks Your Mind,* by Debbie Shapiro

~ ~ ~

# INDEX

≈

# ACKNOWLEDGMENTS

There are many people who deserve thanks for the advent of this book. For those I have forgotten to mention, Infinite Love & Gratitude to you!

To my friend and teacher Jeri Love—your guidance through this incredible journey of writing has been invaluable. I'm in awe of your wisdom, organization, and dedication. You are my rock, and I'm infinitely grateful to you for helping me transform my inspiration and thoughts into a book. I couldn't have done this without you. Thank you for going the extra mile. Thank you! Thank you! Thank you!

Thank you, Louise Hay, for recognizing the vision and giving me an opportunity to share it. I will forever remember your kindness and open heart in allowing me to teach you and your friends The LifeLine Technique in San Diego. I agree—it's truly all about timing, and I'm so grateful and honored to be a part of the Hay House family.

To editorial director Jill Kramer, copy editor Alex Freemon, and creative director Christy Salinas, along with the other wonderful employees at Hay House, thank you for your patience and guidance during the process of making this a beautiful Hay House book.

Next, thanks to Dr. Thomas Bayne: Your foresight, big ideas, and unending passion have motivated me to be my best.

I thank Dr. Ingrid Maes for challenging me to go beyond my limits, helping me to see that there are no limits. I am no longer afraid, and I have you to thank for that!

Thanks to Bob Sandidge and Anne Ward of CreativeCore: I don't know what Tom and I would have done without you. Everything is perfect, and it was part of the big plan that our paths have crossed. The latest update of The LifeLine Flow Chart is beautiful and a true expression of the inner beauty you both radiate.

Thank you, Jeffrey Sofferman and David Schiffman, for the greatest friendships a person could ever envision. I'm blessed to have you both in my life. Thank you for your support, guidance, and unconditional love. You guys are the best!

Thank you, Cindy Kaplan: Your gift of be-ing has inspired me to be my best. I'm in awe of your presence as a friend, aunt, and the queen bee of The Way to Optimal Health, and I am forever grateful to have you in my life.

Thank you, Harlene Newman, for always saying the right thing at the right moment. You have an incredible skill for transforming lemons into lemonade.

Thank you to the thousands of people who have entrusted me along your journey toward optimal health. I'm infinitely grateful for the opportunity to be a part of your healing path. You have helped me heal, and I have grown so much as a result of our encounters.

A special thanks to Dee Michell, for showing me unending courage, love, and dignity throughout your life. Your journey has impacted me in a way that I'm unable to purely express. You will always be in my heart.

Brian Goedhart, thank you for teaching me how to flow effortlessly and to live without judgment. You are the wizard of the *wind.*

Thank you, Dr. Roy Gonik, my beautiful friend. My life is so much richer with you in it. You are a gifted teacher and I treasure our friendship.

Thank you, Dr. Keith Jordan. You are so special to me. Luddy was a good boy.

To Kimball Paul, I extend my gratitude for your wisdom and grace and for sharing your infinite knowledge of *The Way.*

Thank you, Ruth Bender, my friend and editor. Your skills of editing are only exceeded by your heart and the authentic way you live your life.

To my mom and dad, I am so blessed to have chosen you. Thank you for giving me life. Your compassion, kindness, and authentic way of living have molded me into the person I am today. I'm so proud to be your son and to spread the Infinite Love & Gratitude you nurtured me to embrace within myself.

Thank you, Kenny, Paula, Rachel, Marc, and Yoni Weissman, for your unyielding support and love. A special thanks to you, Paula, for your incredible editing skills and wonderful feedback. It was so helpful, and this book would not have been as beautiful without your insight and special touch.

Thank you, Howie, Nicole, Alex, and Jacob Weissman. Howie, you have been a great teacher and friend. I have learned so much about myself, and I am forever grateful. I love you.

To all my aunts, uncles, cousins, and especially my great-aunt Ethel, I give my thanks. You are all so wonderful, and I feel so privileged to be a part of such an amazing family. What makes our family amazing is that we hold family traditions and connection as a top priority. It is something that has been handed down through generations, and I am thankful to be connected to such a rooted and extended family tree. I love you all very much!

Thank you, Martini/Anderson family, for being the bonus to life. I feel so fortunate to be a part of your loving family.

Thank you, Floyd, Zen, and Buddha (our cats), for your unconditional support and love. Your Taoist ways have awakened me to the subtle nature and joy of life. *Meow!*

I humbly express my Infinite Love & Gratitude to my daughter, Joya Ruth. Your mom and I are so blessed that you have chosen us as parents. I have a whole new appreciation for love with you in my life. You have helped me to recognize that every moment is a miracle waiting to happen.

Thank you, Sarit, my beautiful wife, friend, and lover. You are living proof that Infinite Love & Gratitude is what it's all about. Thank you for sharing life's journey with me. I look forward to the many adventures we'll share. Thank you for your encouragement, for loving me for who I am, and for supporting me to own my power. With your tender and compassionate love, I am able to reach for the stars. This book would not have been possible without you! I love you infinitely with all of my heart.

# ABOUT THE AUTHOR

**Dr. Darren R. Weissman** is the developer of The LifeLine Technique, an advanced holistic system that releases subconscious emotions and patterns that lead to symptoms of stress. The LifeLine Technique integrates 14 modalities of natural healing into one unified system. Darren earned his B.S. degree in human biology at the University of Kansas, and his doctorate in chiropractic medicine at the National College of Chiropractic. He received additional intensive training in acupuncture, homeopathy, and other forms of energy medicine in Sri Lanka.

Darren's other postgraduate studies have included applied kinesiology (AK), Total Body Modification (TBM), Neuro Emotional Technique (NET), Neuro-Linguistic Programming (NLP), NeuroModulation Technique (NMT), Chinese energetic medicine, natural healing, and many other forms of energy healing. In addition to running his private practice, he trains other healing arts practitioners and laypersons in the use of The LifeLine Technique and the power of Infinite Love & Gratitude. His mission is world peace through love and gratitude. Beyond his healing arts work, Darren lives a passionate life with his wife, Sarit; and their daughter, Joya Ruth.

# NOTES

# NOTES

# NOTES

# NOTES

# NOTES

# NOTES

# NOTES

# NOTES

We hope you enjoyed this Hay House book.
If you'd like to receive a free catalog featuring additional
Hay House books and products, or if you'd like information about the
Hay Foundation, please contact:

Hay House, Inc.
P.O. Box 5100
Carlsbad, CA 92018-5100

**(760) 431-7695 or (800) 654-5126**
**(760) 431-6948 (fax) or (800) 650-5115 (fax)**
**www.hayhouse.com®** • **www.hayfoundation.org**

*Published and distributed in Australia by:* Hay House Australia Pty. Ltd., 18/36 Ralph St., Alexandria NSW 2015 • *Phone:* 612-9669-4299 • *Fax:* 612-9669-4144 • www.hayhouse.com.au

*Published and distributed in the United Kingdom by:* Hay House UK, Ltd., 292B Kensal Rd., London W10 5BE • *Phone:* 44-20-8962-1230 • *Fax:* 44-20-8962-1239 • www.hayhouse.co.uk

*Published and distributed in the Republic of South Africa by:* Hay House SA (Pty), Ltd., P.O. Box 990, Witkoppen 2068 • *Phone/Fax:* 27-11-467-8904 • orders@psdprom.co.za • www.hayhouse.co.za

*Published in India by:* Hay House Publishers India, Muskaan Complex, Plot No. 3, B-2, Vasant Kunj, New Delhi 110 070 • *Phone:* 91-11-4176-1620 • *Fax:* 91-11-4176-1630 www.hayhouse.co.in

*Distributed in Canada by:* Raincoast, 9050 Shaughnessy St., Vancouver, B.C. V6P 6E5 • *Phone:* (604) 323-7100 • *Fax:* (604) 323-2600 • www.raincoast.com

Tune in to **HayHouseRadio.com®** for the best in
inspirational talk radio featuring top Hay House authors!
And, sign up via the Hay House USA Website to receive the Hay House online
newsletter and stay informed about what's going on with your favorite authors.
You'll receive bimonthly announcements about Discounts and Offers, Special Events,
Product Highlights, Free Excerpts, Giveaways, and more!
**www.hayhouse.com®**